The Historic Gardens of England Series

Historic Gardens of Herefordshire

Opposite: *Herefordshire Tracts,* vol 2, Hereford City Library

The Historic Gardens of England Series

Historic Gardens of Herefordshire

Timothy Mowl

Jane Bradney

For Sir Roy Strong

The publication of this volume has been made possible by a grant from
THE LEVERHULME TRUST
to cover all the necessary research work

Spanish Chestnuts, Croft by Betty Pennell. *By kind permission of Betty Pennell*

First published in 2012 by Redcliffe Press Ltd.,
81g Pembroke Road, Bristol BS8 3EA
T: 0117 9737207
E: info@redcliffepress.co.uk
www.redcliffepress.co.uk

ISBN 978-1-906593-91-9

British Library Cataloguing-in-Publication Data
A catalogue record for this book is available from the British Library

Designed by Stephen Morris, smc@freeuk.com www.stephen-morris.co.uk
Printed by HSW Print, Tonypandy, Rhondda

Contents

continued

Acknowledgements

As with the last eight books in this series, my first thanks go to Professor Sir Richard Brook and his Trustees at the Leverhulme Trust, whose generous funding of the research has made the Herefordshire travelling and garden visiting a pleasure rather than a financial worry. Their generosity has made it possible for Dr Jane Bradney, a former PhD student of mine and resident of the county, to be appointed as consultant for *Herefordshire*. She has undertaken all the research and co-ordinated the site visits in a meticulously professional manner. I should also like to thank again Dr Clare Hickman, Research Fellow of the project, who has overseen the writing and research of the book with her usual efficiency. Clare has now moved on to Oxford University and her role has been taken by Marion Mako, co-author with me of *Cheshire* and *Somerset*. She has dealt expertly with the last-minute glitches, picture permissions and editing.

Owners, archivists, historians, friends, colleagues and Bristol University MA Garden History students and postgraduate researchers who have been particularly helpful include Lucinda Aldridge-Blake, Pelham Aldridge-Blake, Mike & Anne Allen, Gillian & Mark Archer, Stephen Astley, Elizabeth & Lawrence Banks, Pete Barnes, Dr Dianne Barre, Cinna Belloc-Lowndes, Lady Bridget Bengough, Anthony Brookes, Edward Bulmer, Russell and Ros Catley, Carole & John Challis, William Chase, Nathan Cheesman, Mimi & Ben Chester-Master, Pat Churchward, Mrs Jeremy Clay, Peter Clay, Edward & Tamsin Clive, Bertie Comerford, Angela Conner, Simon Cooter, Penny Corbett, Harry & Katherine Cotterell, Liz Cousins, David Crichton-Watts, Veronica Cross, Christine Curtis, Major David Davenport, Michael Deacon, Lucie Dingwall, Robert Doran, Simon Dorrell, Domenica Dunne, Sir Thomas & Lady Henrietta Dunne, Kate Edwards, Anne Evans, Brian & Chris Evans, Adrian Farmer, Dr Kate Felus, John & Jocelyn Finnigan, Rupert Foley, David Forbes, Christopher Francis, Fiona Fyshe, Helene Gammack, Geoffrey & Bettie Gartside, Helena Gerrish, Roger & Jane Gouldstone, Rhys Griffith, Ian Grisenthwaite, John Handby, Edward & Victoria Harley, Philip & Linda Harley, Diana Harrison, Jane Hawksley, Sandy Haynes, Donna Helme, James Hepworth, James Hereford, James Hervey-Bathurst, Professor Mark Horton, Jeffrey Howarth, Dr David & Helen Humphreys, Julia Ionides, Mark & Alexandra James, Chris Jones, David Jones, Noel Kingsbury, Angela Lawson, Hilda Lee, Roger and Vanessa Lee, Mike Lewis, Michael Liversidge, David Lovelace, Dr Laura Mayer, Bronwyn McArthur, Dawn McBarnet, John & Janet MacPherson,

Ian & Jen MacKie, Francis May, Keith Meehan, Lesley Malone, Sir Richard & Lady Fiona Mynors, James Page, Heather Pegg, Ronald & Betty Pennell, Marianne Percival, Dr Sophieke Piebenga, Steven Redding, Clive Richards, Dr Neil Rimmington, Nicholas & Sarah Rogers, Paul & Lizzie Rumph, Sarah de Rohan, Miriam Seal, Melissa Seddon, Paul Segrot, Andrew & Rosie Simpson, Edward Simpson, Brian Smith, Anna Spreckley, Dr Paul Stamper, Lorna Standen, Nicholas & Carmel Stephens, Tom Stuart-Smith, Lesley Tanner, Judith Temple, Tom Wall, Charis Ward, David Wheeler, Erica White, David Whitehead, Hannah Wilks and Susan Wood.

I must thank Michael Richardson of the University's Special Collections for bringing many important texts to my notice, and also Hannah Lowery for help in searching out primary sources, while Jamie Carstairs undertook the archival photography from the University's collection with precision. John Sansom and his daughter Clara Hudson have been encouraging and enthusiastic publishers, and Stephen Morris has achieved another elegantly designed volume. Alexandra Denman has proofed the typescript most conscientiously, and Douglas Matthews has produced yet another definitive index. I must also thank Martin Bradney for his input regarding logistics, assistance with photographs and for support to his wife, Jane.

Herefordshire has been researched alongside my teaching of Bristol University's MA in Garden History, so I must thank my postgraduates for their lively encouragement. My agent, Sara Menguc, has continued to support the project with her affectionate enthusiasm. My wife, Sarah, and daughter, Olivia, went with me to check out The Feathers Hotel in Ledbury that was later to provide the perfect base from which to visit the southern quadrants of the county. In the north, just over the border in Shropshire, a room above De Grey's tea rooms with a view of the Market Place at Ludlow was equally accommodating. My son Adam has supported me through regular texts and emails from London, where he has been researching for his PhD at King's College. Finally, I should like to thank Sir Roy Strong, to whom this book is dedicated. He has followed my academic career closely and given several of my earlier books on architectural history thoughtful and enthusiastic reviews. It is a pleasure here to record my gratitude for his continued encouragement and kindness. I now leave the orchards of this lush western county for the wide-open skies of Cambridgeshire.

Timothy Mowl, Bristol, May 2012

Introduction

Border county of landscape aesthetics and mellow fruitfulness

One of the most spectacular views of the Herefordshire landscape can be gained from the British Camp on the Malverns (*colour 1*), a stepped rectangular extrusion, transversely set across the southern hills. The view is breathtaking, out west to Herefordshire and back east to Worcestershire. The Camp is just one of a series of Iron Age hill forts – Croft Ambrey at Croft Castle, Coxhall Knoll overlooking Brampton Bryan Castle and Backbury Hill – which are potent visual reminders that this is an ancient county. Each has had its influence on landscape and garden designers, with Charles Francis Annesley Voysey's conscious alignment of his house and gardens at Perrycroft on the British Camp, and John Beale's adoption of Backbury as the ideal place from which to appreciate unadorned Nature. The architect Robert Adam was also inspired in the 1770s to respond creatively to a hill fort at Coxhall Knoll, commanding Lord Oxford's park at Brampton. It was thought that the camp was the site of the British chieftain Caractacus' last stand against the Roman invaders, a subject dramatised in William Mason's best-selling poem, *Caractacus*, which was first published in 1759 and ran through four more editions before being adapted for the stage in 1777.[1] In the eighteenth-century picturesque spirit of setting associational ruins as eye-catchers in the landscape, Adam attempted to dramatise the ridge with a wonderful, but sadly unexecuted, design (*1*) for a towered and battlemented Romanesque fortification.[2]

It is no coincidence, therefore, given the views, that Celia Fiennes, who set out on one of several excursions to visit an uncle in or before 1696, entered the county at Malvern: 'I rode up upon the top of one of the highest [hills], from whence I could discern the Country above 40 miles round'.[3] From this 'Ridge of hills [that] was formerly esteemed the divideing [between] England and Wales' she looked out over Herefordshire, which appeared to her 'like a Country off Gardens and Orchards, the whole Country being very full of fruite trees etc., it looks like nothing else, the apple pear trees etc., are so thick even in their corn fields and hedgrows'.[4] This dependence upon fruit production was challenged in the next century by Lord Bute, who proposed a tax on cider: four shillings on every hogshead. Cider was, of course, the lifeblood of farmers, so the proposed tax caused outrage in the cider-producing counties, especially in Herefordshire. Riots broke out in 1763 and, as a consequence of his continued unpopularity, Bute resigned as prime minister. The Cyder Act was repealed in 1766 and celebrated by members of the Herefordshire Society in London. The vignette of a joyous trumpeting angel, which appears on the title page of this book, is taken from a letter and a song published by the Society in that year:

Come jolly *Hodge*, and *Will*, lay by your Pike and Flail,
For *Susan's* gone to fetch our largest Milking-pail
Brimfull of brave old Cyder, such, as Bute never knew;
Tis Liberty we'll drink until the Skies look blue.
Then let the merry Bells all ring
In every Village round,
And nought but Joy and harmony
In every Place be found.[5]

Interestingly, Fiennes was aware that Hereford and Shropshire were originally 'Weltch Countys',[6] hence the need for the Marcher Lords who administered, independent of the Crown, a semi-autonomous legal system in this frontier country with its reputation for wildness and unrest. This

1 Robert Adam's 1770s unexecuted design for a Romano-British-style eyecatcher at Brampton Bryan. *By courtesy of the Trustees of Sir John Soane's Museum*

accounts for the string of Marcher castles set dramatically along its western boundary, which include the ruins of Clifford Castle, birthplace of Henry II's fated mistress, Rosamond Clifford, and Wigmore Castle, scene in the fourteenth century of elaborate tournaments. It might also explain the preponderance of country houses given the title of 'Court' in the county, as places where legislation was enacted and fines meted out; a Court is more usually indicative of a Regency or early nineteenth-century property. As well as castles built to withstand sieges, Herefordshire is rich in small, fortified houses, which are often surrounded by defensive moats. The most beautiful of these, which was probably retained in its park as an eighteenth-century picturesque incident, is the fifteenth-century Lower Brockhampton House (2), defended by a timber-framed gatehouse and embowered by orchards. This siege mentality is also symbolised by Offa's Dyke, the great earthwork thrown up to protect the Saxon kingdom of Mercia from the Welsh in Powys, which can be seen at its most dramatic at Knighton.

So Fiennes had identified the two principal characteristics that define Herefordshire: its agrarian, fruit producing tradition, which encouraged men like Beale to return to his home county and write about its orchards in the Commonwealth and Thomas Andrew Knight to produce the *Herefordshire Pomona* in 1811, and its location on the dangerous edge of civilisation. These characteristics were to shape, not only its political and social history, but also its garden history. Designed landscapes are relatively few and far between in a county at the outer reaches, and when they are present they

2 The romantically moated Lower Brockhampton House was to be a focal point in a proposed 1769 landscape design by Thomas Leggett

respond to the natural contours of the countryside rather than aim to impose artificial ornamentation on the terrain. This approach, of course, is the essence of the Picturesque in late-eighteenth-century landscape theory, and Herefordshire was, through Richard Payne Knight of Downton and Uvedale Price of Foxley, in the vanguard of the aesthetics of this movement.

The county's sense of isolation is perpetuated today by the national motorway network, which features in Herefordshire only in the M50, an under-used and quiet spur from the M5 near Strensham Services. It is an idyllic stretch through gently rolling countryside, enriched by ploughed fields of red soil, which carries little traffic and then stops abruptly at Ross-on-Wye. Any forays further west or north have to be made on minor roads. This inaccessibility has historical resonance, as the river Wye was unreliable for transport because of fluctuations in level. In 1793 the London to Hereford coach took a minimum of thirty-six hours to complete the journey, while the much shorter trip from Hereford to Worcester still took six hours.[7] It might go some way to explain why the county has relatively few landscapes by Lancelot 'Capability' Brown, who seems to have spent most of his working life travelling between commissions, which were being supervised by his clerks of works. The great park at Berrington Hall, south of Ludlow, that he laid out for the Hon Thomas Harley, is one of his finest minimalist achievements, a perfect compliment to the austere neo-classical parent house designed by Brown's son-in-law, Henry Holland junior. At Berrington and at Moccas Court, maps and entries in his bank account prove Brown's involvement, but this is not the case at an intriguing relic landscape of Brownian character, Eywood in the north-western quadrant of the county close to the border with Wales. All we know is that Brown stayed there briefly because of ill health.

In 1775 Brown set out on one of his mammoth tours, which took him from Lancashire, into Shropshire and on to Carmarthenshire. Before riding to Trentham in Staffordshire he stopped over at Eywood, which belonged to the Earl of Oxford, brother of Thomas Harley of Berrington. It is not known whether he formulated any plans for Eywood, but when he later reached Trentham he wrote to the Hon George Rice of Newton Castle, Carmarthenshire, where he had just been advising: 'My Health ... is not of the best kind but I assure you not the worse for my Welsh journey. The Day I left you I was very ill. I found the Judges were at Hereford which determined me to go to Lord Oxfords & the post Boys were so obliging as to take me through a River that filled my Chaise with water. However I am thank God much better than I was at Herifordshire'.[8] Lord Oxford's seat was already surrounded by a beautiful park when Bishop Pococke, the eighteenth-century counterpart to Celia Fiennes, saw Eywood on his travels in September 1756: 'We then passed by Haywood, where Ld Oxford has a large house and a fine lawn, with a beautiful piece of water and great woods on the hill over it'.[9]

Certainly, by 1795, there were three pools at Eywood, and today there are two: the Garden Pool to the south of the house site and the larger Titley Pool to the east. The park is also surrounded by great tracts of

3 The ruins of Eywood, where Lord Byron pursued Lady Oxford, stand in rough pasture surrounded by remnants of eighteenth- and nineteenth-century planting

woodland, principally Garden Wood by the Pool and Beech Wood behind the house. Sadly, the house, which succeeded Lord Oxford's eighteenth-century mansion in an 1898-1908 remodelling by Oswald Milne, was demolished in 1954, but classical fragments still rear up among the extensive earthworks (3) and the stable court survives, as well as an eighteenth-century brick Dovecote on the ridge behind the house. Other serious Herefordshire losses in the 1950s are Aramstone, Rotherwas, the bones of whose formal gardens survive as earthworks, and Perrystone Court, while Stoke Edith was gutted by fire in 1927, after which its rebuilt shell was erected and then knocked down again.[10] Here there are remnants of extensive gardens and plantations, some of the most important of the latter replanted by the late Andrew Foley and his forester, Bede Howell. In strict garden history terms, however, there can have been no more grievous loss than Uvedale Price's destruction of his grandfather's 'old-fashioned garden'[11] at Foxley, which is shown in an early watercolour by Robert Price (4). This included a 'summer-house', designed by James Gibbs, 'with a luxuriant Virginia creeper growing over it'.[12] Price bitterly

4 Robert Price's 1783 watercolour of Foxley records the house constructed for his father, with its formal garden and a pavilion that was later demolished by Uvedale Price. *Private collection*

regretted this youthful act of wanton vandalism in his 1810 *Essays on the Picturesque*, when he wrote: 'I destroyed it, not from disliking it; on the contrary, it was a sacrifice I made against my own sensations, to the prevailing opinion. I doomed it and all its embellishments, with which I had formed such an early connection, to sudden and total destruction'.[13]

Fortunately, much survives at Eywood, where the landscape is best approached via the Herefordshire Trail, from which there are views up the park; from there two ha-has can be made out in the fields, suggesting a segregation of livestock, and also the remains of a lime avenue, which is clearly shown on the first edition Ordnance Survey map. Closer to the house there are indications of a circular bastioned area with box hedging, probably associated with the Edwardian house, and an earlier shrubbery, which links the gardens with the walled Kitchen Garden across the lane at the back of the house. The stone-edged paths in this deeply yew-shaded area lead to a tunnel under the lane, which is fronted by a classical entrance. The limestone façade and general character of this archway are close in style to an Orangery at Eywood that has, like the house, been demolished, but which was sited at the entrance to the shrubbery path, looking out towards Garden Pool. A watercolour sketch of the building (*colour 2*) suggests that Sir Robert Smirke might have designed both structures between 1806 and 1807, when he was working at the house for the 5th Earl of Oxford.[14]

The four layers of period design at Eywood – the original park, a possible Brownian remodelling, the Regency pleasure grounds and a later Edwardian reshaping of formality around the house – are typical of many sites in the country, and it is only through walking the terrain that such chronological design nuances can be detected. This is an approach where the *Historic Gardens of England* series is distinct from other county guides and gazetteers. Herefordshire already has its own intensely scholarly and informed survey of sites carried out by the local historian David Whitehead.[15] Instead of limiting new scholarship, Whitehead's book has been a positive influence, sending us to sites we might have missed, such as The Vern below Dinmore Hill, where we can now reveal that James Russell followed Percy Cane, working in the mid-twentieth century.

In line with the custom of previous volumes in this series, we have generally omitted the many deer parks identified by Whitehead in order to concentrate specifically on gardens and designed landscapes. For this reason the park and garden of Kentchurch Court, which is included on the English Heritage Register of parks and gardens largely because of its medieval deer park, is absent from this volume. In contrast, Brown's interest in the peripheries of the deer park at Moccas Court, with its outstanding collection of ancient oaks, and the ravishingly located deer park of Brampton Bryan, where ornamental sweet chestnuts stride out in avenues, have demanded our attention. The Brampton Bryan avenues may have been introduced to repair some of the destruction caused by the biblical storm that blew on the night Cromwell died in September 1658 when the park's owner, Sir Edward Harley, lamented Satan's choice of path across his park as he conveyed the Protector's soul to Hell: 'I wish the devil had taken him any other way than through my Park, for not content with doing me all the mischief he could while alive, he has knocked over some of my finest trees in his progress downwards'.[16] The majestically gnarled survivors of these particular avenues recall the twisted ranks of sweet chestnuts in the landscape park at Croft Castle, north-west of Leominster, sadly compromised on our visit by a temporary installation of telegraph poles intended to suggest the masts of a ship. This artwork was constructed in response to the curious geometric matrix of the planting, which might have been a conscious attempt to recreate the battle plan of the Spanish Armada of 1588, with chestnuts grown from seeds salvaged from one of the Spanish ships.[17]

Whitehead's research into over a hundred of the county's more typical deer parks is outside the scope of this volume, but his publication of first edition Ordnance Survey maps and the biographical material he has unearthed has provided us with a firm foundation on which to construct a design aesthetic for the county in all its periods. Whitehead's book is first and foremost a gazetteer, though he has visited many of the sites. This present study is a specific garden history narrative based on primary source archival research and detailed site investigation. It is, of course, one of the delights of such a venture to explore a site like Eywood that might have been ridden over by Lancelot Brown, as he discussed its capabilities with Lord Oxford, or to ferret around in the ruins of the house where Byron stayed and Richard Payne Knight, when he was not philosophising about the savage beauties of mistress Nature, made more corporeal advances towards Jane Harley, the 5th Earl's wife.

1

Castles, tournaments and chivalric display – in search of early gardens

Wigmore Castle · Bronsil Castle · Hampton Court
Holme Lacy · Rotherwas

MEDIEVAL GARDENS ARE ALMOST IMPOSSIBLE TO RETRIEVE UNLESS THEY survive as ghosts in earthworks or have been recorded on early maps or in written accounts. Romanticised images of them in illuminated manuscripts are just that – idealised symbols of the *hortus conclusus* – and should never be taken as true records of what contemporary gardens really looked like.[1] Even where there is cartographic and textual evidence, it usually dates from the Elizabethan period. Consequently, most early chapters on the medieval period in this series begin with an account of late Tudor and Elizabethan gardens, the exceptions being the Duke of Buckingham's two gardens and orchard at Thornbury Castle in Gloucestershire and the wonderfully atmospheric Beckley Park in Oxfordshire, encircled by no fewer than three moats. While Beckley has no early archive, Buckingham's gardens were described in meticulous detail in an inventory of 1521, taken after the Duke had lost his head, and their walled enclosures survive miraculously in the grounds of the present hotel.[2] Such a survival is rare, however; particularly in a war-torn area like the Welsh marches, where castles were built primarily for defensive purposes rather than for courtly display. Such castles might have had privy gardens and certainly productive orchards and, of course, were often supported by deer parks, but their horticultural environs have escaped description. What might, however, offer some clues as to the appearance and function of such features in Herefordshire is the role of the tournament in medieval England, particularly those pageants held at **Wigmore Castle** in the fourteenth century. Royalty is almost always at the forefront of prevailing fashions and medieval Wigmore was impressively regal in its status under Roger Mortimer.

Wigmore Castle was originally founded around 1068 to secure a narrow strip of the Welsh marches between the river Teme to the north and the river Lugg to the south. For a fleeting moment in the fourteenth century the ambitions of one generation of its owners, the Mortimers, transformed it from a border stronghold into a royal court with all the necessary panoply, including a fine designed landscape. The regal rise of Wigmore began in 1304 when Edward Mortimer died of wounds inflicted during a local skirmish and left his Castle with its barns, dovecote, two fishponds and an undistinguished 'garden' to his son, Roger.[3] The next years of Roger Mortimer's life were spent as a ward of Piers Gaveston at the court of Edward I. The two men remained curiously partnered in history, as Gaveston became the lover of Edward II while Mortimer was the adulterous lover of Edward's queen, Isabella.

Gaveston's life was short and violent. He was murdered in 1312 by men acting for the Earl of Lancaster, one of the many nobles antagonised by his manipulation of the King. Gaveston's unofficial position of confidante and favourite was not vacant for long. Hugh Despenser, a hereditary enemy of the Mortimers, stepped in, using his relationship to manoeuvre for the vacant title of Earl of Gloucester. Like Gaveston, Despenser alienated some of the most powerful lords, including Mortimer. Rebellion left Mortimer a prisoner in the Tower, but he escaped to France, returning to Court in 1326 with his mistress Isabella, Queen of England and daughter of the King of France. They landed in Suffolk with 700 mercenaries, forced Edward aside in January 1327 and set up the young Edward III as a puppet king. Isabella was her son's official council, but for the next three years Mortimer pursued his ambition to become the unofficial king of England, making Wigmore a place of courtly entertainment.

In late August 1328 Mortimer celebrated socially advantageous marriages

5 This 1731 engraving of Wigmore Castle shows its close proximity to the Abbey, marked 'Priory', in the Moor below. *University of Bristol Library, Special Collections*

for two of his daughters at Hereford. The presence of the juvenile king Edward transformed his tournament there into a Round Table. The first revival of licensed tournaments, which often included such an evocation of the Arthurian legend, had been established by Edward I to celebrate his victories over the Welsh. Round Tables had been held at Kenilworth and Warwick in 1279, Warwick in 1281, Nefyn in 1284 and Falkirk in 1302.[4] Royal accounts of the period document the transportation of tournament scenery, a canvas tent and pegs and poles from Wigmore; later, four dozen lances were purchased in Hereford, as Mortimer moved on to his second Round Table of the year at Bedford.[5] In 1329 Roger celebrated his elevation to the title of Earl of March with a tournament at Wigmore Castle. Roger took the part of Arthur and Queen Isabella, seated next to him, of Guinevere.[6] Guests were accommodated in the lodging towers, which faced west towards Wales, while the Earl of March looked down from his private chambers at the top of the Castle across the seasonal lake of Wigmore Moor. Even now this valley is dotted with grey pools in winter (*colour 3*), the remnants of a lost glacial lake. The atmospheric ruins of Wigmore's Augustinian Abbey are sited on the northern shoreline and can be seen clearly from the Castle. The Abbey was established around 1172 on land given to the monks by Hugh Mortimer, becoming the family mausoleum where three generations of Mortimers had been buried by the time of Roger's tournament.

Work by Natural England to buttress the Abbey ruins at Wigmore during the last decade has produced a Gothic folly in the garden around what is left of the Abbot's domestic range. The grounds, which include a Cloister Garden divided into quadrants with a statue of St Joan at its centre, and a pyramidal-roofed Summerhouse giving views out across the Moor and to Wigmore Castle, have been created from scratch by an owner whose Mortimer ancestry only came to light when the property was purchased.[7] Rampant climbers are a big feature of this atmospheric garden, perfectly in tune with its medieval complex, and include Rosa Kiftsgate, Paul's Himalayan Musk and Rambling Rector. The owners hope to commission from Clare Austen a rose named Wigmore Abbey to scramble over the newly stabilised Abbey ruins.

When, at the end of the seventeenth century, the antiquary John Aubrey jotted down some initial thoughts for his proposed natural history of Herefordshire, he was still impressed enough by Wigmore Abbey and the Mortimers to draw parallels with Wilton House and the earls of Pembroke in his published volume on Wiltshire.[8] Similarly, the visual connection between the Castle and Abbey at Wigmore attracted the attention of Samuel and Nathaniel Buck when they included the Abbey in the engraving of the Castle for their *Antiquities* (5). It was also noted by local artist James Wathen when he painted the scene in 1796.[9] Both images record the Castle much as it is today, but with more of the lower bailey towers surviving; the Abbey, marked 'Priory' in the Bucks' view, can be seen to the north in the distance. In the fourteenth century the transient glacial pools of the Moor would have provided an aesthetic touch to a medieval landscape of power and status that combined heavenly, temporal and regal power. The solemn force of this landscape composition was lightened, not only by the tournament, but also by the exuberant hunting which Mortimer offered his guests in the recently created 'park next to Wigmore castle containing about 300 acres in which there are about 100 fallow deer, bucks and hinds'.[10] One deer park was close by the Castle, with a deer pasture to the east, while another was at nearby Gatley Park.[11] Nineteenth-century field names such as Great Lawns and Little Lawns indicate the original function of the enclosures for assembling and feeding the deer. Yet only a year after the Wigmore tournament, all was lost, as Mortimer was implicated in the murder of the young Edward III, found guilty of treason, stripped of his estates and hanged at Tyburn.

It is interesting to speculate as to what garden and landscape features might have been created as backdrops to these tournaments and where in the environs of Wigmore Castle these pageants might have been held. What is clear on approaching the Castle from Wigmore village is that the fortification is built almost precariously on a narrow ridge above the plain. The pathway by the gaunt parish church extends along the side of a level field, which must have been the outer bailey of the Castle, and then rises up to the double ditch of the moat and the curtain walls, or what is left of them, with the gatehouse beyond. An English Heritage notice-board displays an illustration of the 1731 Samuel & Nathaniel Buck engraving of the site, stating that this is how Wigmore appeared in the early twelfth century, when it is quite obviously how it looked in 1731. The Buck view records the Castle much as it is today but, like the Wathen watercolour, with more of the inner bailey walls surviving. The notice has another misleading strapline: 'A romantic garden on a Herefordshire hilltop'. Presumably this means the wild garden that has grown up around the ruins. Wigmore Castle certainly has 'spectacular views of the surrounding countryside' and is 'a haven of native birds, plants, and animals', two other claims on the board. The terrain between the inner bailey behind the walls and the keep above is far too steep for any significant privy garden to have been laid out. This suggests that the garden mentioned in the early fourteenth century was a productive area located in the outer bailey or beyond, where it is known that, as well as the deer parks, there were fishponds, a dovecote and a rabbit warren.[12] It is just conceivable that a pleasance might have been constructed on the flat fields in the vale below the Castle near to where the tournaments were held, but there is no surviving record of one.

The staging of medieval tournaments required several miles of open countryside where knights could ambush and sortie in the mêlée, which was a free-for-all combat, initially conducted on horseback and then on foot, with hand-to-hand fighting. Interestingly, in view of Wigmore's role in such pageants, according to the antiquary William Dugdale, the first English casualty in the sport was Hugh Mortimer, who was killed at Worcester during King Stephen's reign.[13] Another element of the tournament was the joust, which took place in paled or roped-off lists backed by portable scenery and commanded by temporary grandstands and tents, in which the courtiers would be dressed for battle and also take refreshment. What is clear is that all this activity must have taken place in the vale, which may have been made artificially more picturesque by the damming of the Teme at Burrington Bridge to the north-east, thereby increasing the water in the Moor close to the Castle. It is known that the Earl of Leicester's castle at Kenilworth in Warwickshire was similarly dramatised by water, where the great Mere surrounded it on three sides. The original approach to Bodiam Castle in Sussex is now also proven to have been via a causeway across a lake.[14] The spectacle of jousting knights silhouetted against the backdrop of shimmering water, with Wigmore Castle rising above, must have looked like an illustration out of Froissart's *Chronicles.*

While the moats at Wigmore are now dried up, and there is little surviving on the ground to indicate the presence of a medieval garden, the atmospheric earthworks at **Bronsil Castle**, in the landscape of Eastnor Castle near Ledbury, are far more rewarding. The 1731 Buck engraving of the south-west view of the Castle (*6*) and its inscription reveal that the quadrangular fortification was 'encompass'd by a Double Ditch', the earthworks and watery moats of which survive on the site today.[15] The engraving clearly shows a grass walk extending around three sides of the

Castle, which is confirmed by two later maps by Edward Moore of 1726 and J Davis of 1808.[16] The Moore survey, drawn up for Thomas Reed, shows the double moats fed by a stream that enters the estate from the north-east and is developed by damming into a small tributary heading due north to create two large ponds; one of these remains today.

The hedged fields close to the Castle have names which indicate arable productivity, but two to the south-east are marked 'Park Field' and 'The Park', suggesting they were deer enclosures, and one to the far north-east on the perimeter just below the Malvern Hills is named 'The Old Orchard'. It is known that in September 1460, two months after he had been defeated at Northampton in the War of the Roses, Henry VI granted Richard Beauchamp a royal licence to impark 200 acres of meadow, 500 acres of pasture and 600 acres of wood at 'Estenore'. Beauchamp was also granted leave to 'build a tower in the said park of stone and mortar, and to crenellate, embattle, and provide with turrets and machicolations the said tower, and to make deer leaps in the said park at his will'.[17] Despite the continuing national unrest, Beauchamp chose the sheltered slopes below the Iron Age fort on the summit of Midsummer Hill for what John Leland would describe in the sixteenth century as 'a castelle having fair towrres' that occupied 'the clyving of an hille'.[18] The enclosures marked on the Moore map will be the surviving vestiges of Beauchamp's fifteenth-century deer park.

At this point in the early eighteenth century Bronsil was already ruinous and presumably uninhabited; there is no sign of any ornamental garden. Interestingly, the later Davis map (7) shows the recently built U-shaped domestic complex, which survives today facing the causeway bridge over the moat, with its own hedged garden taken out of the 'Mowing grove and orchard'. While the regimented trees lining the moats on the map have all now grown wild and are interspersed with Victorian rhododendrons, the northern arm has a yew walk about twenty feet wide. This is the clearest sign that the grass between the moats was used for promenades; more than that cannot be ventured.

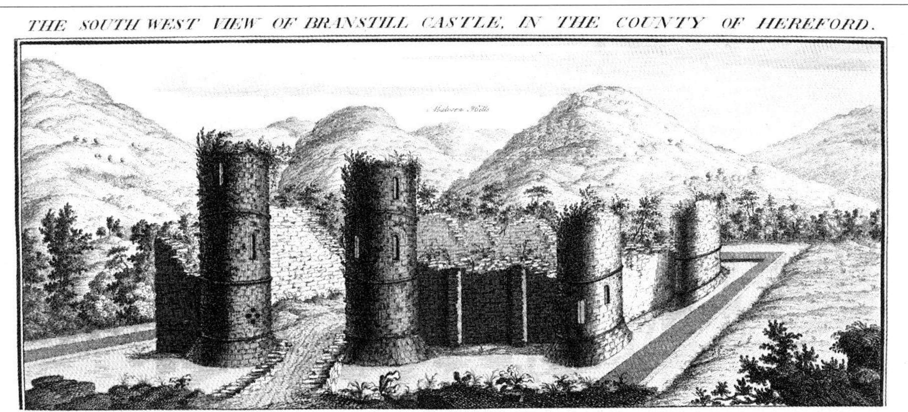

6 The raised grass bank between the moats at Bronsil Castle is likely to have been used for promenading. *University of Bristol, Special Collections*

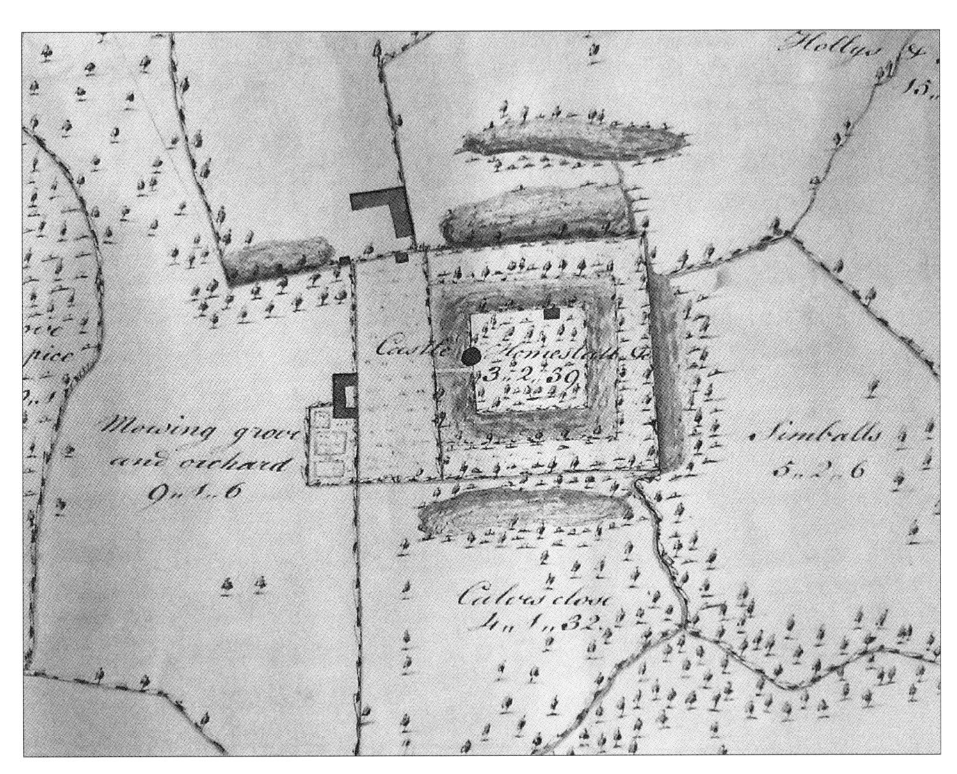

7 Regular tree planting around the moat at Bronsil suggests that the Castle was being treated as a picturesque incident in the landscape when it was surveyed by J Davis in 1808. *Kind permission of Mr James Hervey-Bathurst*

The third site in this early period is equally tantalising, though there are clues in a portrait of Sir Thomas Coningsby, which is thought to have been painted in 1572 by George Gower, and another by Thomas Bate of about 1692, of a later Lord Coningsby. Both canvases have landscapes in the background, Gower's enlivened by a sketch of a river with an arched bridge and towers. Bate has his sitter, attended by his pair of greyhounds, reclining under a tree in a coppice with an oriental poppy growing out of the bank. At least two-thirds of the painting is treated as a landscape with, in the distance, a towered house surrounded by a walled enclosure. The house, with its attendant buildings, is recognisably **Hampton Court**, just outside Leominster, the grounds of which were to be remodelled by Lord Coningsby after 1692 into one of the most extensive and spectacular water gardens in the county. Leonard Knyff recorded this great reshaping in two beautiful oil paintings, one of 1699 and the other undated, and, as a consequence of these and the vast scale of the works, most commentators on the site concentrate on this important formal garden phase at Hampton.[19] However, it might be that some elements of the layout were developed from an existing Elizabethan garden created by Sir Thomas Coningsby on his return from a 1573 visit to Italy with the poet Sir Philip Sidney, whose cousin, Philippa Fitzwilliam, Coningsby was later to marry. That this is likely is suggested both by the Bate painting, which shows Hampton before its remodelling, and the presence of an ornamental fountain (*8*) in 'Hampton Court square', drawn in 1684 by Thomas Dingley for his *History from Marble*, which was later published by the Camden Society in 1867.

It can be safely assumed that Gower's portrait (*colour 4*) of the dashing Thomas Coningsby was painted to mark his coming of age, as the inscription records that he was 21 in 1572. He is engaged in the sport of falconry, with a falcon's hood in his left hand, while in his right he swings a lure to attract the bird, which Gower has painted hovering overhead. The vignette in the distant background probably represents the capital, with the gabled houses of old London Bridge set against a backdrop of church

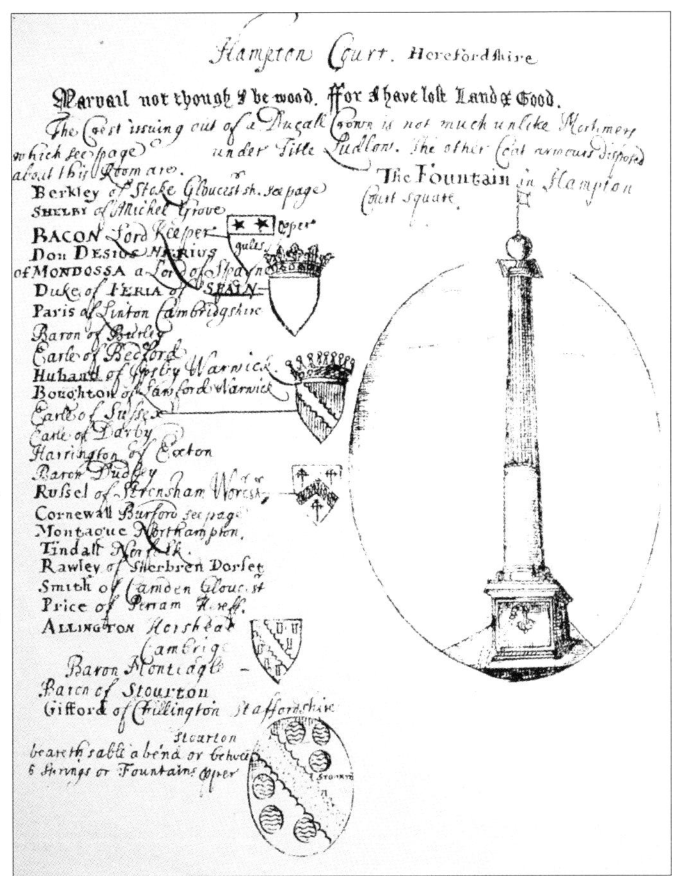

8

For his 1684 *History from Marble*, Thomas Dingley drew the Elizabethan courtyard fountain at Hampton Court.
Reproduced by permission of Herefordshire Record Office

towers. Gower, who was appointed Serjeant Painter to Queen Elizabeth in 1581, lived in the parish of St Clement Dane's at this time.[20] The London setting puts the young Coningsby firmly in the Court milieu, enjoying an elitist sport, something which at least one contemporary account of his character confirms:

> A person of great estate and of a temper equal to his fortune he was liberal without extravagance reserv'd without moroseness a great master of Economy hating luxury and avarice with equal violence his house or let us call it a colledge was full of the sons of Gentlemen who at his expence were instructed in the arts of Riding fencing and other manly exercises nor was Sir Thomas wanting to instruct them in the proudest methods of living being pleased to make them his companions.[21]

This sounds as if, like the Duke of Newcastle at Bolsover Castle in Derbyshire, Thomas Coningsby was more likely to have built a riding school than spent lavishly on an elaborate garden. However, his fountain in 'Hampton Court square', closely modelled on a contemporary example at the royal palace of Nonsuch, and which was presumably sited in a courtyard of the house, suggests that he may have indulged in garden making.[22] Both fountains were constructed of columns surmounted by ball finials; the one at Hampton is shown in the drawing with a spout emitting water from the plinth. Moreover, Coningsby was later described as 'an Italianate knave', a term of derision in the sixteenth century for someone returning from the Grand Tour with the fixation that nothing at home could live up to Italy.[23]

Certainly Coningsby shared the interests of his Herefordshire contemporary Sir John Scudamore of **Holme Lacy**, who was a keen horseman and a man of culture, and of Sir John's son, Sir James Scudamore. Both men were influential members of Elizabeth's Court. Holme Lacy was described at the time as 'not onlie an Academia, but even the verie Courte of a Prince'.[24] Unfortunately, it is not known whether the brick house that Sir John's grandfather had built in the 1540s had a significant garden. Nothing is known of the grounds until Sir James' eldest son John, who was to become 1st Viscount Scudamore in 1628, inherited in the 1620s.[25] However, given Sir John's chivalric and cultural interests, and particularly those of his son Sir James, it is likely that Holme Lacy had an elaborate Elizabethan layout. Like Coningsby, Sir James attached himself to Sir Philip Sidney and became a great courtier knight at the Elizabethan tilts held every year on 17 November to mark the Queen's Accession Day. He is said to have been the model for Scudamore in Edmund Spenser's *Faerie Queene* and was eulogised by George Peele in his 1595 poem *Anglorum feriae*:

> L'escu d'amour, *the arms of loyalty*
> *Lodg'd Skydmore in his heart; and on he came,*
> *And well and worthily demeaned himself*

In that day's service: short and plain to be,
No Lord nor knight more foreard than was he.[26]

As JC Loudon was to write much later in his 1822 *Encyclopaedia of Gardening* when describing 'the old garden' at Holme Lacy, the name Scudamore was still associated with the Elizabethan pun, 'Escuedamors, Ecuyer d'Amours, squire or assistant in love matters'.[27] By this time the family had retreated to their Kentchurch Court estate on the river Monnow, where there once hung a striking portrait of Sir James. He stands in a woodland clearing emblazoned in a Greenwich suit of armour, his jousting lance in his hand ready for a tilt.[28] It is not known whether the parkland setting is idealised or a real place within the landscape at either Holme Lacy or Kentchurch Court. Sir Roy Strong believes that the romantic sylvan backdrop probably represents Scudamore's idea of himself as a Knight of the Crown, perhaps the Shepherd Knight, a tradition first evolved by his close friend and mentor, Sidney.[29]

The George Gower portrait of Thomas Coningsby also offers an emblematic view in a notional landscape, but the later Bate portrait of Lord Coningsby is a conscious attempt to place the nobleman within his own demesne (*colour 5*). As such, it is a remarkably prescient painting, for this approach was not generally current until at least the 1740s, when artists such as Arthur Devis began to exploit the new fashion for portraits of owners and families painted as they relaxed at leisure in their estates.[30] The view of the house is taken from the ridge to the north-east, on the north side of the present A417, in what was originally the Hampton deer park; it is marked as such on the 1889 Ordnance Survey map. It shows the north elevation of the Court with its central, keep-like tower commanding ranges of service buildings, both gabled and turreted, fronted by a walled enclosure punctuated by gate piers. The detail is too indistinct to allow a faithful analysis of exactly what existed in garden terms on this north side of the house in 1692, but it roughly approximates to the Kip and Knyff engraving of that sector in the 1707 *Britannia Illustrata*, though much altered owing to the recent formalising of the grounds.

One last early site in the county invites yet more speculation. This is a forlorn place at Dinedor beside a soulless conjunction of roundabouts and light industry, a petrol station where one obtains the key for the chapel, and a sewage treatment works. This is what is left of **Rotherwas House**, once an impressive brick and timber-framed building, which was replaced in the 1730s by an eleven-bay, classical block designed by James Gibbs; the house was gutted in 1913 and subsequently demolished in 1926.[31] This left a long, narrow rectangular site parallel to the surviving stable block and chapel, which is clearly visible in aerial photographs (9). Visible too is the original medieval fishpond, since turned into a small lake, which veers off from the gravel track towards the sewage works.

The stables give some idea of the grandeur of Gibbs' lost house, but it is the chapel that offers a clue as to who lived at Rotherwas in the sixteenth century and who might, therefore, have laid out the garden whose earthworks are still discernible from the air. The chapel interior is chalky white, with fine late-Victorian fittings by Edward Welby Pugin. These include a stained glass window of St Winifred levitating above her holy well in Flintshire with Sir Roger de Bodenham, clad in chivalric armour, giving obeisance on one knee. The inscription reads: 'Dedicated to St Winifred in thanksgiving for the recovery of Sir Roger de Bodenham at Holywell where he found health for Soul & body alike & after a short infidelity returned to the Church of Christ'. His health cure visit was in 1606, long after he had built the chapel upon inheriting the property in 1583; a tie-beam in the roof has the date 1589.

Bodenham added a stone range to the existing timber-framed mansion in which was the 'fair Parlour ful of Coats of Arms' seen by Thomas Blount in the 1670s.[32] Part of this room, now known as the Rotherwas Room, has been recreated at the Mead Art Museum, Amherst College, Massachusetts.[33] This is panelled in walnut with an ornately carved Jacobean chimneypiece. Blount also writes of a 'fair gatehouse of Brick' near the 'now disused' chapel, which suggests that the original mansion

9 This aerial view of Rotherwas shows the platform of the lost house and its attendant garden. Stylistically, the formal layout could be Elizabethan, but is more likely to date from the early eighteenth century. *Woolhope Naturalists Field Club. Photo: Chris Musson*

had courtyards like Hampton.[34] It is likely, therefore, that Bodenham's Rotherwas had an ornamental garden laid out roughly in the area now defined by the surviving earthworks. Blount described Rotherwas as 'a delicious seat...abounding with store of excellent fruit...having also a Park within less than half a myle of the House, where there is a neat Lodge, upon a Hill, which oerlooks the whole County adjacent'.[35] The park was on the northern part of Dinedor Hill, now called Rotherwas Park Wood. So Rotherwas had all the attributes of a landed estate, but are the earthworks the remains of an Elizabethan garden, or those of a formal layout of the late seventeenth century, or perhaps one associated with the 1730s Gibbs house?

A seventeenth-century dating can be challenged, as the estate suffered badly in the Civil War, leaving most of the buildings derelict. The family's fortunes did not revive until Charles Bodenham rebuilt the house in the

1730s, though in 1715 a long avenue of oaks was planted to the north of the house as a memorial to the Stuarts. An Elizabethan dating was put forward in the Ancient Monument Schedule entry compiled for English Heritage in 1996:

> Starting some 125m from the foundations of its NE face, are the earthwork remains of the formal gardens which were probably created to complement Sir Roger's improvements to the old house in the 16th century. The symmetrical layout of the surviving earthworks is typical of the gardens of this period, which would have comprised geometric design of paths and flower beds. The earthwork remains include a terrace which extends across the NE face of the brick mansion, and probably bore the same relationship to the NE face of the early post-medieval house.

The outline of these features can be traced below the long grass when walking the site, but they could be indicators of a sunken garden of the 1730s in that stripped-down geometric style deployed by John Vanbrugh and Charles Bridgeman, with both of whom Gibbs is known to have collaborated. The Schedule entry provides further evidence, as it is couched, of Elizabethan prospect mounts: 'The northern corners of the formal gardens are marked by the remains of two earthen prospect mounds, both 5m in diameter and up to 0.5m high, which may have been surmounted by gazebos providing views back across the garden to the house'. Again, such mounts were a feature of Elizabethan gardens, but they were often used by Bridgeman to dramatise flat landscapes, such as that at Eastbury in Dorset.[36] The one surviving mound is a vestigial tump planted with an ash tree from which, parallel to the brick wall of the Kitchen Garden, a yew avenue extends. The presence of a formal canal on the north-western perimeter of the layout is perhaps the most telling clue to the date of the earthworks. This canal is fed by the fishpond and may well represent an element of what was once a water garden like that at Hampton Court, but of early-eighteenth-century date. Without the evidence of 'an

Elizabethan gate belonging to the earlier garden layout', which was re-sited in the brick wall of the Kitchen Garden, but has since disappeared, there is nothing on the site to suggest that the earthworks are other than a typical garden laid out to complement the Gibbs mansion. If so, we have strayed, chronologically, into the garden phase that will be discussed in the following chapter.

2

Harnessed water, formality and earnest husbandry – seventeenth-century gardens

Croft Castle · Holme Lacy · Caradoc Court · Homme House
Brampton Bryan Hall · Backbury · Hall Court · Newcourt
Wharton Court · Mainstone Court · Moor Court
Court of Noke · Stoke Edith · Hampton Court

HEREFORDSHIRE HAS LITTLE IN THE WAY OF SURVIVING FEATURES OF Jacobean or Caroline gardens, unless one views the earthworks to the south of **Croft Castle** with the eye of faith, as does the English Heritage Register entry, and pronounce them to be 'traces of formal gardens predating the mid C18 alterations'. They may well be coeval with the planting of the great sweet chestnut avenue in the park, but even the date of that is conjectural: either 1620s, Commonwealth, or 1680s; and there is no garden plan of Croft prior to the eighteenth century. There is also no record of the Elizabethan gardens at **Holme Lacy**, and those that succeeded them in the 1630s were, in their turn, eclipsed by the Battle Garden, which is most likely to have been created in the early eighteenth century. However, the 1st Viscount's Caroline garden at Holme Lacy is well documented in the archival, if not in the visual, record, so the features of its layout are known, even if we cannot be precise about where they were on the ground. In one element at least it was significant. In a county that would be at the forefront of Picturesque aesthetics in the next century, the garden reveals an early appreciation of views of the Wye, which meanders in great sweeping arcs due east of the house and doubles back around the parish of Holme Lacy to the north. This orientation helps to identify the location of the tree-lined walk from 'ye bowling green to ye Wye', whose hollows were being repaired in September 1641.[1]

Sir James Scudamore died in 1619, to be succeeded by John, who was created a baronet in 1620. Thereafter, he retired from Court life to Caradoc Court and to Holme Lacy, where he began to plant apple orchards and is said to have introduced the Redstreak variety from the Continent, called by John Philips in his 1708 Cyder, 'the Scudamorean plant'.[2] In 1628 Sir John was made 1st Viscount Sligo in the Irish peerage and soon after began to make improvements to the grounds around the Tudor courtyard house. Fortunately, the 1st Viscount's steward's accounts survive and give a fairly detailed narrative of the work at Holme Lacy. 1632 seems to have been a key year, when the surroundings and the water supply were improved. There was expenditure on 'building the wood house', the 'Terras walke', 'building in the garden', and a sum of money spent in respect of the 'boulinge green'.[3] By 1634 a tourist described Holme Lacy as 'sweetly seated on the hanging of a hill, ascending on the river Wye and curiously wooded'.[4] In 1637 it took three days to clip the hedges surrounding the bowling green, and in June of the same year a mason repaired the banqueting house.[5] Work continued on the bowling green environs and the gravel walks until Scudamore, who was a Royalist, was taken prisoner when the Parliamentarians seized Hereford in 1643; he was subsequently held under house arrest in his London residence at Petty France for four years.

When Scudamore's grandson John, the 2nd Viscount, rebuilt Holme Lacy after 1674 he instructed his mason to utilise both the foundations and the materials of the old house.[6] Seventeenth-century accounts record this as a double courtyard building entered by a great gatehouse and adjoining porter's lodge, the outer court lined with service buildings.[7] Holme Lacy was enclosed in an oval-paled deer park, which is shown on John Speed's 1610 map of the county and on later eighteenth-century maps, particularly one surveyed by Richard and Charles Frizell in 1771.[8] This latter marks the enclosure as 'Homlacy Demesne and Deer-park', with the park extending to a paled fence to the south. Closer to the house

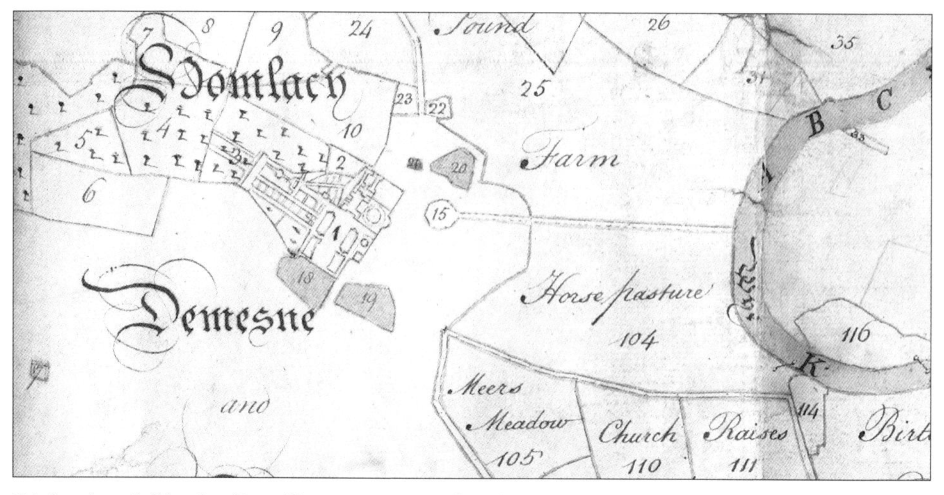

10 Richard and Charles Frizell's 1771 survey of Holme Lacy marks the early-seventeenth-century Bowling Green, with its tree-lined walk leading to the Wye. It also shows the quadrant beds by the house in the area now known as the Battle Garden.
©The British Library Board Add MS 36307 G24

and the formal gardens around it are four ponds and, within the deer park, an octagonal feature marked '15' with a long axial walk leading straight down to the Wye (*10*). This must be the early seventeenth-century bowling green, whose siting within the deer enclosure explains several entries in the accounts, not only for the clipping of protective hedges, but for its paling by Roger Simons in April 1640.[9]

During 1640 the 'allys' were being regularly mown and Simons was commissioned to make garden seats in August 1642.[10] The prevalence of seats for views of the river raises the possibility that Scudamore, or perhaps his son James, laid out a viewing terrace at **Caradoc Court**, near Sellack due south of Holme Lacy, which is perched high above another great arc of the Wye. Little survives of the early house at Caradoc, but overlooking the escarpment there is a pair of seating niches; yet another instance of the growing appreciation for outward-looking views in a period more characteristic of internal vistas within enclosures. This is borne out in part by contemporary wall paintings of rural scenes that decorated the Court before they were destroyed in a fire.[11] One of these landscape friezes in the attic appeared to be a prospect taken from the house, looking north across the Wye to Kings Caple; the very same view that opened up from the niche seats before the scrub grew up from the escarpment and obliterated it.[12]

David Whitehead has deduced from the Holme Lacy accounts that there were three garden enclosures around the 1st Viscount's house: the Great Garden, 'my Lady's Garden', and the Kitchen Garden.[13] These were enclosed by brick walls, with doors for entry, and had walks of grass, gravel and pounded brick laid out in them; fruit trees and vines were grown up the walls, tended by the gardener Brake. Further out in the immediate environs hawthorn hedges were being planted to line the walks. Some of these hedges must have acted as windbreaks, for in April 1640 Brake was 'staking the high hedges'.[14] This would seem to be an early instance of pleaching. The two ornamental enclosures are likely to have been constructed on the south, where the earthworks of the Battle Garden survive today. A note in the accounts for repair work on the house during 1640, when the brick walls were being buttressed and underpinned with stone, provides a clue to the possible location of the banqueting house, which is also mentioned as in need of repair in 1637.[15] To the east of the present Battle Garden, at the south-eastern corner of the ornamental gardens where they connect with the open countryside, is a stretch of brick walling from which projects the base of a building. This has a plinth course of large squared sandstone blocks with brick above. A pyramidal-roofed summerhouse is shown in this location on an engraving published in 1786 in the *European Magazine*, suggesting that the 2nd Viscount may have used the foundations of his grandfather's banqueting house for his own summerhouse. This banqueting house gave views out north and east over the two pools, the deer park and the ridge along which the approach to the house ran before the nineteenth century.

The last feature at Holme Lacy to receive attention in the accounts was a new bridge across a stream in the rabbit warren, which the Frizell map marks as 'Connygar Farm' to the north-west of the deer park. This was being constructed in July 1643, soon after Sir William Waller had captured Hereford for Parliament. The 1st Viscount, who was absent in London, complained that Waller had allowed the woodlands to be wasted, and his wife later petitioned Waller that no more trees should be felled. She had been given assurances that the house would not be slighted, but a tower had been pulled down 'in regard itt might have been some annoyance to the workes'.[16] This refers to the defensive earthworks that had been raised and, in so doing, had destroyed most of the early seventeenth-century gardens. The bowling green must have survived because it was sufficiently far enough away from the house in the deer park.

Robert Whittesley's 1729 survey of part of the manor and park at Holme Lacy marks an octagonal summerhouse at the point where the bowling green enclosure enters the tree avenue.[17] The summerhouse had gone by 1771, for it is not shown on the Frizell map. Whitehead has located the sandstone footings of the building and believes it to have been a timber-framed structure built on a stone base. It is significant that the same sandstone blocks are present in the foundations of the remains of the banqueting house near the Battle Garden. He has also speculated that the undercroft may have been used as an ice house, as it is fairly close to one of the ponds in the park. The 1st Viscount built another structure somewhere else in the park that is referred to in the accounts, which may have been a practical building in which cider was stored. In 1681 the traveller Thomas Baskerville mentioned cider being kept in 'rare contrived cellars', which were cooled by springs to keep the liquor at an even temperature.[18]

There is an intriguing possibility that the bowling green summerhouse may have been coeval with another, very similar structure at **Homme House**, not far away to the east at Much Marcle. This is thought to be a sixteenth-century pigeon house which was later converted into a summerhouse and gazebo; it once commanded a field marked on early maps as 'Pigeon House Field', but is now located in the corner of a walled garden to the west of the house. Although its first appearance on a map is in 1797, a banqueting house is mentioned in accounts for the house in 1686.[19] If it is contemporary with the building in the park at Holme Lacy, then the

11

Recent tree felling has revealed the Gazebo at Homme House to travellers on the A449. Although it is sited in a productive walled garden, it was probably used as a banqueting pavilion

Gazebo was probably raised by Sir John Kyrle, who died in 1660.

It is a most curious and beautiful building (*11*). The main block is an octagon to which is attached a pentagonal staircase tower. The ground floor is mostly blind, but lit by simple Gothic-arched windows and oval portholes in the staircase. The upper floor of the octagon, where there is a Tudor-style, five-centred arched fireplace, has an open arcade of sharply pointed arches giving expansive views out to the hump-backed ridge of the Malverns in the distance. All the stylistic features tally with a seventeenth-century dating except the arcade, whose arches seem closer in style to either eighteenth-century Gothick or Arts & Crafts work of the

12 The early-eighteenth-century Battle Garden at Holme Lacy has been converted into a putting green. Might this angular earthwork be a design by Stephen Switzer, the landscape gardener and writer, given that he wrote about the house in 1729?

late nineteenth century. It is, perhaps, no coincidence that one of Gloucestershire's greatest examples of the Arts & Crafts is Randall Wells' 1902-3 St Edward the Confessor, a couple of miles to the east at Kempley. Like William Lethaby's contemporary Herefordshire church at Brockhampton-by-Ross, it deploys severely pointed arches for its windows, which are close in style to Saxon lights.

After the depredations of the Civil War the usual maintenance work continued on the gardens at Holme Lacy until the 1st Viscount died in 1671. He was succeeded by his grandson, another John, who together with his wife, Frances Cecil, set about rebuilding the house in 1674.[20] Whether they remodelled the Caroline garden is unclear. When the Warner hotel group took over the house in 1995 they produced a guidebook which speculates about the origins of the formal gardens, suggesting that John Evelyn may have had some involvement.[21] Or that the royal gardener George London who, as we shall see, was at Stoke Edith in the late 1690s, might have been consulted. The E H Register entry hedges its bets:

> The date of the formal gardens is uncertain; it is unclear whether they were commissioned by the second Viscount Scudamore (1671-97), and if so being an especially early instance of a style of gardening best seen at Hampton Court before 1702 and in the work of Charles Bridgeman (fl 1709-38), or whether they belong to the third Viscount's time (1697-1716) or even a little later.

Given the survival of the bowling green in the park and the foundations of the banqueting house to the south-east of the sunken lawn it is likely that the structure of the gardens, particularly the great south terrace and the cross axes, is Caroline, and that the only significant alterations to them were the construction of the summerhouse on an earlier base and the shaping of the south lawn. It is known that between 1720 and 1725 Alexander Pope, Lord Digby and Allen Bathurst were advising the widowed Viscountess Scudamore on the reshaping of the grounds to a more informal style.[22] She died in 1729 and, judging by the survival of the Battle Garden (*12*), their advice seems not to have been taken. The grass revetments of the sunken lawn, which give it the appearance of a fortification, hence the name Battle Garden, are typical of the early eighteenth century and its obsession with military iconography.[23] The Revd Stebbing Shaw, county historian of Staffordshire, perceived this when he visited Holme Lacy in 1788:

> The gardens to the south front are all in King William's style of fortifications, surrounded by yew hedges, cut in a variety of forms, according to the taste of that time. Some indeed, have suffered to outgrow their original shape and are really beautiful. As there are so few relicks of these sorts of antiquities now remaining, it is a pity not to have the power of such an inspection sometimes, this is certainly a very fit object for that purpose, and will, in all probability, long continue so.[24]

Both John Vanbrugh and Charles Bridgeman regularly deployed this style for lawns and amphitheatres, as at the bowling green at Claremont in Surrey and the Queen's Theatre at Stowe, Buckinghamshire. Stephen Switzer also promoted it in his contemporary *Ichnographia Rustica* and, more practically, in the bastion walk he designed at Grimsthorpe Castle in Lincolnshire. The Battle Garden is, therefore, most likely to have been laid out by the 3rd Viscount before his death in 1716. The raised walk that runs north-south and forms a termination of the formal gardens west of the house has been known from the nineteenth century as the 'Poop Deck'. There is no reason to suggest that it pre-dates the Battle Garden, or that it has anything to do with Evelyn, as the Warner guidebook implies. The Flower Garden to the west with its central pools was laid out on the structure of the Caroline original in the nineteenth century. The yews must date from the early eighteenth century and are shown in their majestic prime in an early *Country Life* article of 1909.[25] The Orangery in this area was probably built in the 1770s as part of a renewal of the estate undertaken by Frances Scudamore and her husband Charles Howard, 11th Duke of Norfolk.[26]

The development of the grounds at Holme Lacy is mirrored by a similar chronology at Brampton Bryan Castle, that now stands in the grounds of **Brampton Bryan Hall**, in the far north-western corner of the county close to the Welsh border. Their respective fortunes in the Civil War are also matched, though at Brampton Bryan the family sympathised with Parliament rather than with the Crown. As a consequence, the Castle (*colour 6*) was besieged by Sir William Vavasour and defended stoutly by Brilliana, Lady Harley, in the absence of her husband, Sir Robert Harley. As at Holme Lacy, where new defensive earthworks obliterated the gardens, the Castle environs at Brampton were also ravaged by military activity. Copious correspondence survives testifying to Brilliana's shrewd tactical defence of her property, and two of the surviving letters between her and Sir John Scudamore reveal that there was a bowling green in the gardens. Brilliana wrote to Scudamore on 23 August 1643 asking that he meet her envoy, a Mr Phillips, 'in the Bowling Green which is a little on this side of the garden', and later, on 5 September: 'Mr. Moor will do me the favour to wait upon you in the Bowling Green, that by him I may receive what you please to make known unto me, for whose safe return I desire the engagement of your promise'.[27] This exchange came after the church, which 'stood directly before the castle gate, within sixty or seventy paces', had been taken by the Cavaliers on 30 July, and later on 22 August 'when the enemy made their approaches nearer us, cast up breast works in our garden and walks, where their rotten and poisoned language annoyed us more than their poisoned bullets'.[28]

After a succession of parleys in the grounds, the siege was lifted when the enemy troops were called away to fight the King at Gloucester. Perhaps as a reaction to all the stress and hardship of the siege, Brilliana 'suddenly and unexpectedly fell sick of an apoplexy with a defluxion of the lungs', and died three days afterwards.[29] Thereafter, Sir Robert claimed for damages and demanded compensation from Parliament for 'Two Parks wholly laid open and destroyed', one of which was that at Brampton.[30] As we have seen, the great sweet chestnut avenue in the park must post-date this depredation, caused in part by the enemy forces in the Civil War, and also later by the great storm of 3 September 1658, which coincided with Oliver Cromwell's death.

Sir Robert died in 1656, to be succeeded by his son Sir Edward Harley and then by Edward's two sons, Edward 'Auditor' Harley and Robert, 1st Earl of Oxford. All three were to direct works to repair both the house and estate during the next 70 years. Sir Edward was raising a new six-bay house alongside the Castle after June 1663 and, together with his sons, laid out new grounds. Correspondence in 1673 concerned seeds for the garden; a stone roller was bought for the old bowling green in 1686; the entrance drive was levelled and gravelled in 1693, when a paling was also erected to keep animals out of the pleasure grounds.[31] This all sounds like necessary remedial works to the Castle gardens, but a later map of 1722, by an unknown surveyor, but which has been attributed to Charles

Bridgeman, reveals an extensive new layout.[32] There is an intriguing letter of 1692 from Robert Harley to his father which mentions George London's visit to Stoke Edith: 'If it were worth so much money he would go over to Brampton and see the situation, and could make a draught of what he thought the place capable of'.[33]

The 1722 map (*colour 7*) is a survey of how the gardens looked at that time, not a design for a new layout. So at some point between the 1693 letter and 1722, the grounds had undergone a complete reshaping. If this was carried out in the 1690s, Sir Edward would have supervised its construction. He died in 1700 and, although both of his sons – Edward 'Auditor' and Robert – were engaged in looking after the estate after their father's death, Robert was the eldest by three years and it is likely that he would have taken the lead. Robert, by that time 1st Earl of Oxford, died in 1724, just two years after the survey was taken; his brother outlived him until 1735. The ODNB entry for Sir Edward Harley, written originally by Gordon Goodwin and later revised by David Whitehead, states categorically that Harley 'took considerable pains to establish a fine garden adjoining his new house'. On balance, the layout is therefore likely to be pre-1700, when London is known to have been in the county. It is a fairly simple scheme, retaining the seventeenth-century bowling green to the east of the Castle, where the Kitchen Garden is today, but introducing a T-shaped canal, the northern arm of which crosses the walled orchard. This is developed from the Teme in a stream, which enters the pleasure grounds at the 'place behind the house' and terminates in a dovecote. The gravelled entrance drive to the house, mentioned earlier, is shown, while a topiary-lined walk cuts obliquely in front of the Castle and its adjoining bowling green. This is clearly visible in the 1731 Buck engraving (*13*) of the Castle in their *Antiquities*.

It may well be that, in addition to the bowling green, the 'lower Garden or Orchard', as it is marked on the survey, was an earlier feature retained in the new works. There are stretches of brickwork in the walls that are laid in English bond with diapers in fired headers, suggestive of a

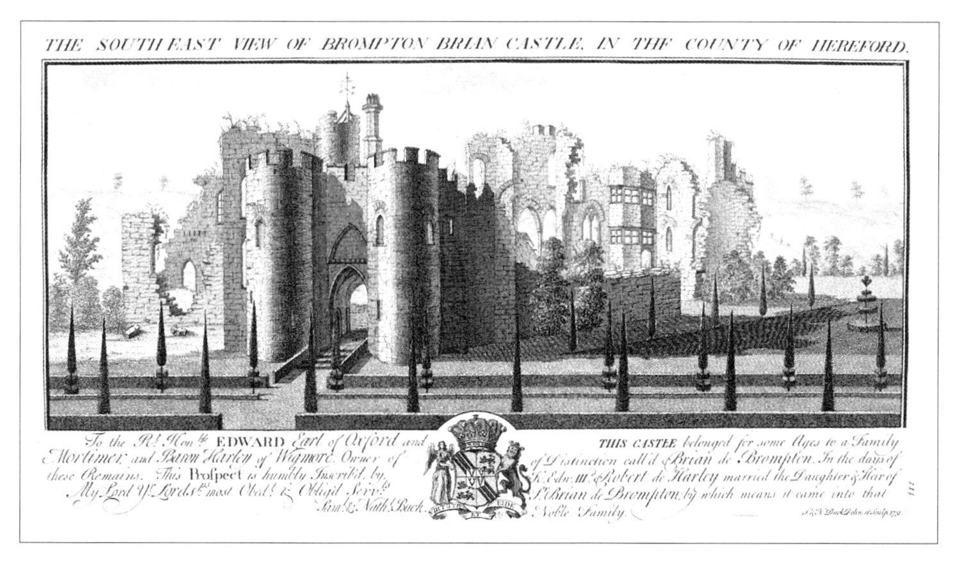

13 This 1731 engraving of Brampton Bryan Castle is reproduced in a stained glass window commemorating Brilliana, Lady Harley, who withheld a siege there in the Civil War. Some yews and a section of raised walkway survive of the formal gardens depicted by the Bucks. *University of Bristol Library, Special Collections*

late sixteenth- or early-seventeenth-century date, rather than the Flemish bond characteristic of the end of the seventeenth century. Sir Edward had an account with a Worcester bookseller, Mr Rae, and in 1657 he bought Ralph Austen's *Treatise on Fruit Trees* (1653).[34] Accounts of 'Wall fruit planted at Brampton' on 6 November 1740 record that the enclosure was still being used productively in the next century.[35] 'The West Wall the end next the bottom of the Canal' was planted with several varieties of pears, while pears, cherries and plums covered the 'East Aspect Wall from the Corner to the Water Gate'. Some of the walls still retain lead fruit labels including 'Large Elruge' and 'Violette Hative', both varieties of nectarines.

We have seen how Sir John Scudamore introduced the Redstreak apple to Holme Lacy, the draught from which was known locally as 'the *Vin de Scudamore*'.[36] This craft of cider making, supported by the careful production of rare fruit varieties, warrants a digression on Hereford's most noted authority on apple growing: John Beale, whose seminal book, *Herefordshire Orchards, A Pattern For all England*, was published in 1657. In the true pansophist spirit of the Commonwealth he dedicated it to 'the sedulous advancer of Ingenious Arts, and Profitable Sciences, And the Principall Contriver of Generall Accommodations, Samuel Hartlib'. Beale was later to produce a lengthy text on fruit trees, which Evelyn included as an appendix – *Pomona* – in his *Sylva* of 1664.[37] Evelyn mentions 'the most excellently learned Mr. Beale' in a footnote to the preface of *Pomona*, though it is clear that almost everything he writes is taken directly from Beale. This is typical of Evelyn, who had already used Beale's evocative description of the landscape around **Backbury**, word for word, for his unpublished manuscript the 'Elysium Britannicum', without giving him any acknowledgement. Beale's self-effacing nature prevented him from claiming the credit due to him in his own lifetime. Even the title page of his own *Herefordshire Orchards* has only the initials 'I B', rather than his full name. Beale's undoubted influence on the circle of correspondents drawn together by Hartlib has only recently been assessed, as has his impact on garden history in Herefordshire.[38] The latter assessment concerns his extraordinary prescience about the scenic value of unadorned Nature and how it might inform our design of gardens and landscapes. Beale had this perception from the top of Backbury Hill at Old Sufton, to which he often retreated to stay with Henry Hereford, a local hermit who lived under the lee of the hill. It will be more instructive to discuss Beale's early advocacy of the God-given beauty of natural landscape in a later chapter on the development of the Picturesque aesthetic. Here, it will be appropriate to consider his more practical devotion to cider-apples in a county of orchards.

Beale delights in the humble pleasure that orchards offer, for both their aesthetic and their productive qualities:

> I need not tell you how all our villages, and generally all our highways (all our vales being thick set with rowes of villages) are in the spring-time sweetened, and beautified with the bloomed trees, which continue their changeable varietyes of Ornaments, till (in the end of Autumn) they fill our Garners with pleasant fruit, and our cellars with rich and winey liquors.[39]

He continues to outline the benefits of orchards which 'do not only sweeten, but also purifie the ambient air, (which I conceive to conduce very much to the constant health and long lives, for which our County hath been alwayes famous:) and for that they fence our habitations and walks from the stroke of winds and storms in the Winter, and afford us shelter & shade in the heat of Summer; and (if I may acknowledge grate-full trifles) for that they harbour a constant aviary of sweet singers'.[40] There follows a digression on soil, apple varieties, grafting and the correct way of orientating and planting out an orchard.

Letters concerning the building of **Hall Court** at Much Marcle and the planting of an orchard there for John Coke survive to confirm that all this was common practice.[41] The house was built between 1608 and 1610 on a site facing the Malverns that was already stocked with orchards, as there are references to 'haying' in the little and long orchards.[42] In January 1609 Coke's wife Marie, who was in charge of progress at the estate, wrote to her husband to inform him that most of the timber frame for the house had been raised, while 'Your new orchard is almost set up with stockes; and on Wednesday I purpose to see the bayberries set'.[43] Letters also record payments to Thomas Gannon for '3 dozen stocks sett at Halecort' and to James Glover for '3 days worke lopping crabtrees at Hallcourt'.[44] The purchase of stocks and grafts feature regularly in the accounts for Hall Court; in 1615 a note was added to the accounts: 'grafted this year 1615 in April Pembroke quinces, King's codlings, Cambridge Piermains, Harvey apples russet & yellow, French pears from Whitchurch, winter queenings, apple quinces, French plumbs from Spring garden at Whitchurch of divers sorts, & pippins from Cambridge'.[45] Hall Court still has its walled garden to the front lane, where in 1610 privet, box and roses were being planted. Today, swathes of geraniums, delphiniums, bleeding heart, catmint, lady's mantle and geums are preferred. To the north of the house the orchard still produces fruit.

After dealing with practical, horticultural matters, Beale goes off on a tangent about patriotism and parkland trees, name-dropping by initials all those Herefordshire squires who have promoted 'the best expediencies of all kinds of Agriculture', including 'The Lord *Scudamore*', who is a 'great preserver of woods against the day of *Englands* need'.[46] 'This is,' Beale argues, 'the Countrey where *Rowland Vaughan* began his Waterworks', yet another of his 'admirable contrivers for the publick good'.[47]

Mention of Rowland Vaughan warrants another short digression on his *Booke*, which was published in 1610, and the layout of his garden around **Newcourt**, near Bacton, just north of Abbey Dore. Sadly, there is nothing left above ground of either house or layout along the drive from the B4347 at Moorhampton Bridge to Newcourt Farm and beyond, but the water meadows on the west side of River Dore between Peterchurch and Bacton give some idea of Vaughan's 'manner of Winter and Summer drowning' of the land to 'make these *grounds* (*especially if they be drye*) more Fertile *Ten for One*. As also a demonstration of a *Project* for the great benefit of the *Common-wealth* generally, but of *Hereford-shire* especially'.[48] This was proudly stated on the title page of Vaughan's 1610 *Booke*, suggesting that the series of sluice gates, weirs and leat – the 'Trench-royall' – was an extremely early, possibly 1590s, revolutionary agricultural irrigation scheme more characteristic of the mid-seventeenth century.[49] While this was an extraordinary land management project, it is neither a designed landscape nor an ornamental garden. However, the 1897 edition of Vaughan's *Booke* is illustrated with a naively drawn representation of Newcourt, presumably taken from a contemporary map (*14*). This shows not only the main courtyard house, with what looks to be a pump in the centre, and attendant buildings such as the 'Slauter House', the 'Mill House', the 'Brew House' and the 'Kitchin', but also the Dore, two tributaries and a walled garden enclosure. This last has productive beds, an elaborate parterre garden with grass walks and two over-scaled pot plants. In a prescient remark from the *Booke*, Vaughan argues that if the whole country adopted his system of drownings, 'it would profit the kingdome in a yeare two Millions: which would maintaine an *army-royall* to the honour of *Great Brittaine*'.[50] Such predictions were not lost on the next

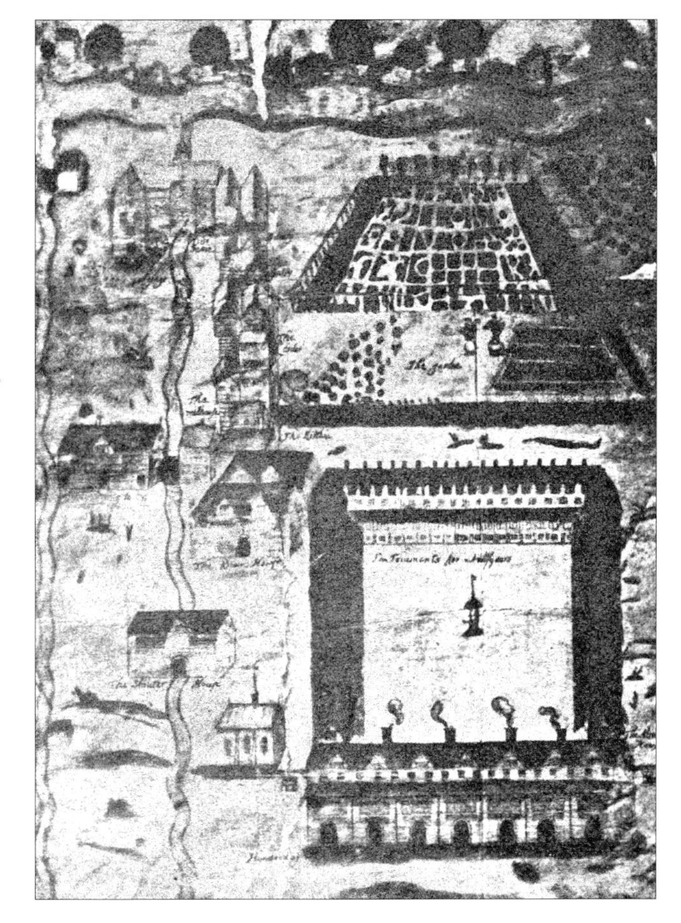

14

Rowland Vaughan's *Booke* of 1610 contained two engravings. One illustrated his complex system of irrigation for agriculture, while the other recorded in a naive style the designed landscape that may once have existed around Newcourt. *Reproduced by permission of Herefordshire Record Office*

generation of improvers, led by Samuel Hartlib, Cressy Dymock, John Blith and, in a Herefordshire context, John Beale.

Water and its harnessing, both for productive and ornamental purposes, is a common theme in Herefordshire and the presence in the county, already noted, of George London has encouraged speculation as to his possible influence on several late-seventeenth-century garden layouts, particularly those that incorporate canals and pools. Before his work at Stoke Edith, which is documented, is discussed, it will be instructive to consider several surviving garden layouts that deploy water, if only to prove that such sites are ubiquitous and are often developed from existing moats. This is the case at Wharton Court, near Leominster, Mainstone Court at the Trumpet crossroads near Ledbury, Moor Court at Pembridge and Court of Noke at Staunton-on-Arrow. Hampton Court, the county's most spectacular water garden, which is very likely to have been inspired by London's practice, will be reserved as the climax to this chapter.

Wharton Court is thought to date from about 1604, but it was rebuilt in 1659, when a porch was added with four stone niche seats decorated with oak sprays, and the tall compact form with its distinctive Commonwealth roofscape was achieved. To the rear there is a romantic moated island, which might have been created in the Commonwealth as both an ornamental and a productive feature, or it might conceivably have been the remains of the original moat of the Jacobean house. The same might be said of the water surrounding **Mainstone Court**, which was originally an Elizabethan house, later rebuilt in about 1820. There the moat has a distinctly regular plan and has been likened by Whitehead to John Harborne's 1620 water garden at Tackley in Oxfordshire, which was illustrated in Gervase Markham's 1623 *Cheap and Good Husbandry*.[51] There is no doubt that these water features were used for keeping and breeding fish, but the canal (*colour 8*) which survives at the demolished **Moor Court** appears to be primarily ornamental and is thought to have been inspired by Dutch practice current at the time. This, however, is a hare that was set running by a visit to the estate by members of the Woolhope Club in 1870. While the Club has done much to chronicle the archaeological, architectural, landscape and garden history of the county, its early reports must be seen as the products of informed local naturalists gripped by the twin late-Victorian passions for geology and conifers. As such, they are important first-hand records, but some of their attributions and suppositions should be treated with scholarly caution. In the case of Moor Court, the Revd Charles Robinson speculated that 'in the canal that runs hard by and the quaint geometrical arrangement of the garden paths there are other indications that Moor Court has once been occupied by some native of the low countries'.[52] Robinson's 1872 account was derived from the earlier visit to the site by the Club, which was principally concerned with the trees on the estate.

The water garden at **Court of Noke** is in another league. It dramatises a beautiful late seventeenth-century, seven-bay brick house with a tall, hipped roof. The setting is idyllic, even when, as on our visit, the moat is drained for repairs (*colour 9*). As with other sites in this chapter, the layout at Court of Noke is difficult to date. In May 1997, Mr and Mrs Edward Bulwer commissioned an archaeological report from Christopher Currie, which was subsequently published by the Woolhope Club.[53] This argues that the canals were likely to have been created by George Mason, who lived there from 1673 to about 1718. A more precise dating within that occupation is probably 1700, when it is known that Mason rebuilt the house and must have reshaped any existing fishponds into the more formal canals to complement his new building. These are first recorded on the 1841 tithe map, which shows the T-shaped canal to the north and east of the house with other canals and ponds parallel to the river Arrow, from which the water is derived. The more precisely angular form of the water courses must post-date the 1840s; the several ponds are shown, united into one continuous canal-like water, on the 1884 Ordnance Survey map.

The development of the new house and great gardens at **Stoke Edith** is far better documented though, unlike Court of Noke, very little survives from this period on this atmospheric site, the 1690s house built by Paul Foley having been destroyed by fire in 1927.[54] The estate is signalled first by a late Palladian lodge, gate piers and railings on the A438 Ledbury to Hereford road, and then, further on at a sharp bend, a great neo-Classical lodge with paired Tuscan Doric columns and a dome (*15*). These are known to have been designed by William Wilkins and built between 1792 and 1796. Between the two lodges, the road leading up to the site of the house passes a railed semicircular-arched well and the Georgian box-like nave of the church, which has been crudely grafted onto a spindly earlier tower with a needle-sharp spire. In the buddleia bushes beyond are the ruins of the service buildings of the lost great house, its central hall one of James Thornhill's greatest triumphs of painted *trompe l'oeil* decoration. High above the ruins a transverse grass terrace, aligned east-west, strikes out south in a rising enclosure, now

15 The Hereford Lodge at Stoke Edith is irreverently, if understandably, nicknamed 'the Cotton Reel'. It is a powerful neo-Classical design of the 1790s by William Wilkins

fenced for rearing game birds. These are the once formal axes of the garden laid out by William Andrews Nesfield after 1853, which will be considered in a later chapter. But what of the original Elizabethan house, Paul Foley's new mansion of the 1690s that replaced it, and George London's impact on the gardens at that time?

The first visual records of the Elizabethan house and grounds are two surveys of Stoke Edith made in 1680 and 1684, both by William Deeley, taken before Foley began to make major improvements to the estate.[55] They are drawn in an engagingly naïve manner and are very similar in their depiction of the estate, though there has been an improvement in the gardens around the house between the two dates. The earlier survey (*16*) records a gabled, five-bay house with two walled forecourts, one gravelled and one green, with a walled orchard to the side commanded by a raised grass terrace on the west and two pyramidal-roofed summerhouses at the eastern corners. The wider landscape is divided into an upper and lower park, an orchard and the 'Knotnol Poole', which survives; there is a

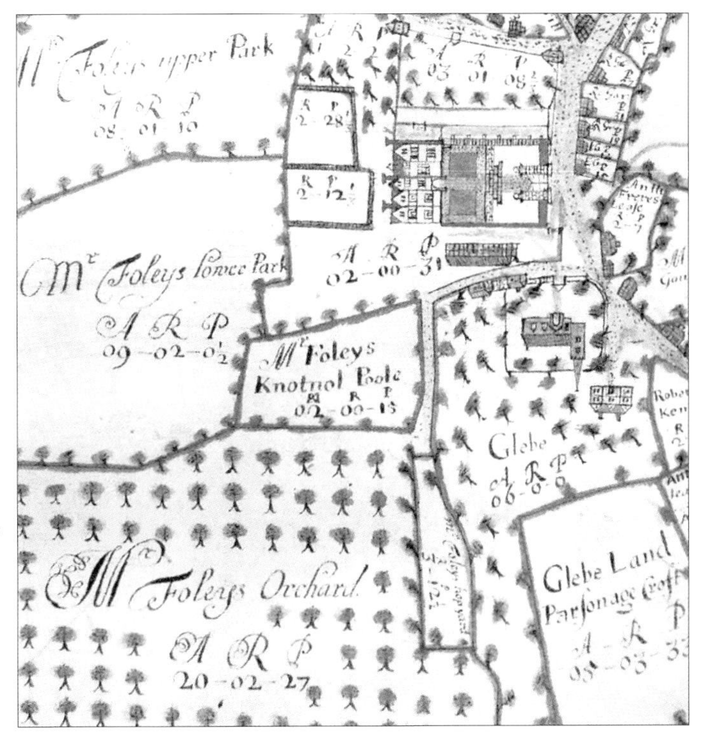

16

A detail from William Deeley's first survey of 1680 of Stoke Edith, carried out for Paul 'Speaker' Foley. It shows the walled formal gardens around the house and the wider parkland beyond.
Private collection

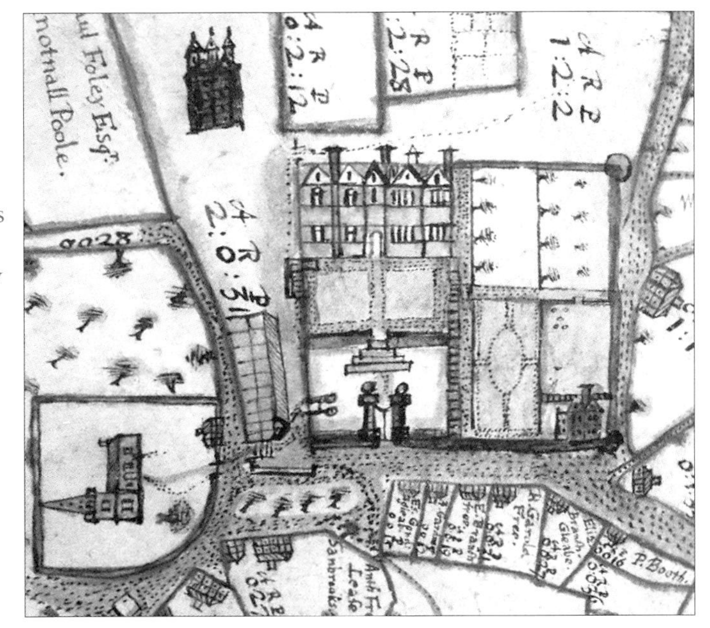

17

Deeley's second survey of 1684 records Paul Foley's improvements around his new house at Stoke. These include a new summerhouse and an extraordinary turreted building in the park.
Private collection

'Conybeare Walk' to the south of the house. On the later survey (*17*) the walled garden has now been divided into four sectors: a simple grass plat with paths, what looks like a bowling green, and a two-part orchard. At the south-east corner there is a substantial gabled summerhouse with a central chimney; the smaller garden building at the north-east corner has disappeared. Most intriguingly, there is another, much taller, gabled building in the park to the north-west, adjacent to the pool, which could be a banqueting house with 'types', or rooftop pavilions for viewing the hunt. Was this an Elizabethan hunting lodge that was omitted from the earlier map, or is it a new structure built between the map dates as part of Paul Foley's drive to remodel his grounds?

Foley seems to have begun his improvements by forming a deer park, which was enclosed by licence in January 1688. Thereafter, the archival record is silent until, as we have seen earlier in connection with Brampton, George London visited Stoke Edith in July 1692. Whether or not Foley followed London's advice, or set about improving to his own design is not known; certainly there are several references in the accounts to London sending a man to Stoke to help supervise the works.[56] Yet, despite their joint efforts, nothing substantial seems to have been achieved when Celia Fiennes visited in, or just before, 1696: 'It's a very good house of Timber worke but old fashion'd and good roome for Gardens but all in an old form and mode, and Mr Folie intends to make both a new house and gardens; the latter I saw staked out, so it will be to no purpose to say any thing of it as its now, only the good Barns and Stables that are now covered with slate, the fine Bowling green walled in and a Summerhouse in it all new'.[57] The new 'Summerhouse' would seem to be the more substantial structure that replaced a smaller building on the 1684 survey. If this is the case then it was hardly new in 1696, which suggests that Fiennes' visit might have been earlier. However, what her letter does prove, unequivocally, is that, by the time of her visit, Foley had remodelled his walled enclosures, but still not embarked on major works in the gardens, nor had he begun to rebuild the main house. He had, however, started planting avenues in the wider parkland.

Foley's steward, Paul Booth, wrote to his employer in 1693, confirming that an elm avenue and a formal terraced garden had been set out. 'Mr London's man' had also instructed Foley's gardener, Robert, in laying out a coniferous walk and 'in the setting of the large firres in their places appointed for them all through the walk, and all the lesser spruce firres, pines and scotch firres within 15 elms length'.[58] Unfortunately this work ground to a halt when soil conditions deteriorated for 'the ground further in the walk was not fit to plant such things in, it being poure cold ground'.[59] A 1766 survey by John Bach done for Paul Foley's great grandson, Thomas, 1st Lord Foley of the second creation, reveals the location of London's avenue.[60] The upper and lower parks were planted with a double avenue of alternating deciduous and coniferous trees known as the Tarrington Walk, the avenue planting described by Booth. It would have complemented the existing tree-lined Coneybeare Walk to the south of the house, which had been made to appear more impressive once the adjacent orchard was grubbed up.

In 1694 ground in the garden was levelled and a basin was created. Booth was also busy calculating the volume of iron, presumably to be supplied from one of Foley's many connections with the industry, required for new railings, as well as the number of bricks for three sides of a walled enclosure.[61] A plan associated with these calculations suggests the bricks were for a new fruit garden, while another indicates that it was to be sited to the north of the house, where the natural slope would enhance growth.[62] Low-growing fruit such as raspberries were to be planted between the more familiar wall fruit of figs, cherries, plums, apricots, sweet almonds, medlars, quince and winter and summer pears. Inside there were hotbeds, a heated melon ground and beds for strawberries, as well as a tool shed that doubled as a storage space for 'roots' whilst an encircling water channel eased the task of watering such a complex.[63] The same labour-saving design had been used at Brampton and was recorded in the survey drawn up for Robert Harley in 1722.[64]

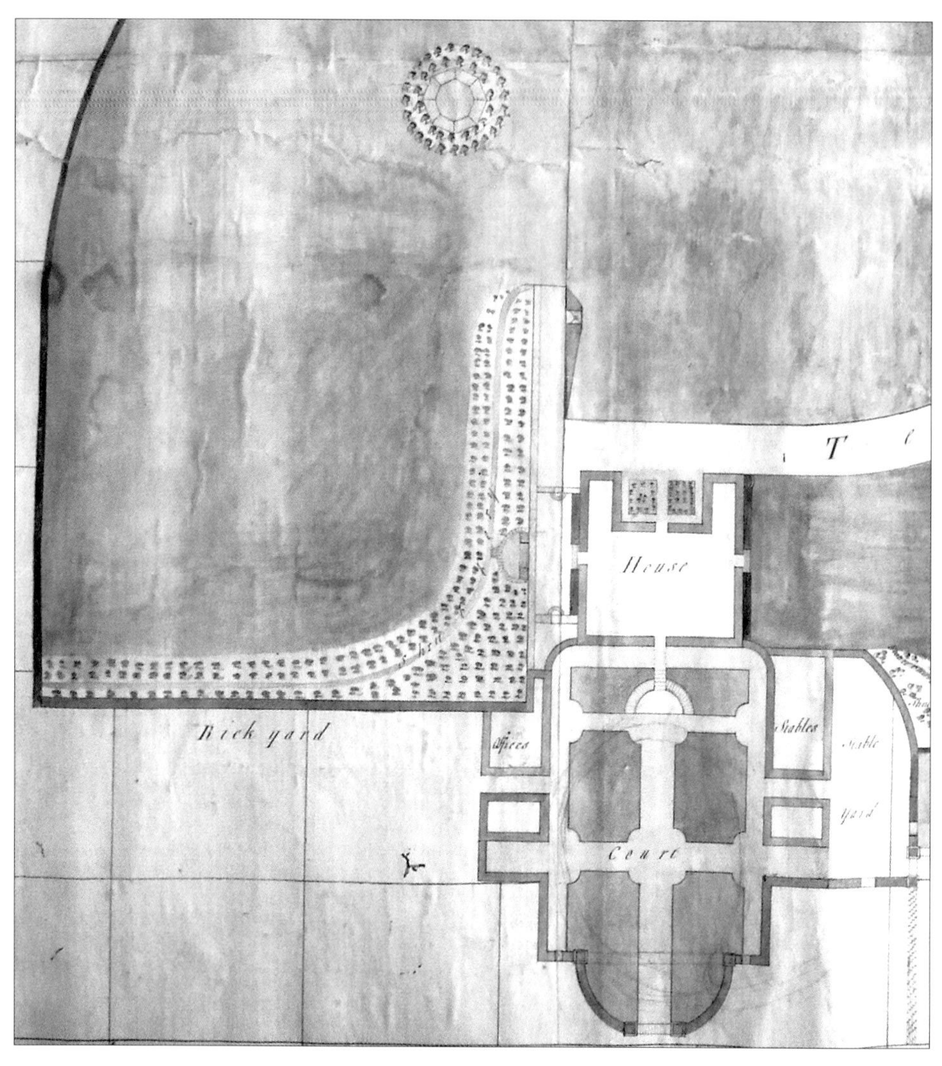

18 In 1766 John Bach produced a survey and also a landscape design for Stoke Edith. The shrubbery in this detail may have been the setting for the scandalous liaison between Lord Peterborough and Lady Ann Foley that prompted the 2nd Lord Foley to petition for divorce in the 1780s. *Private collection*

When Fiennes returned for her second visit in 1698 she found 'to this front [north] which is to be the entrance large opening iron spike gates which lookes into their Grounds and Meddowes below it of a great length with rows of trees to the river [Frome]'.[65] Fiennes made her third and final recorded visit to Stoke a year or two after Foley's unexpected death in 1699 following a fall from his horse. The gardens, which were now accessible from the new house, had taken shape very much as indicated in the undated plan of the walled fruit garden and the pool, and in the later Bach survey and proposal, though by this time there had been attempts to soften the terraced formality (*18*). There was now a much grander descent from the house along

> staires two wayes all iron work and meete halfe way and joyne in the next descent on gravel which is in a halfe moon, and so design'd to be left in a low place with a cascade beneath and the gravel walke and grass walks to go by it and beyond it in many rows of trees, the walled gardens and walks one below another; this terrass gives a vast prospect of the country it being scituated on the ascent of the hill, many rows of trees in meadows below it adds to its beauty, being all within his own ground.[66]

Fiennes also saw a 'fountaine bason just faceing the balcony doore that leads to a terrass paved with black and white marble and iron palisadoes; it has a long space and broad for walking, and two enclosed on each side by same iron work a step up or two these doores from the Ladies closet and the studdy'.[67] In conjunction with these garden works Foley rebuilt the old house, principally between 1695 and 1698, but it was still not finished when Fiennes made her last visit some time between 1701 and 1703. Whitehead's analysis of Booth's cash-book charts the construction with careful precision.[68]

In spite of London and Wise's design predilection for waterworks in general and canals specifically, Stoke seems only to have had the benefit of the basin between the house and the walled fruit garden, and the cascade below the terrace; there were no formal watercourses in the wider grounds, which were simply punctuated by tree avenues. However, London and Wise's signature design was to be achieved in Herefordshire, for which London was paid £80 in 1692,[69] by the 2nd Lord Coningsby at **Hampton Court**, which must rank as the county's most spectacular formal gardens and one of its greatest losses.

Fortunately for posterity, no fewer than three beautiful paintings survive of the great layout, two of about 1699 painted by Leonard Knyff and the other of about 1705 by John Stevens.[70] A little later, in 1707, the two Knyff oils were used to produce an engraving published in Jan Kip and Knyff's *Britannia Illustrata* (19) and a further illustration of the layout appeared in the third volume of *Vitruvius Britannicus* in 1725. A detailed analysis of the 1725 view must wait until the beginning of the next chapter, as it concerns the work done at Hampton after 1717 under the supervision of Stephen Switzer. Here the discussion must focus on the earlier oils and engraving to ascertain what Lord Coningsby had achieved by 1705.

That London and Wise were intimately involved with the design and supervision of the landscape at Hampton is proved by a letter written to Lord Coningsby at the House of Commons by his father-in-law, Captain Ferdinando Gorges, from Eye Manor on 23 January 1692.[71] Its spelling and syntax are somewhat erratic, but Gorges had seen Bercroft, one of Coningsby's employees, in Leominster and had been shown by him a letter concerning the garden works at Hampton, which included information about 'the trees and Mr London's plot for the makinge [of] a garden in the pidgion house close'. Apparently Coningsby was vexed that Bercroft had not acted more swiftly upon his commands to set the work in train and Gorges responded by urging Bercroft to 'send away immediately to Mr: ffolies for Mr London's man & to put the trees in the grownd'. It is clear that 'Mr London's man' had already been at Hampton, deciding where to plant the new trees, and had baulked at cutting down fruit trees in the Chapel Orchard to provide planting space there. He had determined to develop the Pigeon House Close instead, though Coningsby had 'seemd to designe two garden yr one in the pidgion house close & the other in the Chaple orchard'. These then were the initial stirrings of what was to become a spectacular landscape that, with his wealth from Court appointments, particularly as Paymaster-General of William III's army, Coningsby laid out to the north and south of his house. In this venture he may well have been aided by the architect William Talman,

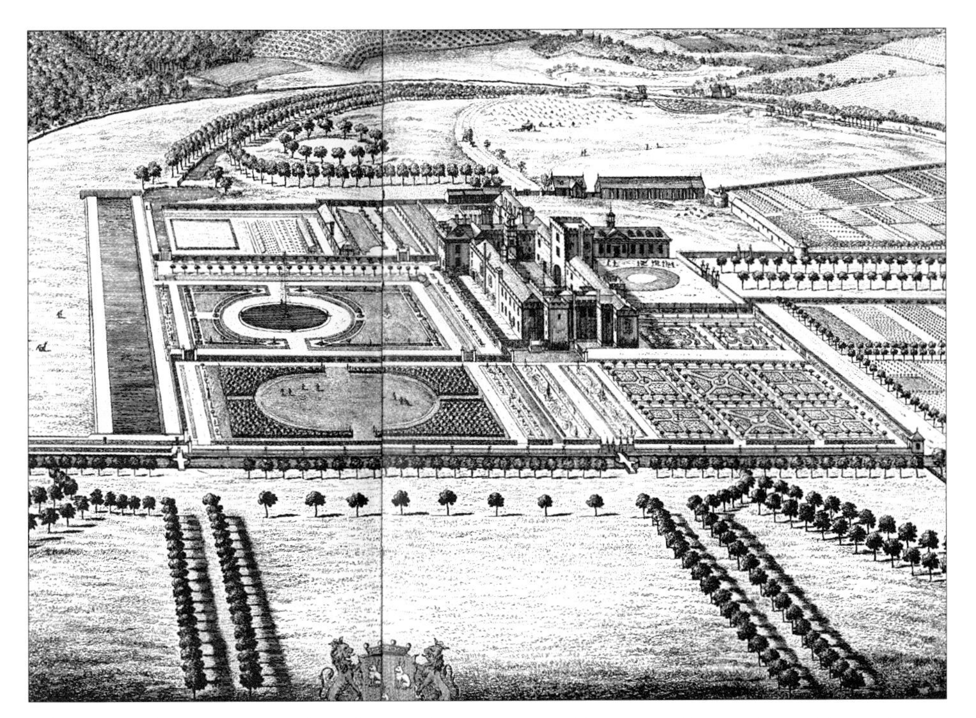

19 The most elaborate formal garden in the county, at Hampton Court, from Kip and Knyff's *Britannia Illustrata* of 1707. The complex had been swept away by the time John Byng visited in 1784. *University of Bristol Library, Special Collections*

who enjoyed a close collaborative partnership with London, especially when architectural features were required.[72]

Knyff captured the formal spectacle of compartments, parterres, topiary, canals, bridges and avenues set out in the lee of Dinmore Hill in the two bird's-eye perspectives that both hinted, more strongly than usual, at the importance of the surrounding countryside to the setting. The south-east view sets the house and its pleasure grounds within the wider parkland, its perimeter defined by the river Lugg and the Humber Brook, beyond which are woods and the hills towards Leominster, while in the north prospect the house is completely dwarfed by the landscape to include the deer park and its duck decoy, which is mentioned in the painting's inscription. Understandably, when Kip prepared the engraved plate for *Britannia Illustrata*, which was published in 1707, he concentrated more closely on the house and its gardens. Interestingly, given its date of publication, the view does not show the extension of the trans-

20 The canted outlines of the former Neptune Fountain at Hampton Court reappear miraculously in parch marks on this aerial view. The circular garden closer to the house may be contemporary with Sir Joseph Paxton's Conservatory.
Woolhope Naturalists' Field Club. Photograph by Chris Musson

verse canal on the south into an angular pool, as recorded on Knyff's oil of the south-east prospect, nor the elaborate Neptune fountain which centres it on Stevens' later painting of the south prospect.[73] There is no doubt that the pool was made, as it shows up in parch marks on aerial photographs (*20*) taken in 1995. There is also proof that the fountain was constructed and survived well into the 1750s. It is mentioned in a letter of 1758 from Tom Lyttelton to Mrs Montagu:

> In the middle of [the garden] is a piece of water of about an acre, cut into two square lines, in which, to the astonishment of the beholder, you see Neptune upon his throne, and twenty Tritons waiting behind him. The carver has express'd great fierceness in his countenance, and well may the god who shakes the earth with his Trident, be angry at being confined in a Pool, which would scarce hold two hundred fish.[74]

Most of today's 40,000 annual visitors to Hampton Court, if they are not discouraged from entering by the silly dictatorial signage on the walled garden – 'Don't Drink the Water in the Garden it's River Water!!' – inspired by children's book illustrations, will have no idea that this was the site of the most impressive seventeenth-century formal garden in Herefordshire. However, those who make it past Stephen Dorrell's modern garden, head for the cedar-shaded south lawn for refreshment in Sir Joseph Paxton's Conservatory, and take time to study the excellent guidebook to the gardens, will begin to appreciate the vast scale and magnificence of the lost layout.[75] Furthermore, if the site is walked – always a prerequisite for understanding a landscape, whether extant or lost – the south-east canal can be discovered, dramatised now by a later cascade, close to the point where Talman built his summerhouse. Sadly, in typical late-eighteenth-century style, the vacant lawn extends right up to the walls of the house and out, via a ha-ha, into the parkland beyond.[76] Nothing survives of a layout that must once have rivalled its royal namesake in Middlesex. The analysis of Hampton's formal gardens is, however, not quite complete. It must wait for the opening of the next chapter, for it concerns the appearance at Hampton in 1719 of one of London and Wise's protégés, who was to have a significant impact on landscape design in general, and the management of hydrostatics in particular, in the early years of the eighteenth century.

3

Lost prospect towers and an unsung Rococo Garden

Hampton Court · Bernithan Court · Langstone Court · Hill Court
Castle Ditch · Canon Pyon Great House · Shobdon Court · Wood Bank

THE FIRST AWAKENINGS OF INFORMALITY IN THE EARLY DECADES OF THE eighteenth century are generally thought to have been driven more by the literature of the period than by actual practice in gardens and landscapes. While John Vanbrugh and Charles Bridgeman were developing a stripped-down formalism of geometry, underpinned with military iconography appropriate to an age of triumphalism, writers such as Joseph Addison and Alexander Pope were calling for a loosening of the formal shackles and a softening in the planting. But one *Windsor Forest*, with its delight in unadorned Nature, did not make a landscape movement and, indeed, Pope's early designs, by the Thames at his own garden in Twickenham and at Marble Hill, displayed a strictly formal structure of axial paths and regimented planting. It would take the genius of William Kent to create that joyful combination of classical buildings and natural-seeming plantations that would become known as the English landscape style and which would be copied throughout Europe. At the forefront of this move away from the confines of formality close to the parent house was Stephen Switzer, who had been trained by London and Wise, but who was about to launch himself as a writer on garden aesthetics and agricultural improvement, and as a landscape practitioner in his own right. His appearance at **Hampton Court** signals a tentative move towards informality outside the rectilinear formal gardens (*21*), which had been created by the

2nd Lord Coningsby. Coningsby was to live until 1729, albeit in an increasingly litigious and erratic frame of mind, so he will have been responsible for any changes wrought in the landscape at Hampton between the completion of the great water garden and his death.

A letter from Lord Molesworth to Coningsby, written on 26 May 1719 as Molesworth arrived at his house near Dublin after a stay at Hampton Court, suggests Switzer's involvement in a later phase of landscaping at

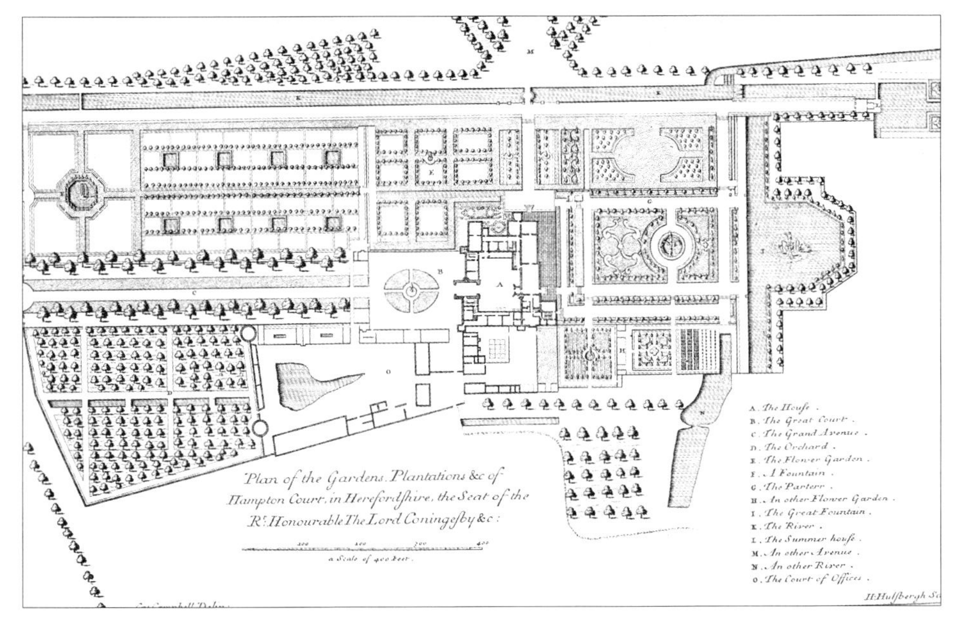

21 The 2nd Lord Coningsby's ornamental water gardens at Hampton Court from *Vitruvius Britannicus*. The layout was separated by walls from the wider landscape, where Stephen Switzer was devising a more practical waterworks.
University of Bristol Library, Special Collections

Hampton and identifies the contemporary work at Bushy Park as an influence on what was to be achieved in Herefordshire.[1] Molesworth thanks Coningsby for all his favours and asks: 'remember me when you have got ye designs of ye water contrivances at Bushy Park'. It would seem that both men were keen to see the Bushy plans, to aid practical improvements at their respective houses. After a digression on the lush growth of his fruit in Ireland, Molesworth returns to garden design:

> I acquainted our 2 L Chief Justices & some other gentlemen improvers with Mr Switzers abilitys, & his design to visit Dublin they seem very fond of him & really I believe his comeing over assisted by what favour & countenance I can give him will answer his end. But by his not meeting you at Hampton Court I suppose my Ld Cadogans departure has made him alter his project of seeing this country.

This raises several interesting questions in the light of Switzer's dedication to Coningsby of the second volume of his *Ichnographia Rustica*, which was published in 1718. The dedication and Molesworth's remark about Switzer not being able to meet Coningsby at Hampton implies that there already existed a professional relationship between the two men. As his biographer, William A Brogden, argues, Switzer did indeed work at Hampton in the wider landscape, creating a practical waterworks. He was

> to some degree responsible for the kitchen quarters of the garden, but his principal work was the new river (like natural rivers sometimes serpentine, sometimes straight, and sometimes irregular) dug in the park north of the house and garden. It runs roughly parallel to Hall Brook, which joins the River Lugg at the foot of the garden, but is on higher ground and thus provided a head of water for the fountains in the garden, and acted as a reservoir for the hitherto unwatered lands north of the park.[2]

Brogden's interpretation is based on remarks made by Switzer in his 1729 *Hydrostaticks*.[3] In discussing England's contribution to 'the raising of Rivers and Carriages for the Overflowing of Meadow and Uplands', Switzer cannot let the point pass without establishing his own credentials: 'I must beg leave to assume to myself the Credit of an Undertaking of this Kind, performed some Years since for the Earl of *Coningsby*, at *Hampton-Court* in *Herefordshire*; which, though not brought above two Miles, may (considering the Difficulties that attended this useful, but

1 The Iron Age hillfort of the British Camp, a mark of the county's ancient origins, as seen from the gardens at Perrycroft

2

A few limestone blocks and a tangle of iron are all that remain of the Eywood Orangery, painted here by Rachel Harley.
By kind permission of Edward Harley

3

Pools still form in winter, recalling the glacial lake that added scenic consequence to the medieval setting of Wigmore Castle and Wigmore Abbey

4

On reaching his majority in 1572, Sir Thomas Coningsby was depicted with the trappings of status and wealth. *©National Portrait Gallery, London*

5

Thomas, 2nd Lord Coningsby, seated in his demesne at Hampton Court, with a distant view of the house and its walled enclosures. *National Museums, Northern Ireland, Collection Ulster Museum*

6 The ruins of Brampton Bryan Castle, scene of Brilliana, Lady Harley's Civil War heroics, provides today a suitably picturesque embellishment for a garden on the Marcher borders

7 This 1722 survey records Brampton Bryan Castle hemmed in by house, church, bowling green and one arm of a T-shaped canal. Today the Cow Meadow retains its name, while the planting between church and the Castle is now known as the Wilderness.
By courtesy of the Trustees of Sir John Soane's Museum

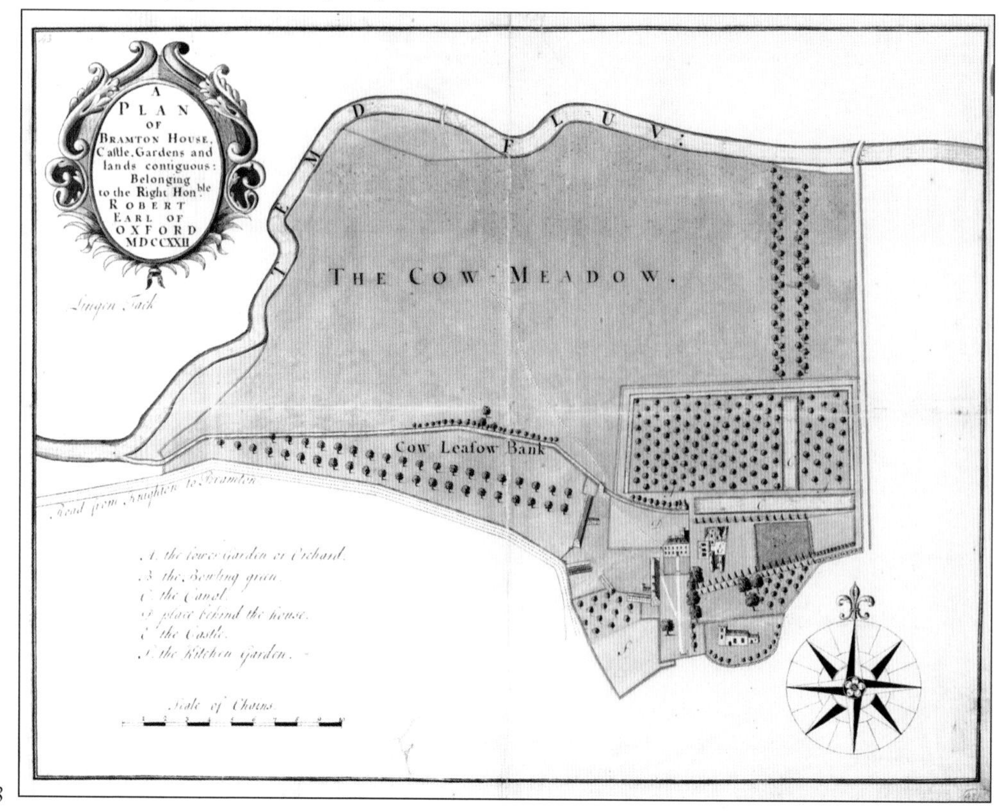

8 The pools and canalised Curl Brook aroused speculation in the nineteenth century that a Dutch designer was responsible for the layout at Moor Court

9 Archaeological investigation suggests that the plinths in the canal at Court of Noke were for statuary to frame the pedimented door of the house

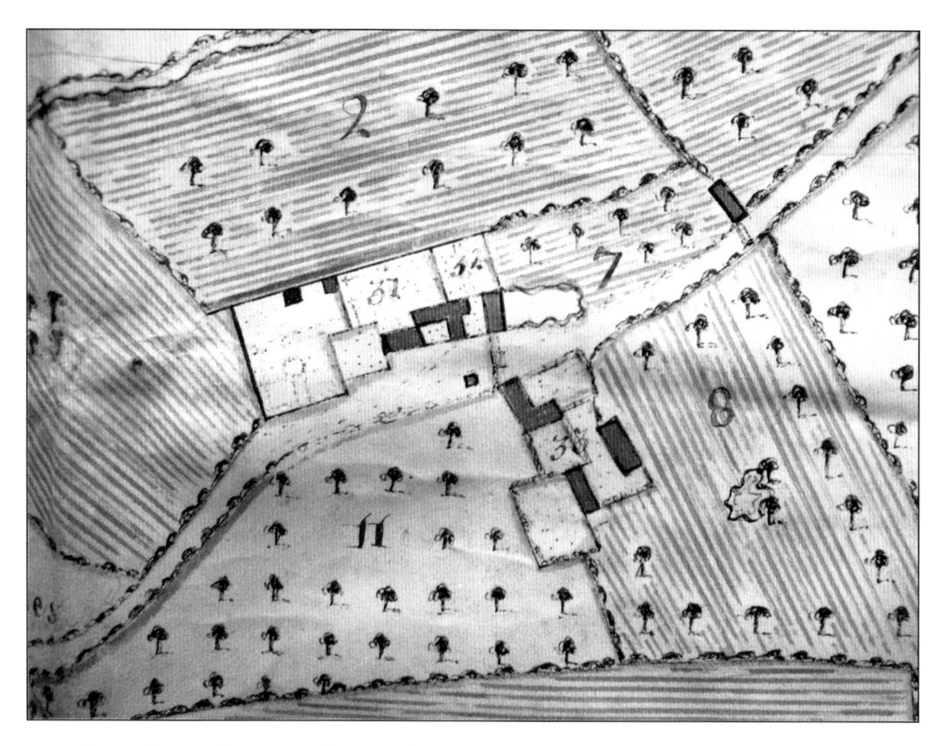

10 The walls, pools and garden platforms that surround Bernithan Court mirror exactly Thomas Green's 1780 survey.
Reproduced by permission of Herefordshire Record Office

11 The walled setting of Langstone Court, shown on Walter Green's 1758 survey, survives intact

12 Yew and holly still frame the spiral walk which gave views out over The Great House before it reached the Summerhouse at the top of Pyon Hill

13

Richard 'Dicky' Bateman had his portrait painted wearing oriental costume to reflect his current interest in Chinoiserie. *Birmingham Museums & Art Gallery*

14 Bateman's letters reveal that he was making changes to Shobdon's Canal Pool around 1753

expensive Work) be reckoned amongst some of the greatest Undertakings that were ever attempted in this or any other Country by a private purse'.[4] The new river he refers to is likely to be the Humber Brook, marked as such on the 1889 Ordnance Survey map, which winds through the deer park to the north-east and crosses into the Court environs to run parallel with the formal gardens and link up with the Lugg. The work was 'begun and finished in eight or ten Months, was conducted by many Windings and Turnings through high and almost impenetrable Rocks....and over other Variety of Earth, Clay, &c. in a Drain or Carriage about five yards wide'.[5] This project for improvement calls to mind Richard Vaughan's meadow drownings at Newcourt, especially as the Hampton scheme had 'laid the Foundation for the watering of two or three hundred Acres of Land, that is, and may be very well improved from five or six Shillings, to twenty or thirty Shillings an Acre at least'.[6]

Whether the existing canal in the pleasure grounds is a relic of this watercourse or, as argued earlier, the perimeter canal of the water garden, is not clear. If, indeed, the new river was developed to produce a head of water for the Neptune fountain, which was depicted by Stevens at some point between 1705 and 1710, it puts Switzer's involvement much earlier than the Molesworth letter of 1719. Significantly, the most important of the Bushy Park waterworks was the Diana or Arethusa Fountain, which was constructed in 1712-13 under the supervision of Sir Christopher Wren. Switzer's involvement at Hampton would seem, therefore, to have been confined to the functional waterwork, even if, with its serpentine windings, it was making an ornamental gesture towards the growing informality. The rural and extensive gardening that he was promoting in his three-volume *Ichnographia Rustica* had little impact on Hampton's formal gardens, which survived, walled off from the surrounding parkland, until the mid eighteenth century. Switzer continued to advocate *La Grand Manier* of Le Nôtre,[7] when it was deployed on a vast scale close to the house, but at the same time he was arguing for the improvement and ornamentation of the wider landscape setting. However, when Lord Torrington visited the place in 1784 the gardens had been swept away and the park was being cleared:

> we turn'd to the right to visit the old seat of Hampton-Court, long possess'd by the Coningsby family and lately come into the dominion of Ld Mallden. It is a venerable old mansion, built round a paved court....it is fronted by a steep wood, with the River Lugg flowing thro the garden....Ld M...has been here, he had not the (what shall I call it) curiosity to...open it, when the keys were delivered to him; or a wish to stay in this princely place longer than to give orders for the demolition of its beauties. Here I faint at narration. And wish I cou'd not say that all the noble timber of the park is fell'd or felling, 10000£ worth last year, and 1200£ more to fall this; every tree is mark'd: I feel for the dryads of the grove, and lament that I cannot suspend the axe.[8]

It was one thing for the owners of the grandest estates to indulge in Switzer's ideas of gardening in the 'grand manner' and unite their formal gardens with newly improved landscapes further afield, but this was not an option for the lesser gentry.

Indeed, several houses built in Herefordshire either in the late seventeenth or early eighteenth century had to be content with the safe, homely enclosures that characterised gardens in the Elizabethan period. One such is **Bernithan Court** at Llangarron, which was raised by the Hoskyns family around 1695 on the site of a medieval house. It is a typical, compact design of five bays and a tall, hipped roof. Its original gardens were also fairly standard in that they comprised four enclosures, one of which at least seems to have been ornamental: the first, with a network of paths set around a circular pool and two garden buildings; the wider landscape was of cultivated fields and orchards. What is strikingly atypical, however, is that this layout survived until at least 1780, when it was depicted on a survey (*colour 10*) by Walter Green.[9] A reference in the text around the side of the survey refers to the 'Fountain

22

Floral emblems surround a wildly mustachioed Green Man on the late-seventeenth-century gate piers in the walled garden at Bernithan Court

Court Garden', which is presumably the enclosure with the paths, pool and buildings. One of these is known to have been a three-hole privy, while the other may have been a small summerhouse.[10] Today, the walled enclosure to the garden front of the house survives, punctuated with elegant gate piers, strangely topped with Green Man finials (*22*), while further out the pool also survives.

Bernithan shares a stylistic affinity with nearby **Langstone Court**; they are in sight of one another across fields, but separated by the Garren Brook, which flows into a languorous loop of the Wye at Goodrich just south of Ross-on-Wye. It is likely that the same architect designed both houses;[11] certainly the same surveyor, Walter Green, made a survey (*23*) of Langstone in 1758 that records the walled enclosures around the house, which survive almost intact today.[12] The date of building is also close to that of Bernithan. Walter Gwillym the younger inherited Langstone in 1698 and was dead by 1706, so he must have built the house within that

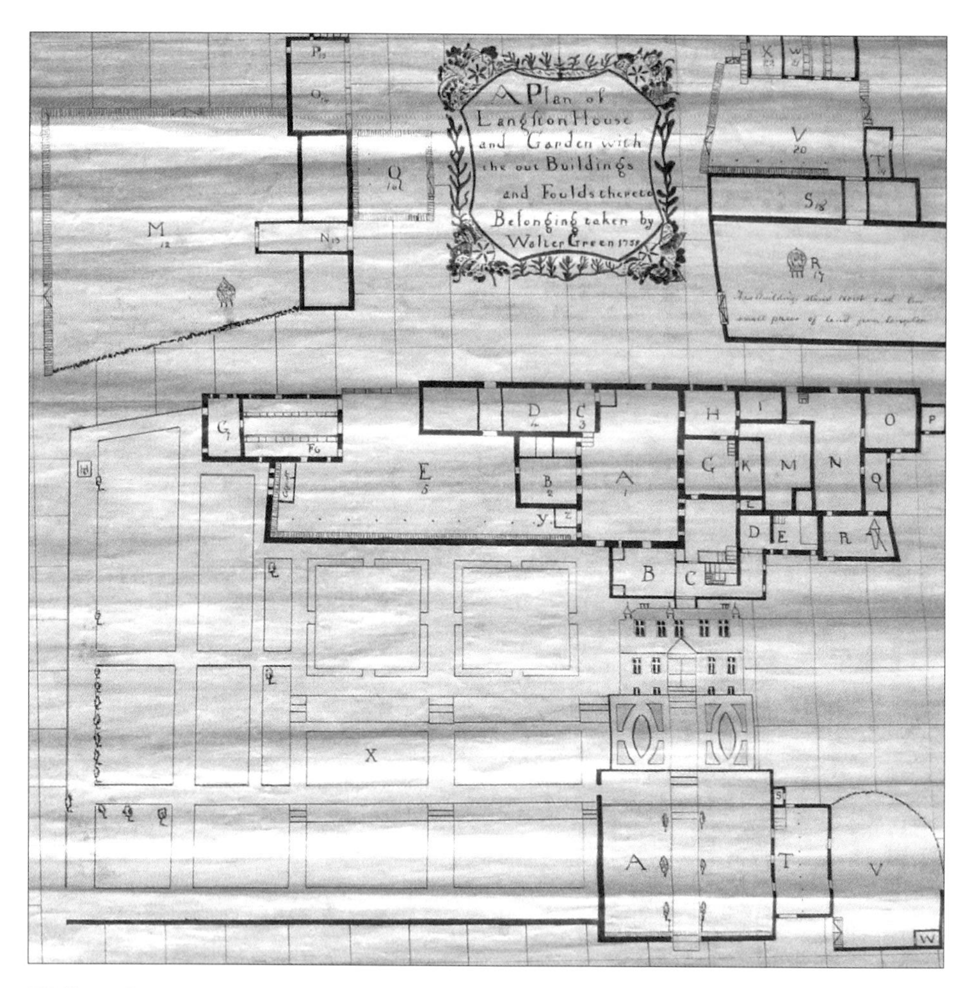

23 William Green's 1758 skeletal representation of the grounds at Langstone Court belies the profusion of flowers in the several compartments to the side of the house.
Private collection

brief period; furthermore, the Hoskyns intermarried with the Gwillyms. The setting of Langstone could not be more idyllic, with the house raised up on a platform commanding a three-part terraced garden flanked by a gabled barn (*colour 11*). A low wall punctuated by gate piers defines the perimeter of the enclosure, where steps lead down into a wilder area of meadow and later specimen trees. This extends to the Garren Brook, which meanders through the meadow, in which there is a curious building said to have been a stand for viewing the hunt in the fields beyond the Brook. At the other side of the walled enclosure is a much larger area marked 'garden' on the survey. In 1758 this was divided into a series of rectangular sectors linked by descending steps, while the farthest section had oblong beds, presumably for vegetables. At the top corner a square building marked 'H' was a summerhouse. A few trees are marked in the outer beds, but there is no evidence of an orchard, which is curious given that, in his manuscript notes for a history on the county, John Aubrey identified Gwillym's father, also William, as an expert on cider apples.[13] However, it may well be that there were orchards beyond the formal gardens, in the wider landscape which was not included in the survey.

A country house of far greater magnitude was built for Richard Clarke in about 1700 at **Hill Court**, near Ross-on-Wye. This has associations with John Kyrle, the Man of Ross, which will be covered in a later chapter, which discusses Herefordshire as the birthplace of the Picturesque movement. It is also an important twentieth-century garden that will find its place in the penultimate chapter of this book. Here it will be important to identify yet another inward-looking series of courts and a large walled enclosure that were constructed around the house as it was being built. John Cornforth has written three articles on the house, which chronicle precisely its development over the eighteenth and nineteenth centuries.[14] The bricklayer Robert Wayman was paid on 21 September 1700 for 'all the bricke worke in his house walls and draine and the sum of £11 in part towards his great court walls'; he was paid again a year later for building the garden walls.[15] The entrance forecourt has been opened up, which has shattered that sense of early enclosure. The gate piers are probably eighteenth-century in date and were originally sited at the east end of the tree avenue. They were moved to their present position in 1933 when the gates were being made as a 21st-birthday present for Guy Harold Trafford. Sadly, he never saw them in place, for he was killed in a car accident on his way to Queen's College, Oxford. However, the Walled Garden survives, now replanted in eighteenth-century style, though there is another pair of eighteenth-century gate piers, and the octagonal Dovecote is original.

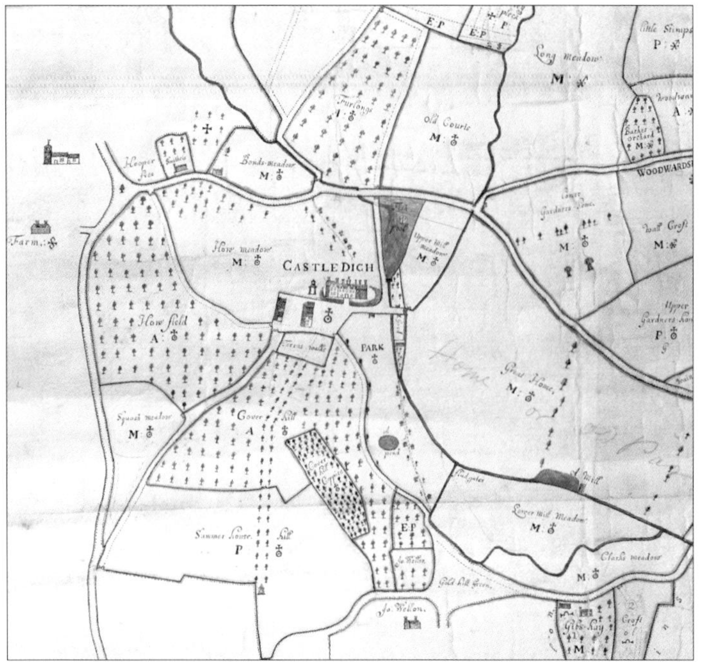

24

The 1726 survey of Castle Ditch marks the dog-legged, tree-lined avenue which led from the terrace walks by the house to the summerhouse on its hilltop. *Kind permission of Mr James Hervey-Bathurst. Photograph by David Lovelace*

However, at several early-eighteenth-century gardens in the county there are signs of a more cautious move out into the wider landscape than occurred at Hampton Court. One of the earliest of these seems to have been at **Castle Ditch**, the original house of the Cocks family, before it was submerged in the great lake that dramatises Sir Robert Smirke's early nineteenth-century Eastnor Castle.[16] Fortunately, John George surveyed 'Castle Dich' in 1726 and his map (*24*) shows that it stood in How Meadow, ringed by a watery moat (the ditch), which separated it from its service buildings and pigeon house.[17] It was skirted to the east by a stream and a 'Fish pool', and there were orchards to the north and west. The remains of Castle Ditch are said to occupy the island in the lake to the north-east of the present Castle. The main feature of the early garden was an angled walk lined with fruit trees that connected the 'Terras walks' by the house with a pyramidal-roofed summerhouse on the top of the appropriately named 'Summer house hill'. The hill immediately to the south of the Castle is still known by this name today, although the prospect house has disappeared. Significantly, although this was a conscious attempt to

25 The Great House at Canon Pyon before the addition of semicircular bows. The line of the raised walks is still evident in the garden, but the dovecote has been demolished. *Reproduced by permission of Herefordshire Record Office*

dramatise the landscape with a building and, therefore, to extend the visual bounds close to the house, there was no remodelling of the house environs. The park remained quite separate from the patchwork of orchards and fields that surrounded Castle Ditch.

The same tentative approach to the siting of garden buildings away from the parent house in a sylvan setting, an approach that would gradually develop into the Arcadian landscape, is apparent slightly later at The Great House at **Canon Pyon**. There is a beautifully drawn survey with vignettes of the garden, which, although undated, identifies its maker, Isaac Taylor, as the author of the 1754 county map of Herefordshire.[18] The survey shows the complex of compartmented gardens around the main house and a walk from them through an orchard, a pasture and a strip of 'Vicar's Land' up to 'Pyons Hill'.[19] One of the pencil vignettes depicts the Great House commanding a raised terrace walk punctuated by urns, and also a dovecote (25), while another shows tall hedges, one framing an allée terminating in a

Palladian archway topped by more urns. Overlooking the gardens in the first view, high on its hilltop, is a battlemented octagonal summerhouse.

All the features present in the views are consistent with a much earlier date, of the 1730s rather than the mid 1750s, and suggest that George Sawyer, who died in 1753 and whose monument by Louis-François Roubilliac is in the parish church, created the gardens. Although the monument is a fairly tame affair – a draped marble urn set against a concave wall – its design suggests that Sawyer was a man of taste and sophistication who might have laid out such a garden. There is a further clue to possible authorship on the Great House itself, which sits serenely in beautifully manicured gardens, where the outlines of the former terraces can still be seen. Indeed, the axis to the Palladian archway is preserved, though now leading to a modern Gothick seat. Although the original garden front of the house has been altered by the addition of two semicircular bays, the earlier rainwater heads are still *in situ*. They are inscribed: 'G S 1737'. They record the date of the house, as well as the owner responsible, George Sawyer.

The Summerhouse survives today, though in a ruinous state. It is not visible from the house, the trees having grown up around it, but access is via a private pathway alongside a cultivated field of rich red soil, and then into the woodland, where a circular path lined with old yews winds up to the summit. The Summerhouse bursts into view in a clearing ringed by great horse chestnuts and more yews (*colour 12*). The twenty-foot high building, constructed of finely laid brick in Flemish bond, is raised on a stone basement and still has sections of plasterwork clinging to the interior walls, recording its polite function as a place of genteel retreat.

That inveterate traveller, Dr Richard Pococke, the wandering bishop, spotted another prospect summerhouse in September 1756, which has so far eluded discovery. While on his way from Sutton, a few miles north of Hereford, to 'Willington', which is presumably the modern-day Withington, he passed a place where 'a tradesman of Hereford has a house, and a summer house on top of the hill, on each side of which are some oaks extending over the top of the hill, and being cut up, and only some small bough growing out, they have a most singular and beautiful effect'.[20] The only hill in the vicinity is to the south of Thing Hill Grange, a fourteenth-century hall house, which might have provided the status required for a local tradesman to cut a figure as a country gentleman.

In the same September, while travelling from Wales towards Hereford, Pococke fetched up at **Shobdon** and, at last, he found a landscape garden that satisfied his passion for the Rococo.[21] Lord Bateman's seat was

> built on a rising ground from which there is a fine view of the country....There is a fine lawn at the back of the house, adorn'd with clumps and single trees; terminated with a portico, which appears like a small temple. Up the side of the hill to the north also is a lawn and plantations, and on it is a building, consisting of a large arch and one smaller on each side; they are made out of three Saxon arches of the old church very highly adorned, and over them are two reliefs in a very bad taste, taken out of the same building, and beyond it is the old font which is Gothick and was adorned with ancient reliefs; further to the west clumps of trees form a sort of avenue up the hill, and lead to very fine rideings through the top and sides of an agreeable hill, which commands a most glorious view of a rich country. Near the house an old mount of a fortress is improved into a bowling green with a summer-house. To the south of the house is a piece of water and wood below it, through which are several walks, and a piece of water appears through them like a river.[22]

Shobdon had, therefore, all the necessary attributes for an eclectic or 'Rococo' garden: a series of structures in mixed style – classical, 'Saxon' and Gothick – the site of an ancient fortress to give it an added antiquarian interest and, in terms of pure landscape design, lawns, walks, rides, tree avenues, plantations and a sheet of water masquerading as a river. Pococke's description reads like the visual counterpart of a contemporary watercolour by the artist Thomas Robins, who painted two gouaches of Lord Bateman's uncle Richard's Grove House, Old Windsor.[23] There, to both classical and Gothick buildings, Richard Bateman had added more exotic Chinese touches. Indeed, as his portrait by de Tournières reveals (*colour 13*), in which he is depicted dressed as a mandarin standing somewhat self-consciously in front of a Chinese garden building, Bateman was obsessed with Chinoiserie in the 1740s before his close friend, Horace Walpole, persuaded him to revert to the more patriotic Gothick. In a later letter of 24 September 1762, Walpole wrote to his friend George Montagu: 'I did not doubt but you would approve Mr Bateman's since it has changed its religion; I converted it from Chinese to Gothic'.[24] He was still claiming his influence over Bateman as late as 1781 in another letter, this time to the 2nd Earl of Stafford: 'I am as proud a disciple as of having converted Dicky Bateman from a Chinese to a Goth. Though he was the founder of the Sharawadgi taste in England, I preached so effectually that his every pagoda took the veil'.[25] However, could it be that Bateman's experiences at Shobdon, particularly in respect of the Arches, influenced him more than his friend did?

That Richard Bateman was responsible for the elaborate gardens at his own house at Old Windsor is not in doubt, but his authorship of the eclectic garden at Shobdon is less certain because he did not own Shobdon. He merely looked after the estate both for the 1st Viscount Bateman and, after he inherited in 1744, the 2nd Viscount, who was Richard's nephew. Fortunately, no fewer than 363 letters survive from both Richard Bateman and Lord Bateman to the Shobdon agent Benjamin Fallowes and, while they do not prove that Richard designed the gardens, they chart his overriding influence in what was built and planted at Shobdon between 1739 and 1767.[26] Furthermore, there are strong similarities in design between Grove House and Shobdon. A letter of 23 December 1752 from Richard Bateman to Fallowes even suggests that he viewed Shobdon as a smaller version of his own garden by the Thames: 'At my return from Old Windsor I found yr letter I am very glad to hear you have so good luck in making yr water at Little Windsor. I shall have a great pleasure next summer in seeing it'.[27] This copious correspondence details the work on the grounds, including the construction of the Portico, the summerhouse

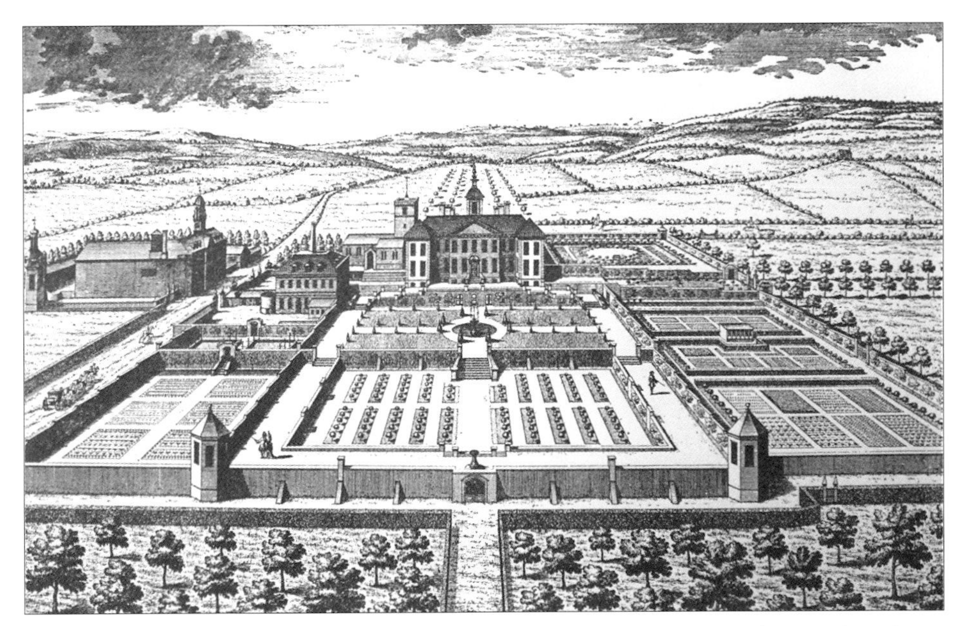

26 The enthusiasm for wall fruit depicted here suggests a certain artistic licence, but the engraving is an accurate record of the scale and layout of the formal gardens at Shobdon Court in the 1740s, when Richard Bateman became custodian of the estate. *University of Bristol Library, Special Collections*

on the bowling green, which had been laid out on the site of the former castle, work to several pools, some unidentified garden buildings and a fountain, all of which were in progress during the three decades which the letters span.

The mid-eighteenth-century improvements at Shobdon were all undertaken outside the confines of the original formal gardens that had been laid out around the late-seventeenth-century house. These are shown in an engraving (*26*) published in the second, 1715, volume of *Britannia Illustrata* and, while they were much smaller in scale than the celebrated water gardens at Hampton, they were nevertheless an important example of the Franco-Dutch fashion. Insistently walled, with steps linking each descending area of the gardens, they were laid out in simple flower and vegetable beds, though the enclosure immediately below the house had grass plats defined by conifers and a basin with a fountain. There were two pyramidal-roofed summerhouses on the outer wall in axis with the house and there were further garden buildings on the eastern perimeter wall. Tree avenues radiated out into the park to the east, while a double avenue ran north from the house to where the Shobdon Arches define the ridge today. This north-south axis was altered when Dicky Bateman began to direct operations in the 1740s. The eclectic garden was laid out principally in the parkland to the east of the house with the Portico and its attendant flower garden providing the focus for views out into the landscape on the east.

The main approach to the house was along Berry Lane from the village to the south. This is now a private drive that rises on an embankment to the site of the house; it passes the Swan Pool on the right and a straight canal on the left (*colour 14*). The drive then continues between the stable block and the present house, built out of the former Agent's House and service buildings, to the church. This is not the building shown in the early engraving, as it was rebuilt under Dicky Bateman's direction in 1751, though the medieval tower was retained. For such a sublime example of Rococo-Gothick it is extraordinary that the architect remains elusive. There are elements of Batty Langley Gothick, as well as shades of both William Kent's Gothick and that of Henry Flitcroft.[28] It hardly seems to matter; it is a breathtaking interior and wholly justifies the demolition and re-use of the former Angevin chancel arch and two doorways with their carved tympana that were set up as the Shobdon Arches (*colour 15*). Whether this was an early instance of architectural salvage and conservation is not clear; the presence of the Norman font noted by Pococke, since reinstated inside the church, suggests that it was rather a case of ornamenting the landscape with architectural incidents, as at Grove House. Significantly, the Arches look like a Gothick folly from a distance because Bateman ornamented the parapet with crocketted pinnacles in neo-medieval style.

To the north-west of the house the castle site was utilised for a circular bowling green overlooked by a summerhouse. The enclosure survives today alongside light industrial buildings, ringed by some veteran oaks of vast girth, though the garden building has disappeared. The views from it, out towards Hay Bluff and the Black Mountains, are spectacular. But it was to the east that both Dicky and Lord Bateman directed their attentions, creating a new landscape that was part Arcadian and part emergent Gardenesque. Indeed, in its deployment of shrubs, roses and flowers in circular beds it mirrored contemporary designs by Thomas Wright, but anticipated the ground-breaking flower garden at Nuneham Courtenay, laid out by William Mason, by at least twenty-five years.[29] The correspondence proves that both Bateman and his nephew were actively pursuing plants for this area of the grounds and directing the gardener where to plant them.

In 1747, Dicky was informing Fallowes of plants that were being sent down from London:

> By the carrier next will come a hundred roses and fifty honeysuckles. I would have a Rose and a Honeysuckle planted alternately between every one of the trees down from the House on each side of the gravel walk of the Portico within the box edging. There will be more Roses & Honeysuckles than will be wanting for this work. Let him plant them where I told him in the Kitchen Garden. If you don't understand entirely how I mean to have these Roses planted down the side of the South Parterre, write to me before they are planted that I may explain it more.[30]

All of this busy planting has now disappeared, but there are some writhing oriental planes on the terrace and the Portico (27) still stands in splendid isolation on axis with the house site, in a thicket of conifers and sweet chestnuts in the middle of a ploughed field. Significantly, its four columns are Ionic – the same order that Dicky Bateman used in the 1730s for his temple on the circuit walk at Grove House.[31] In Grove House's self-contained flower garden, flower borders extended from the corners of the temple to a circular planting bed, the whole a mixture of roses, jasmine, honeysuckles, stocks and pinks. It is likely that Bateman was aiming for the same effect at Shobdon. In March 1749, he was still sending

27 The recently restored Portico at Shobdon was once the focal point of a circular flower garden; it now stands isolated in a thicket

seeds from London, this time to line the walks and to be planted in the woodland between the house and the Portico:

> A great quantity of seeds will come down this journey let the Gardiner sow them directly with great care. There are about 1000 little roots of Lillies of the Valley let him plant them at the corners of the corners & a long the edges of the different walks of the great garden within the wood & also the 300 roots of the single white Hiyacinths the same. The other things must be planted with care in the Kitchen Garden.[32]

The Kitchen Garden features again in December, when Lord Bateman writes to Fallowes: 'By the next week's wagon I shall send a Box of Foreign Seeds some very scarce ones so I would have you prepare some Beds in the Kitchen Garden to sow them'.[33] It may be that the seeds were obtained from Mark Catesby, who in the 1720s, supported by 'encouragers' including Dicky Bateman, had been collecting in the Carolinas and had introduced several new exotics including *Wisteria frutescens* (American kidney bean tree) and *Catalpa bignonioides* (Indian bean tree).[34]

There were other similarities between Grove House and Shobdon. A 1774 survey of the estate appears to show a peripheral walk,[35] while in the park Dicky Bateman was trying to introduce other architectural incidents as well as the Arches. In July 1761 he was vexed about a delay: 'I am very desirous to have the Building in the Garden finished before I come down, so I would desire you would hurry it as much as possible & employ the people Mr Pember mentioned to you',[36] while two weeks later he was urging that:

> The work may be finished before I come into the county if you please I cannot conceive there is a week's work to do, as I want the room finished to make use of it... Ask Mr Pember how many yards of green and white will be wanting for the chairs and the couch that are to be in the Bench, as I chase to send it from London and there is no blue and white linnen here to be got of the sort I intended for it.[37]

The building was still not finished in September of that year, but these entries suggest that garden structures were being added to the 'Gothick gateway in Park', 'Pavillion tetrastile in lawn' and 'Rustic entrance' that Edward Knight noted in his usual shorthand on a visit in 1760.[38]

While authorities like Mark Laird and John Harris have written perceptively on the mid-century vogue for flower gardens, assessing the undoubted importance of Dicky Bateman's Grove House and Mason's Nuneham Courtenay, the eighteenth-century garden at Shobdon has never been given its due. Lack of visual records have not helped, but it must be seen as a mid-point between Grove House and Nuneham, where Bateman took the metropolitan ideas that had informed his design on the Thames and transported them to the wilds of north-west Herefordshire.

In a county of wild frontiers and picturesque scenery it is not surprising that the Rococo Garden, with its eclectic mix of styles and its floral busy-ness, hardly features. So it is to the Wye that we must return to end this chapter of tentative moves towards informality in landscape design. Yet again a prospect tower, offering views out across its great arcs, signals the true significance of garden and landscape practice in the county, that of the aesthetics of the Picturesque. Here, at least, we have a visual record of Mr Purchas' house and garden at Fownhope, painted from the foot-path to Holme Lacy in September 1798 by James Wathen. Geoffrey Lipscombe saw the complex in 1799 and recorded in his journal:

> Mr. Purchas conducted us through his brewery and shewed his vast repositories of wine, Accompanying these attentions with an air of so great humour, and such pressing invitation to partake of refresh-ment, that we took leave of this hospitable gentleman with regret...[the brewery]....was sheltered by a vast rock which rises boldly behind it. Mr. Purchas has cut steps up the hill, planted with juniper bushes, and other shrubs, thrown a screen of firs along a field on the right, and built a castellated prospect house on the brow of the steep.[39]

Wathen's watercolour (*colour 16*) of what is now known as **Wood Bank**, on the B4224, just before the B4399 branches off left to Hereford, shows the main house with its attendant service and industrial structures, most of which have now disappeared. In the painting, behind the house, a zig-zag path rises up via an obelisk-shaped structure to a two-storey castellated viewing tower painted white to act also as an eye-catcher. The lias stone and brick remains of the Prospect Tower survive deep in the woods, where breaks in the tree line give spectacular glimpses out over the Wye towards Holme Lacy, with Dinedor Hill on the horizon. The zig-zag path has recently been repaired (*colour 17*), but the conical building has long since gone. Mr Purchas' Tower reaffirms the scenic draw of the Wye and the Herefordshire countryside and is the perfect preparation for

Uvedale Price's Foxley, where another prospect tower commands an expansive panorama. However, even though the Ragged Castle at Foxley was built by Uvedale's father, Robert, about 1740, continuing the chronology of this analysis of mid-eighteenth-century enthusiasts for landscape views, Uvedale's remodelling of the estate was not carried out until the later decades of the century. His Picturesque experiments, both practical and aesthetic, were, in part, a response to the vapid parks of Capability Brown, who had died in 1783. It is, therefore, to Brown's Herefordshire commissions, scant though they were, that we must now turn.

4

A failure of artificial Nature in the face of real scenery – the Brownian park

Brockhampton Park · Berrington Hall · Moccas Court
Allensmore Court · Cagebrook House · Kinnersley Castle · Garnons

LANCELOT 'CAPABILITY' BROWN'S PROFESSIONAL LIFE FROM 1751 TO 1783 WAS one continuous journey, taking him the length and breadth of England in the creation of ideal parkscapes for leisure, profit and sport. At his death, aged sixty-seven, no fewer than 170 estates had been shaped by his personal design, while over 4,000 landscape parks had been created by a new generation of landscapers inspired by him. In view of this legacy, it is surprising there are so few Brownian landscapes in Herefordshire, let alone ones personally shaped by the great practitioner himself. There is no proof that Brown designed the park at Eywood, even if he did visit the Earl of Oxford there in August 1775,[1] and his involvement at Moccas Court can be challenged. A scatter of landscape parks, which includes those at Allensmore, Cagebrook House, Kinnersley Castle and Garnons, have connections with one his followers, the nurseryman and landscaper designer John Davenport, while Thomas Leggett, another disciple, produced a plan for **Brockhampton Park** (*28*) that was never implemented.[2] This is inscribed to Bartholomew Richard Barneby and dated 1769, so it pre-dates Brown's first commissions in the county, but it is resolutely drawn in his style with shelter belts, tree clumps, a circular carriage drive sometimes threaded through plantations, a pleasure ground in front of the house with gravel paths for walking and divided from the parkland by a ha-ha, and a serpentine lake in the valley. Leggett is known to have worked as William Emes' clerk of works on several estates in Cheshire and the plan bears hallmarks of Emes' style, particularly the elongated lake.[3]

Leggett's ambitious plan was to remain a paper proposal, whereas at **Berrington Hall**, north of Leominster, Brown was to create one of the most beautiful landscape parks in the country (*colour 18*). This was due, in no small degree, to the complementary skills of landscaper and architect.

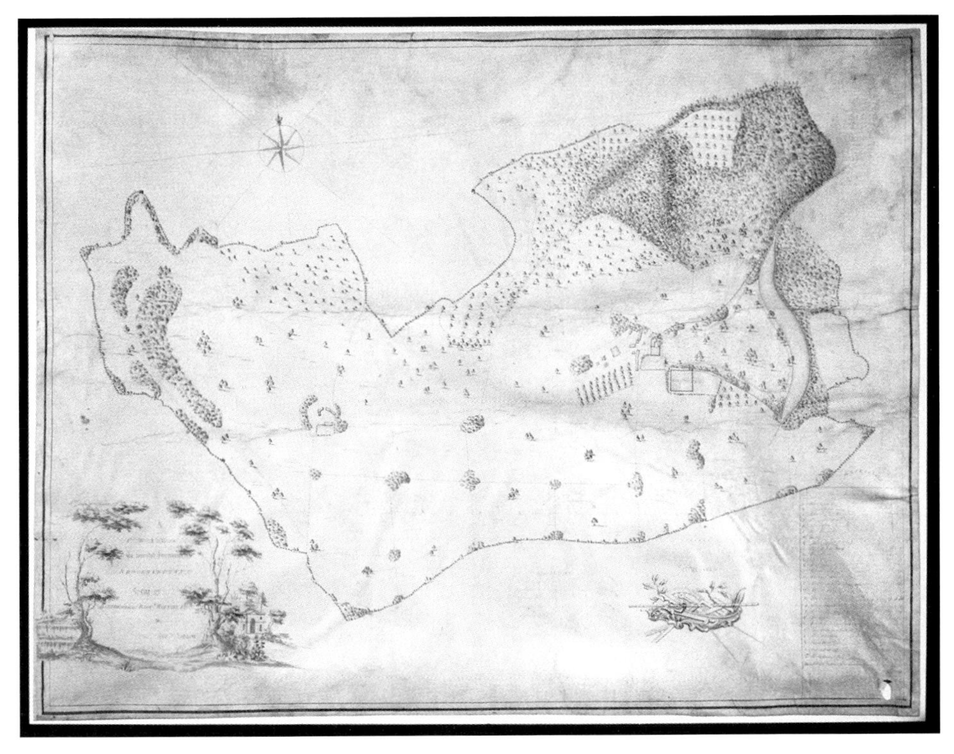

28 The natural topography of the Brockhampton estate meant that the Barneby family had little to gain from implementing Thomas Leggett's somewhat pedestrian design in the Brownian style. ©*National Trust*

In Brown's designs the main house was an integral part of his carefully composed landscapes. On occasions Brown himself was commissioned to produce designs for a new house, but much of his architectural work was executed by Henry Holland, a master builder from Fulham, and later by Holland's eldest son, also Henry. In 1771 Brown went into an informal partnership with the younger Holland, handing over to him the architectural side of his practice, and in 1773 Holland married Brown's daughter,

29 Victorian planting around the house confines the expansive views that were the essence of Brown and Holland's collaboration at Berrington Hall. Holland widened the central section of the portico to provide vistas across the ha-ha to the lake

Bridget. So by the time he was brought in by Thomas Harley to remodel the park at Berrington, Brown was already in partnership with his son-in-law.

The landscape writer and poet, William Mason, writing later to Humphry Repton, Brown's self-styled successor, perceived the importance of designing both landscape and ornamental buildings, including the parent house, in concert:

> I also am uniformly of the opinion, that where a place is to be formed, he who disposes the ground and arranges the plantations ought to fix the situation at least, if not to determine the shape and size of the ornamental buildings. Brown, I know, was ridiculed for turning architect, but I always thought he did from a kind of necessity having found the great difficulty which must frequently have occurred to him in forming a picturesque whole, where the previous building had been ill-placed, or of improper dimensions.[4]

This is what makes the park at Berrington so effortlessly beautiful. Brown had no need to reshape the terrain to enhance an existing house; house and landscape were redesigned as one to produce that 'picturesque whole' identified by Mason. The house sits like a giant garden building overlooking a Claudean landscape dramatised by the 'Great Water', created from a tributary of the Lugg and fed by springs, with greensward and pasture enlivened by sparse, solitary trees and thicker plantations, while on the perimeter a shelter belt defines the park boundary. Eighteenth-century mobility within the park was provided by paths for walking, rides for horses and drives for carriages; at Berrington the A49 slices across the estate, giving present-day motorists that rare experience of actually travelling through his landscape. In Brown's day there were two roads through the park; the main thoroughfare between Leominster and Ludlow was along what is now the B4361, which is shown on Isaac Taylor's 1754 map of Herefordshire.[5]

Thomas Harley often stayed with his brother, the 4th Earl of Oxford, at nearby Eywood, and it is presumed that he rode over to the Berrington estate, which he had bought from the Cornewalls in 1775, with Brown to discuss its remodelling. However, Brown did not supply a landscape plan until 1780, by which time Holland had produced designs for the house; his plan and estimate date from 1778.[6] Berrington Hall is one of the masterpieces of late-Georgian architecture in the country, its pared down classicism perfectly in accord with Brown's austere landscape. Furthermore, there are signs that Holland conceived his house not only as an incident to be seen from the landscape, but also as one connected with its surroundings by subtle architectural nuances. These are most evident in the south portico (*29*), the central intercolumniation of which is double the width of the space between the paired Ionic columns either side, so that it offers uninterrupted views out towards the Black Mountains and Radnor Forest. This concept is also evident in the flanking wings, which have seat niches with coffered semi-domes for shelter to catch the morning sun and evening sunset (*30*). The niches would seem to be an integral part of Brown's treatment of the pleasure grounds around the

30 Holland's elegant seating niches offer perfect observation points from which to enjoy Brown's minimalist landscape

house, which were laid out with 'close walks' that are shown on the 1844 tithe map.[7]

Brown's Account Book charts the work at Berrington,[8] but there are later entries in the papers maintained by Harley's agent, James Crummer, which concern Christian Sanderson.[9] Entry 146 in the Account Book records two journeys made to Berrington by Brown's foreman Samuel Lapidge in May and June 1780 'to take a Survey of the Grounds for the plan of alterations'. For this plan, which may have been prepared by John Spyers,[10] Brown received £400 on account in July 1781. He received another £400 in February 1782, and £300 on 31 May. The account was settled with a final payment of £500 in September 1782. However, Sanderson, who was probably acting as Brown's clerk of works, was at Berrington from 1780 to 1783, and again after Brown's death until 1806.[11]

One of the surprising elements of Holland and Brown's joint design of house and grounds is the triumphal-arched Lodge, which has been described as 'surely unique' and perhaps represents a reminder of Harley's success as a banker in the capital, where triumphal arches marked 'the old

Roman gateways into London until the 1760s'.[12] However, the reasoning behind such a close placement of a gatehouse to the main house is more likely to be a reflection of local architectural practice in north Herefordshire and Shropshire, where earlier timber-framed houses, such as Lower Brockhampton and Stokesay Castle, have attendant gatehouses. The Lodge is set obliquely to the rear elevation of the house and thus encourages the visitor to walk directly to the Dairy wing with its niche seat and then on to the lawn in front of the south façade to take in the views across the parkland. As with so many of Brown's lakes, the Great Water flows out into the distance, its true extent masked by fingers of water that recede into the planting and out behind an island in the middle. Poor maintenance of the banks, which are overgrown with reeds, has reduced both the scale and the impact of the water, while some of the contrived views across the landscape have been lost. A Brownian landscape needs constant pruning if its sharp outlines and framed views are to be preserved. But the extent of the park is defined on the south-west by a shelter belt, along the periphery of which the Moreton Ride, a Brown carriage drive, was laid out to give views out towards Croft Ambrey Fort in the west. The ridge to the east is similarly dramatised by the Long Wood, which is threaded by a ride that cuts back across the park to the Keeper's Lodge at the south-eastern end of the lake. On the eastern side of Long Wood the Stockton Ride snakes from the A4112 at Stockton along the contours north to the Hundred Lane at Ashton, close to the north lodge into the park; it is not known whether this is an original feature.

Many of the original elements survive today, making Berrington one of the most complete Brownian landscapes, despite the current lack of careful maintenance around the lake. Fortunately, Lord Torrington visited Berrington on 30 June 1784 and gave a good account of the new house and the parkland in its manicured prime:

> In 4 miles from Leominster, we quitted the turnpike road to see Berrington Castle, a house of Mr Harley's; and nothing cou'd be

> seen to form a stronger contrast, in most particulars with our morning visitation [to Hampton Court]; that, is old, grand, and gloomy; this is gay, just finish'd and furnish'd in all the modern elegance, commanding beautiful views, a fine piece of water, and is throughout a scene of elegance and refinement...We pass'd a most agreeable hour in our survey of this place.[13]

By that time Brown was dead. On 5 February 1783 he went to call on his old friend Lord Coventry at his town house in Piccadilly, and on returning home he fell to the ground and collapsed. He died at his daughter's house the following evening. Berrington was one of his last commissions and possibly the most satisfyingly minimalist of his entire output. However, its legacy was short lived in a county that, perhaps because it was already enriched with dramatic natural scenery, did not require Brown's talents for artificial landscapes. It was appreciation of this real Nature that was to exert such a powerful influence on Uvedale Price and Payne Knight, who in the mid-1790s were to denigrate Brown's achievements whilst promoting the new Picturesque aesthetic. There were, however, some minor experiments and unexecuted designs in the Brownian style undertaken before the polemics of 1794 shifted taste away from manicured minimalism to a more earthy delight in rough Nature.

One of these is the landscape, as opposed to the deer park, at **Moccas Court**, across the river from Monnington-on-Wye. The authorship of the Court, a serene brick villa perched high above the Wye with a view from its semicircular bay to The Scar (*colour 19*), a crimson rock face arcing around a bend in the river, is not in doubt. Robert Adam produced designs for a house in 1775 for Sir George Cornewall, but these were not carried out; instead it was constructed between 1776 and 1783 to designs by Anthony Keck.[14] What is not certain is how much influence Brown had on the emergent landscape around the Court, and what Humphry Repton might have achieved in the 1790s long after Brown's death. The keys to unravelling these attributions is a landscape survey (*31*) by Brown

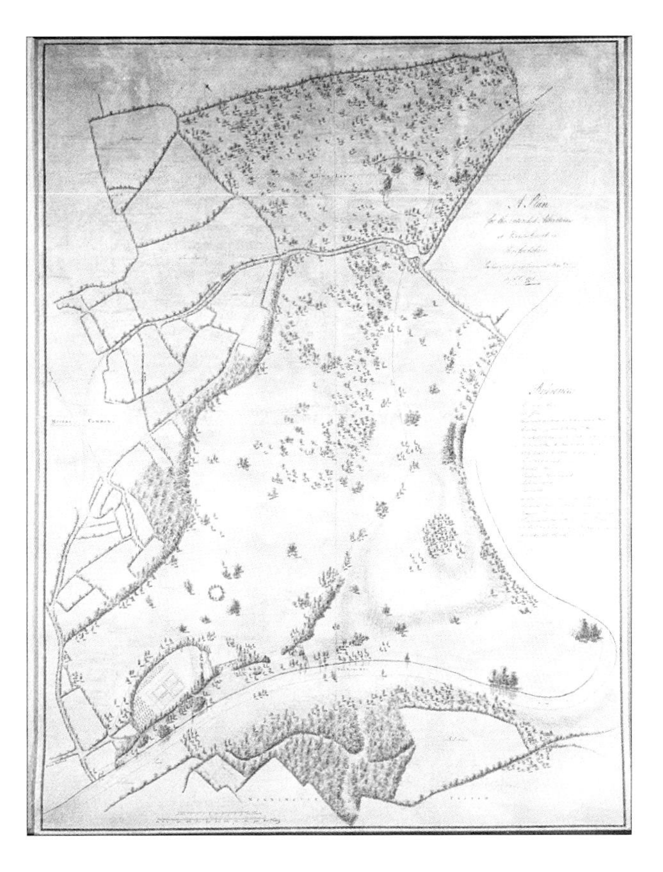

31

Brown's design for Moccas aligned parkland views on the house from a carriage drive, before opening up in a broad sweep at the rear to take in the River Wye. *Getty Center for the History of Arts & Humanties, Santa Monica*

dated 1778 and a view of Moccas taken from 'Brobbury Scar' (*32*) by James Wathen ten years later.[15] Brown's first biographer, Dorothy Stroud, claimed that Brown supplied plans costing £100, 'but was not responsible for their actual execution'.[16] This payment is logged in Brown's Account Book, but he does not appear to have received further monies and, indeed, the Wathen view shows a somewhat desultory landscape with its hedgerows and fields still intact. There is none of the scattered tree planting in the park, the clumps framing the Scar, or the tree-lined carriage drive snaking across the landscape towards the deer park shown on the Brown plan.

Another undated, and unsigned, watercolour (*colour 20*) shows Cornewall and his wife surveying their land, still unimproved, from the Scar.[17] This must be close in date to another estate map prepared in 1772 for Cornewall by John Lambe Davis, who was paid £124 for it in April

32 James Wathen's 1788 monochrome sketch of Moccas shows an unimproved landscape, suggesting that Brown's plan was not carried out in his lifetime. *Hereford City Library*

1773.[18] This shows the ground plan and layout of the house that preceded the Keck villa and which is illustrated in the undated watercolour. The main feature of the complex of formal enclosures around the house is 'The Walk', laid out parallel to the Wye. Cornewall's account books, which are preserved in Herefordshire Record Office, chart his work in copious detail and suggest that he supervised the early landscaping himself.[19] Significantly, there are references in the 1780s to a gravel walk and, more surprisingly, to payments for work mending roads.[20] While the landscape retained its system of fields – Great Church Field, Church Yard Meadow, The Warren – it was threaded with roads, or at least drives. These are curious in that Brown always gave priority to mobility within his landscapes, but his plan does not include them. At least one commentator has suggested that this network of drives, particularly in the Upper Park at Moccas, is indicative of Repton's input.[21] However, the map proves that they were always a feature of the estate long before Cornewall consulted Repton between 1792 and 1795. Repton's contribution to the landscape, and that of his partner John Nash, who is likely to have designed the lodges for the entrances, will be discussed in the following chapter.

Mystery also surrounds the landscape at **Allensmore Court**, south-east of Clehonger, the sad remains of which are reached by a footpath in the churchyard that crosses a stream into what is now called Kiln Field. This is the site of kilns that were used to make brick for the construction of the Court, the Home and Green Farms. A carriage drive once ran through this field connecting the Court, another house by Keck, which was demolished in 1958, with the parish church.[22] All that is left now is a fragment of the walled garden, a 5-acre lake and the Birch Wood plantation; apart from these vestigial features there is nothing more to suggest that this was once an eighteenth-century landscape park in the Brownian style. However, letters from Davenport, a nurseryman and putative landscape designer from Wem in Shropshire, to Edmund Lechmere Pateshall, written in 1784, prove that a plan was at least prepared, even if Pateshall had not implemented its proposals by the time of his untimely death, aged 42, in 1790.[23]

On 17 February 1784, Davenport wrote:

> I am just favoured with the Honor of yours, and as Business will soon call me into Herefordshire, I will do myself the Honor of waiting on yours – and then a part of your Improvements which you may then propose doing & will with pleasure stake-out and give your Gardener directions in the same as the part you now wish most to be done.....I shall not make any charge to you for that Business, as I much wish what you do about your House to be done in a proper mannor and than you have great pleasure in seeing it, and to do some part one year and some others.[24]

However, by 3 March, Davenport and his surveyor had made two journeys to Allensmore, for which he proposed charging £21, and a further 10 guineas for his 'plan of the intended improvements'.[25] Subsequent correspondence records Davenport's frustration at not being paid for his advice and culminates in a lengthy letter of 1 June in which he defends the level of his charges for the plan – it 'is worth twenty guineas' – also his preferential rates for the procurement of trees and shrubs and their carriage, and anger at Pateshall having called into question his charge for a chaise because he was afflicted with gout.[26] Davenport was, therefore, unlikely to have implemented any of the proposals outlined in his plan without prior payment, and Pateshall must, like Cornewall at Moccas, have supervised any works himself. Indeed, another letter from Sir Hungerford Hoskyns, owner of the Harewood estate near Ross-on-Wye, to Pateshall, although undated, suggests that work was later under way at Allensmore: 'I shall embrace the first opportunity of taking a Ride to view yr Alterations & improvements of which every Body speaks so much in praise, & of which I now and then get a Glimpse from Aconbury Hill'.[27] The hill in question is to the south-east of Allensmore. It is not clear what Pateshall achieved before his death, even after he settled Davenport's bill and continued to buy trees and shrubs from his nursery. However, the lake appears to have been created by Lechmere's son, Edmund Burnam Pateshall, in 1819-20, with advice from his neighbour, John Holder Matthews of Belmont, on how to stock it with fish.[28]

There is an intriguing postscript to Davenport's June 1784 letter, in which he mentions his work for a Mr Green, who seems to have been perfectly happy with Davenport's method of working and the level of his charges. David Whitehead has suggested that this was the owner of nearby **Cagebrook House**, between Clehonger and Eaton Bishop.[29] The close proximity of the Cage Brook with its two mills and the fishpond in the grounds might have been catalysts for an ornamental water garden, examples of which Davenport had either proposed or achieved at Nanteos, near Aberystwyth, at Kyre Park in Worcestershire and at Daylesford in Gloucestershire.[30] Sadly, most of the complex system of leats has now silted up, and the grounds were later remodelled in the nineteenth century, but 'two ornamental lakes with islands' were noted in sale particulars of 1913.[31]

Another Herefordshire site where Davenport might have achieved a water garden is **Kinnersley Castle**. According to a letter he sent to John Geers Cottrell of Garnons, Davenport visited the Castle in December 1792.[32] As with Cagebrook, it is not known what Davenport might have achieved there, but Whitehead has speculated that there are signs of Davenport's interest in shrubberies and waterworks on Letton Lake to the east of the Castle, below the bridge on the Leominster road.[33] He has also identified The Spinney on the south-eastern perimeter of the estate as being a typical 'shrubbery-cum-belt likely to have been introduced by a professional landscaper'.[34] Without further proof of his involvement at Kinnersley this must remain a speculation. So must any input he might have had at **Garnons** (*colour 21*), when Cottrell was planning to remodel the house and reshape the grounds after he had inherited the property in 1790 and married, a year later, a local heiress, Frances Isabella Evans. Although James Wyatt was approached in 1791 to design a new house, the job eventually went to William Atkinson. At the same time Repton was asked to prepare a Red Book, having first visited the estate eighteen months earlier. Although Repton secured the commission and was working closely with Wilkins, Davenport made several visits to Garnons during 1792, no doubt to supply plants and shrubs, and perhaps advise on their planting.[35]

Repton's work at Garnons is indicative of a subtle but important change in fashion from the minimalist Brownian park, highlighted in the county by the wide open spaces of the magnificent landscape at Berrington, to more intimate landscapes. These were to be enlivened with shrubberies and enriched again with garden buildings. While a Brownian park usually encompasses a vast terrain and extends it visually even further, Repton's designs are generally more humanly scaled. His early Herefordshire commissions, when he was collaborating with John Nash, were usually pared-down versions of Brownian parks more fitting for the gentry. Had he been allowed to continue to design these unremarkable but satisfying improvements without constant criticism from the Picturesque aesthetes, the late-eighteenth-century garden history of the country in general, and Herefordshire in particular, might have been markedly different. As it was, a taste for rugged rather than smooth Nature – Edmund Burke's Sublime as opposed to his Beautiful – was to supplant the vapidity of the Brownian aesthetic and alter Repton's own perceptions of his predecessor's achievement.

5

'In the enemy's quarters' – Repton and the pressure of the Picturesque

Garnons · Moccas Court · Stoke Edith · Belmont · Courtfield
Sufton Court · Ross-on-Wye Prospect · Kyrle's Summerhouse · Foxley
Downton Castle · Stonebrook Cottage

THE WYE SEEMS TO HAVE HAD A MESMERIC EFFECT ON HUMPHRY REPTON, as almost all of his commissions in the county were in the Vale of Hereford, with the snaking river as their focus. He may well have perfected the landscape at Moccas, which overlooks the great Brobury Scar in a bend of the Wye, while his other documented works feature stretches of the river or, where it is just out of sight, sheets of water in the parkland which simulate the great waterway. It is likely that this appropriation of, or response to, a natural watercourse in a designed landscape was not something that Repton had automatically perceived, but had learnt while walking along the river in the company of Uvedale Price and some of his friends. Price wrote later:

> I shall always remember with pleasure the hours we spent together on the Wye, and the perfect good-humour and cheerfulness of the whole party; but I could not help observing at the time, (and with much concern,) how lightly you treated the idea of taking any hints from any part of a natural river, towards forming an artificial one.[1]

Stephen Daniels believes that their walking tour may have taken place as early as 1789, after Price had been impressed by Repton's plans for Ferney Hall in Shropshire.[2] This may be the case, but a later letter written by Price to Lord Abercorn on 14 July 1792 suggests that this was the year when they became properly acquainted, two years before the 'stylist war' controversy of 1794:

> I have lately had an opportunity of seeing a good deal of Mr Repton a layer out of grounds, or as he styles himself a Landscape Gardener: you will guess at his manners by his title which I believe is of his own creation, but tho a coxcomb he is very ingenious in his profession, + seems to me to have infinitely more resources, + better principles, than his predecessors: Knight is acquainted with him, + thinks about him as I do, + we both rejoice that he has some respect for picturesque beauty which has hitherto been treated with great indignity. He has been making plans of improvement for some Gentlemen in my neighbourhood at whose houses I saw him, + afterwards went down the Wye with him, + and was happy to find that he really admired the banks in their natural state.[3]

So, although Price had a low opinion of Repton personally, their relations were cordial, with Price taking the lead as the intellectual and aesthetic mentor to a promising student. He was to write in 1810, after the furore had died down:

> From the time I had first the pleasure of being acquainted with you, I wished to be your ally, not your opponent: I flattered myself, that, having considered the same subject in different lights, and by means of a different course of study, we might have been of reciprocal use to each other. I felt great hopes that you might employ your talents (which I thought would naturally lead you in that way) in making experiments in landscape-gardening on the principles of landscape-painting, and the art of painting in general.[4]

This cordiality changed when Repton chose to take, in Price's words, the 'opposite side – to stand forth the defender of Mr. Brown; a circumstance

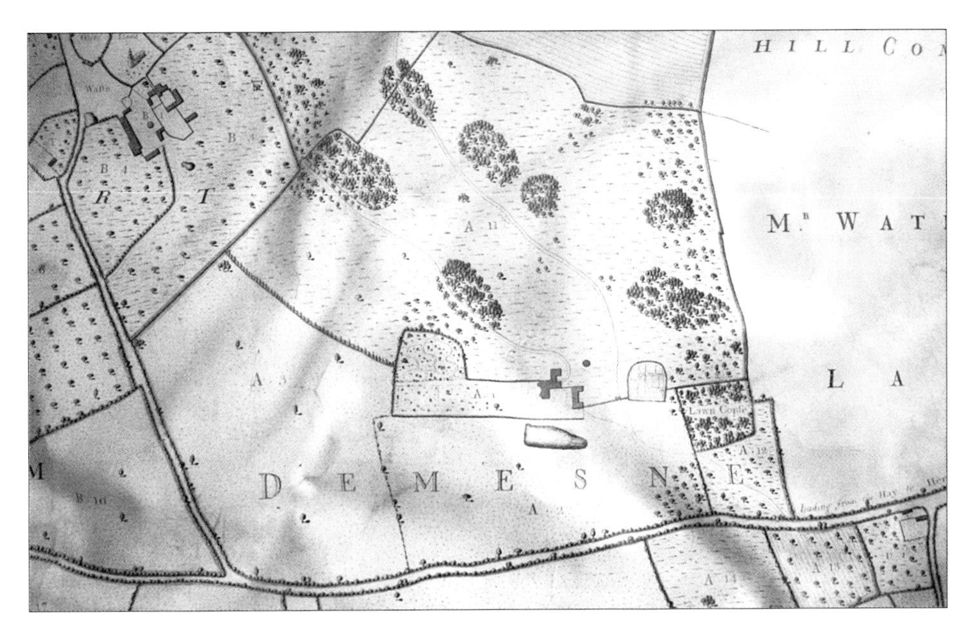

33 James Sherriff's 1784 survey of Garnons shows serpentine walks in a tree-lined enclosure, and a wide terrace by the house, both of which pre-date the involvement on the site in the 1790s of John Davenport and Humphry Repton. *Private collection*

which is sincerely lamented by many of your friends and well-wishers'.[5] In Price's view, Repton had turned into a slavish follower of Brown's designs and methods and had failed to forge his own aesthetic, informed by an appreciation of Picturesque principles: the 'well-wishers', who included Price, 'were desirous that you should stand on your own merits, leaving yourself free to avoid whatever, on more mature reflection, might appear defective in any system'.[6] These perceived defects were, of course, all of Brown's making.

However, Repton had resolutely set himself up in business as a Brown disciple, and so took on his first commission in Herefordshire at Garnons, the adjacent estate to Price's Foxley, with a view to producing a mini version of a typical Brownian park. It is likely that he was introduced to John Geers Cotterell by Price, whose gardener, James Cranston later of the King's Acre Nursery in Hereford, carried out Repton's improvements.[7] The Red Book that Repton prepared for **Garnons** was based on a 10-day visit in February 1791, and was completed at his Essex base in Hare Street,

Romford, in the following July.[8] James Sherriff had already surveyed the Garnons estate in 1784 for John Cotterell, and his map (*33*) is an important record of the park before it was remodelled.[9] Repton acknowledged the existing features and terrain when he wrote in the Red Book that the 'delightful bank on which the house is situated looking towards the south, and commanding the most interesting and varied scenery is such as fully justifies a continuance of the house near the present scite'. His aim was to take advantage of 'the walks which are already in the vicinity of the house'.[10]

The commissioning of architects for the new house is a tortuous story which must, however, be outlined briefly. Repton attempted to introduce, unsuccessfully, his architectural collaborator John Nash, who was to work with him on several Herefordshire projects.[11] John Geers Cotterell knew both Nash and James Wyatt through their current architectural projects in Hereford at the new gaol and the cathedral respectively. In May 1791 Repton was about to call on Wyatt, but he was notoriously unreliable and failed to complete the commission. In the autumn of 1792 William Wilkins visited Garnons and had submitted plans by December.[12] Correspondence between Cotterell and Wilkins continued until 1796, when Repton wrote that he was consulting Nash, after which Wilkins disappeared from the scene. Repton continued to be in touch with Cotterell until 1807, but the house remained unaltered until rebuilt to designs by William Atkinson between 1815 and 1828. What is clear from the correspondence, however, is that Repton was working closely with Wilkins on landscape features and the placement of trees in the park; Wilkins had also designed an icehouse.[13] One letter concerned the entrance to the park,[14] while in another, of 19 September 1792, Repton was exercised by the line of approach to the house and mentioned a Mr Parry, who was presumably the owner of The Weir, which may have been another of his Wye-side commissions.[15] One tantalising reference is to 'the fishing house [which] is a room standing on a cottage to be built in the hollow place by the road side'.[16] Repton was still considering this in December 1807, when he sent plans and sketches for it to Cotterell.[17]

The Garnons Red Book is text heavy and so provides a clear statement of Repton's objectives at this early stage in his career. Under 'Character', he delights in what were to become his twin obsessions – social status and genteel hospitality:

> The Character of a place will take its distinguishing marks from the united consideration of its situation and the extent of territory surrounding. Both these at Garnons require a degree of Greatness which neither the house nor the Grounds at present indicate. It is not necessary to build a palace to produce the character of Greatness, but a house which is the seat of Hospitality and, where according to the custom of Herefordshire, not only the neighbouring Families but even their servants and horses may receive a welcome, must necessarily form such a mass of building as will give an air of Greatness to the general appearance.[18]

At this point Wyatt had been retained as the architect, though Repton had no idea what form the new house would take. He was, however, of the opinion that it should be in the 'Gothic stile' to produce that irregularity of the 'seemingly discordant parts, which produce with skilful management at a certain distance, the effect of a magnificent whole'.[19] His before-and-after sketch of the house is inscribed: 'not having at this time received the promised plan or Elevation. I have here supposed a new house of an irregular gothic stile, merely to shew the effect of the terrace, plantations & Lawn &c, but the house will perhaps be totally unlike that which is intended to be built by Mr Wyatt'. The sketch with the slide in place (*colour 22*) corresponds closely in both the buildings and the planting to the Sherriff map. With the slide pulled back (*colour 23*) it reveals Repton's more elaborate and rambling Gothic house, connected to offices by a loggia. The planting on the hillside behind the house has been retained but thickened, and the horizon dramatised by a viewing tower; a serpentine drive leads down from the hillside to the house. In the foreground, greensward and a new lake have replaced two cultivated fields, while sheep graze about the park in picturesque fashion. The parkland has been extended by the removal of the turnpike further south, as shown on Repton's map (*34*), and a new approach is proposed that will 'enter the park betwixt the plantations, the depth of which will be impossible to distinguish' and then 'burst upon the Lawn at a most interesting point of view', as 'a very extensive park scene presents itself to the west, and as we proceed the house appears in full magnificence'.[20]

After discussing the connection between his proposed new terrace and the existing garden walks in the pleasure grounds, Repton considers the introduction of water to enliven what will still be open parkland. He is not sure that the existing pond 'can retain its situation with propriety', and argues instead for a 'small piece of water' in a 'wet part of a meadow', to 'shew an apparent continuation of River', a corresponding reach of the Wye being 'rendered visible from the house with proper management'.[21] Before-and-after sketches support this expedient (*35 & 36*), and the stretch of water survives alongside the plantation that masks the A438; these are both shown on Repton's map. Views across the park today conform fairly closely to what Repton intended, though it is impossible to see the Wye in its valley between the park and the ridge of hills that form a backdrop to the view (*colour 24*). The new pool acts, therefore, as a deception, inducing the 'stranger to suppose he sees a stretch of the Wye, which he knows must flow at no great distance'; such a deception is allowed because, according to Repton, 'it is the business of Taste to deceive....by which Art endeavours to conceal her own works, and make them appear the products of Nature only'.[22] It is hardly surprising, given such sentiments, that Repton was to incur the ridicule and wrath of the Picturesque aesthetes. Had they read his text, they would also have been sneeringly dismissive of his remark: 'the more wild and romantic continuation of the drive over the hills at the back of the house' would be used less than the main approach because there would be 'difficulty in removing all ideas of danger from the pleasure which such a drive would excite'.[23] Repton's parks were contrived to be safe places in which to enjoy at leisure the

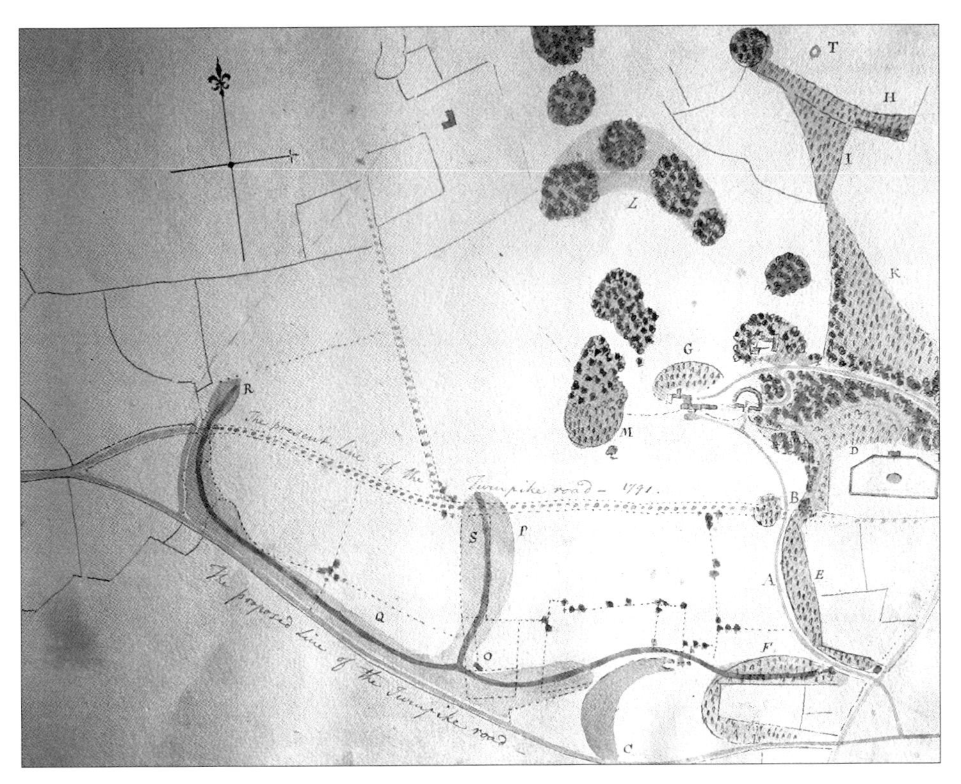

34 A typical Red Book map captures relationships between landscape features rather than providing accurate distances. The curved sweep of water that Repton intended should imitate the Wye is marked 'C' at the bottom. *Private collection*

delights of beautiful Nature, rather than its excitements and danger. These, of course, were just the sensations that Price and Payne Knight hoped to engender in visitors to their estates.

After the complications of designing without a parent house in place, Repton found no such problems at **Moccas**, further north on the other side of the river. Here, as we have seen, Keck had built the Palladian-style villa, though the grounds around it, while improved by Sir George Cornewall, still retained an air of tight formality. There would seem to be no firm documentary evidence that Repton made any major alterations to the landscape shaped by Cornewall, though there has been speculation that he opened up the prospect over the Wye towards Brobury Scar because the mature planting had encroached on the view.[24] Hazel Fryer has suggested that Repton's most important contribution to Moccas was

35 Repton introduces the sluice gate and delineates the regular outlines of the pool to emphasise the artificial nature of the existing water feature at Garnons. *Private collection*

36 In the improved scene at Garnons the pool has gone, to be replaced by a carriage drive and bridge over Repton's proposed imitation of the Wye. *Private collection*

the walk by the river,[25] but Cornewall's Account Book records a payment in 1773 to John Lambe Davis for a survey which shows it in place at that time, long before Repton's arrival.[26] Fryer argues that Cornewall recorded in his notebook that in 1793 he had 'begun the work by Repton's advice from above the river and moved the rails further from the house', but that is another thing entirely.[27] John Phibbs, with no direct evidence but on comparison with other Repton sites, has argued that the network of carriage drives in the park, if that is what they were, had stopping places or 'platforms', from which to take in views.[28] Repton did not, however, refer to features like these in his Red Books until 1800.[29] Finally, Repton himself wrote, in his 1803 *Observations*, of the success of the removal of a 'small quantity of earth' at Moccas, which concealed a view of the river from the house, so it would seem that his work was cosmetic rather than all encompassing.[30]

Whatever the truth of the matter, it is clear that John Nash was involved in designing lodges for the entrances to the park, and that he may well have contrived these with advice from Repton. Edward Foley had introduced Repton to Nash when the architect was remodelling the parlour at Stoke Edith around 1793. For the next five years the two men were to work closely together until they fell out over money.[31] The lodges Nash devised for Moccas are Daw Cottage, which guards the main drive from the B4352, and Bridge Cottage (*37*), south-east of the Court close to a lost bridge over the Wye to Monnington. Designs by George Stanley Repton exist for another cottage and a barn on the estate, but it is not known whether they were executed.[32] Both Nash lodges have the vernacular motifs of latticed fenestration, dormers, tall chimneystacks and rustic porches favoured by him. Daw Cottage is close in style to another lodge thought to have been designed by Nash at Canon Frome Court, north-east of Stoke Edith, and another one at Homend Park.[33] David Verey wrote evocatively in 1955 of the best way to approach Moccas, which was from Monnington 'along Monnington Walk, once a great avenue of Scotch firs planted in the seventeenth century, and over the Wye by a private cast iron "Gothic" bridge to a lodge designed by John Nash, where you will be required to pay sixpence. From the bridge you will have caught a glimpse of the red brick mansion architected by Adam, severely belying its superbly rich interior'.[34]

Whether or not Repton was commissioned by Edward Parry of The Weir, north of a bend in the Wye opposite Canon Bridge, is not clear, although the site was included in Peacock's *Polite Repository* in 1799, which

37 John Nash was concerned about the picturesque detailing of this lodge at Moccas, requesting that the tiled overhang to the main window should match the roof

included impressions that were 'engraved from drawings of H. Repton of scenery improving under his direction'.[35] And, as we have seen, Repton mentioned the owner in a letter to John Geers Cotterell of Garnons. The riverside garden was extensively remodelled in the twentieth century. But with Repton's contemporary work at **Stoke Edith** we are on safer ground, as his Red Book survives,[36] while there is a contemporary poem, admittedly written in a typically unctuous style, congratulating Edward Foley on what had been achieved there by 1799.[37] The landscaping scheme that the 1st Lord Foley achieved included the infamous shrubbery bordering the Ledbury-Hereford road. This was the venue in the 1780s for an adulterous assignation between Lady Ann Foley, soon to become the ex-wife of Edward Foley, and the Earl of Peterborough. Witness statements from Lord Peterborough's prosecution for 'criminal conversation' and Lord Foley's claim for damages at Hereford were reproduced in titillating pamphlets and scandalous newspaper articles. John Davies, a mason and bricklayer from Tarrington who worked for Foley, gave a typical witness

15 Herefordshire's early churches are famous for their Angevin Romanesque carving. The Shobdon Arches were taken from the church when it was Gothicisied under the direction of Dicky Bateman, who preserved them and set them up as an eyecatcher, as part of the eclectic landscape

16 James Wathen's 1798 view of Mr Purchas' House at Fownhope depicts the ziz-zag walk, obelisk and summerhouse behind the factory complex. *Hereford City Library*

17 Views of the Wye from the zig-zag path appealed to Mr Purchas' commercial and aesthetic interests. He landed wine and spirits from Bristol at Fownhope's quay

18 This view of Berrington has all the signature elements of Brown's landscape aesthetics – the ha-ha, tree clumps, shelterbelts and a lake to reflect the contrived minimalism

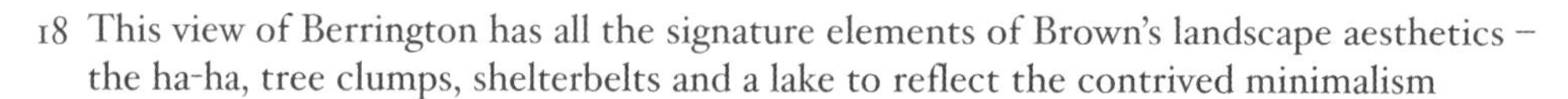

19 The Brobury Scar was a focal point for views across the Wye to and from Moccas Court

20 The Cornewalls, surveying their unimproved estate from Brobury Scar, look across the Wye to Moccas Court and the distant peaks of the Sugar Loaf and Hay Bluff.
Private collection

21 A house and landscape in perfect Regency accord at Garnons, where Humphry Repton worked alongside William Wilkins

24 The view from Garnons towards the Black Mountains as Repton envisaged it, with arable fields replaced by more pictorially pastoral pastureland

22 Repton's unimproved view of Garnons as it was in 1791, when walls protected the serpentine walks recorded by Sherriff and the main approach to the house was in need of remodelling.
Private collection

23 Garnons after Repton's proposed improvements. The foreground has been enriched with a new lake and the grounds dressed with grazing sheep, while the altered line of the hillside drive provides a safer route over a steep gradient.
Private collection

25 In his Red Book for Stoke Edith Repton explained that the pavilion integrated into the rear of the Ledbury Lodge was designed with columns whose proportions were taken from the trunk of a nearby oak tree

26

George Romney's 1786 portrait of John Matthews might have been consciously contrived to emphasise the down-to-earth qualities that distinguished this amateur improver from Richard Payne Knight, depicted as the consummate conoisseur in Sir Thomas Lawrence's famous painting of 1794. *'Dr John Matthews', 1786.*
George Romney 1734-1802.
Tate, London 2011

27 John Kyrle's Summerhouse, hidden away behind the row of shops facing the Market Hall in Ross-on-Wye, has been sympathetically converted for modern living

28

In his youth Uvedale Price was labelled a Macaroni. This undated portrait of him in middle age must have been painted after 1797, when Lady Oxford ceremoniously cut off his pigtail as the recognised mark of Whig opposition to Pitt. *Private collection*

29 This view of Downton Castle shows the battlemented and be-pinnacled terraces added in the nineteenth century, which anchor the house more satisfyingly to its landscape

account. On 30 September 1784 he observed Lady Ann and Lord Peterborough

> in the shrubbery, near the grotto, a few minutes after six o'clock in the evening. That he first heard Lady Ann cry out, two or three times, "O dear! You hurt me!" which induced him to look that way; and, going towards the pales, he look over them, and saw Lord Peterborough and Lady Ann together. That his lordship had Lady Ann round the middle, and that her Ladyship's coats were up; and at the same time, he saw her Ladyship's naked legs and thighs round Lord Peterborough's hams; and her arms round her Lordship's neck.....Being further interrogated by the counsel, he replied, that he was sure his Lordship had sealed her, meaning that he had carnal knowledge of her. That he afterwards turned away, and went on the road, when he met James Moore, to whom he related what he had seen, without suppressing a single circumstance.[38]

The publicity surrounding the affair did not fade away as the *Daily Universal Register* was still running the story amongst its snippets of London news in September 1785: 'Lady Foley and Mrs Arabin have kindly undertaken to plan the intended *shrubbery* behind Gower-street can anyone doubt their *capability*, who reflects with what *art* they have displayed the *beauties of nature* in their own gardens'.[39]

Visitors to Stoke Edith had found the house ill-sited in its park and in need of improvement. In 1788 the Revd Stebbing Shaw remarked that

> the house is large, and wears an ancient aspect, but the principal front is turned from the road, its surrounding shrubs break the ill effect of too great an intimacy with passengers; a bridge communicates with the park over the road, which we passed under. The views from every point are pleasing and picturesque, and from the next ascent the house and parish spire, very high and beautiful, formed a delightful group with the variegated ground adjacent, and finally terminated by the Malvern-hills.[40]

Repton would have concurred with these observations, although for him the most pressing defects at Stoke were the proximity of the house to the road and the manner in which the parish church and adjacent parsonage dominated the scene. He also wanted to change the profile of the ground beneath the south and east fronts of the house to improve the views outwards, and to make some minor planting changes; and in an ideal world he would have covered the red-brick house with stone-coloured paint and sand. Indeed, his first illustration in the Red Book (*38*) shows the house as a white mansion with a far more pronounced portico than existed, with the addition of a lower wing, which would 'connect the house to the offices in a more pleasing manner'.[41] Furthermore, in his sketch the church has lost its spire and the parsonage has been reduced in size and cloaked in greenery, rendering them both subservient, as they always should be in Repton's view, to the main house. In fact, in Repton's ideal picturesque world, it would be prudent to consolidate this living with another and 'to remove the house [parsonage] entirely out of the park, together with all its appendages'.[42]

The following before-and-after views conform closely to those areas of the park that Repton's map marks 'East Lawn', 'West Lawn' and 'North Lawn', which are bordered by shelter belts and, in the case of the West Lawn, dressed with thick tree clumps. These plantations are intended either to obscure unwanted views or to open up the house to views across the parkland, while proposed earth shaping, particularly to the south, would give 'a more pleasing shape to the ground which now falls away too abruptly towards the meadow'.[43] Repton's watercolour (*39*) illustrating this sculpted ground looks remarkably like the valley occupied by the Keeper's Cottage to the other side of Lady Ann's Bridge, suggesting that Foley was following his proposals closely. After further before-and-after sketches of the landscape views, Repton turns to the approach to the house, which he has 'fixed on the line described in the map and marked with stakes upon the spot'.[44] His sketch shows cultivated fields before improvement and a

38 Repton incorporated every alteration, short of demolition, in this pictorial proposal to bring Stoke Edith House out of the shadow of the Parsonage. *Private collection*

39 A perfect illustration from the Stoke Edith Red Book of Repton's contouring of an existing landscape. *Private collection*

sturdy late-Palladian-style lodge when the slide is pulled back. This conforms almost exactly to the Ledbury Lodge (*colour 25*) on the A438, while the Hereford Lodge, mentioned earlier, is a slightly later addition, though marked as a proposal on Repton's map. William Wilkins, who had worked so closely with Repton at Garnons, designed both Lodges between 1792 and 1796.[45]

Under 'The Village', Repton proposed demolishing the labourers' cottages to the west of the house and rebuilding them around a new entrance on the diverted road: 'If their humble dwellings can be made a subordinate part of the general scenery they will so far from disgracing it, add all the dignity that wealth can derive from the exercise of benevolence'.[46] Repton wanted some cottages to be left in the park, particularly in the dell, not just for practical purposes, but because 'the occasional smoke from the chimnies may animate the scene; there is hardly any thing more picturesque and pleasing than smoke curling amongst the trees, and relieved by a dark hanging wood in the deep recess of a beautiful glen like this'.[47] Foley turned to Wilkins for designs for the new village and the architect supplied elevations for seven double cottages housing two weavers, a cooper, a butcher, a blacksmith, a shoe-maker and eight labourers, plus a school and a cider mill.[48] This last, a circular structure surrounded by a colonnade of primitivist Doric columns, made out of tree trunks with the bark left on, was never realised, even though Philips' 1791 edition of his poem *Cyder* was dedicated to Foley and producing the liquor was a real passion at Stoke Edith. It is likely that the cottage by the drive up to the church is a survivor of the two that were built of the original scheme.

Repton wrote about the relatively few opportunities to improve the planting close to the house, yet he did mention in his 1803 *Observations* that a 'pavilion, or covered seat' was integrated into the rear of the new Ledbury Lodge adjoining a 'walk in the shrubbery' and the new plantation nearby.[49] This is consistent with his plan for the new line of the road in the Red Book, which also showed an encircling belt of shrubs or trees. This prompts the questions 'who created the shrubbery – and when?' It may be that Repton consciously avoided any reference to it in the Red Book for fear of stirring his employer's embarrassment following the divorce scandal. Certainly the surviving accounts prove that improvements to the pleasure grounds were being carried out in the 1790s; these went beyond Repton's advice in the Red Book. In 1794 payments were made for shrubbery seats, new stone steps into the shrubbery and for 'making a new door for the stone steps into Shrubbery'.[50] In the following year payments continued for the hanging and painting of a small door at the top of stone steps into the Shrubbery. Other work at this time included the construction of a new 'Garden House', which was fitted out with a writing desk and seat, alterations to a gravel walk near the 'Pavilion', the erection of a paled fence in the 'Lower Garden' and 101 yards of new rail fence for the front of the house.[51] It is not clear who was supervising these works, though it is possible that Repton made additional visits to Stoke to direct the work.

What is not in doubt is that he argued in the Red Book that the belt of trees along the boundary of what, in the seventeenth century, had been Paul Foley's Upper and Lower Park, should be softened. This was the Tarrington Walk, which had been planted by London in 1693. As yet, no record has been found of the felling of this avenue, but it clearly disappeared some time between 1778 and Repton's second site visit in June 1792.[52] He also advocated screening the re-routed road along part of its length with a new plantation, whilst additional clumps on the rising ground beyond the new road would alleviate any 'sameness' in the view.[53] These are the five impressive oval plantations on rising ground to the north of the A438 that were replanted about 1993 by Andrew Foley and Bede Howell, the forester, working on behalf of Abbey Forestry. In the early nineteenth century these tree clumps would have enriched the view from the portico steps of the house, although now they can only be seen from the arable field that was previously the North Lawn. The effect of these clumps, in alleviating what Repton described as a 'uniform sheet of Lawn fringed by a verge of plantations', is a stunning example of how to design a view on a grand scale.[54] Foley's new landscape and his Georgic status was celebrated in Luke Booker's 1799 poem *The Hop-Garden*, which records how aesthetics and productivity worked in tandem on the estate:

> O Thou who, with Esteem unbounded bless'd,
> Sees, round they Stoke's umbrageous woods, arise

> Gardens of od'rous Hop – their stately poles
> Crowning with pendent flow'rs – Gardens which hail
> Thee FOLEY! Their Possessor – to thy Care
> The Muse, that strays those flow'ry scenes among,
> Devotes her artless lay. – Spontaneous flows
> The strain thus foster'd; and, in various mood,
> She, humbly-daring, woos thy gen'rous Smile.[55]

Everything seemed to be going well for Repton in the county until stylistic war broke out in 1794 with the publication of two polemical writings on landscape aesthetics: Uvedale Price's *An Essay on the Picturesque* and Richard Payne Knight's *The Landscape, a Didactic Poem*.[56] Both were intellectual attacks on Brown's landscape practice and his minimalist aesthetic, which had been expressed so well at Berrington, in favour of a more rugged and therefore seemingly natural approach to landscape gardening which, they both argued, should be informed by landscape painting, hence the term 'Picturesque'. It is essential to understand here that the lower case use of the word 'picturesque' relates to anything that could be construed as having the qualities of a picture or, more particularly, a painting, while the upper case 'Picturesque' refers to the aesthetic method of composing a landscape or a view of landscape by certain rules of painterly composition: foregrounds, distances, second distances and perspectives. This approach to landscape gardening was famously satirised by Jane Austen in her contemporary novel, *Northanger Abbey,* in the character of Henry Tilney who, together with his sister, was a devotee of the Picturesque, 'viewing the country with the eyes of persons accustomed to drawing, and decided on its capability of being formed into pictures with all the eagerness of real taste'.[57] The key phrase here, of course, is 'real taste', for that is what Payne Knight and Price felt that Repton lacked in his slavish copying of Brown's landscape style. The controversy and the growing appreciation of natural scenery as a template for landscape design had its roots in William Gilpin's account of his tour of the Wye during the summer of 1770, which was not published until 1782, and perhaps even earlier in the county at

Ross-on-Wye, with attempts by John Kyrle, The Man of Ross, to whom we shall return, to focus contrived views on landscape features. Gilpin's book was entitled: *Observations on the River Wye and Several Parts of South Wales, etc., Relative to Picturesque Beauty*, signalling the importance of the Wye and its potential for Picturesque analysis. He later published his *Three Essays: on Picturesque Beauty; on Picturesque Travel; and on Sketching the Landscape. To which is added a Poem on Landscape Painting.* That appeared in 1792, two years before Price's *Essay*. Repton knew full well, therefore, what to expect when Price and Payne Knight began to prepare their texts, but he was surprised at the personal nature of the attack.

His Red Book for Sufton Court, an estate owned by James Hereford south of Hereford near Mordiford, but close to the Wye, is prefaced by a staunch riposte to contemporary criticism of his work: 'My opinion concerning the improvement of Sufton Court involves so many points, which I deem principles in the art of Landscape Gardening, that I trust you will permit me to take this opportunity of justifying my practice, in opposition to the wild theory of the improvement which has lately sprung up in Herefordshire'.[58] Repton was not standing alone in this theoretical war of words. He had a supporter in John Matthews (*colour 26*), owner of **Belmont**, another estate in the Vale, this time south-west of Hereford, which was perched directly above the Wye (*40*). Matthews is now known to have written the anonymously published 1794 *A Sketch from the Landscape*, a lampoon of Knight's poem, to which was added a postscript addressed to Price. Matthews defended Brown and Repton against the 'unnatural extravagances' of 'these desperate amateurs',[59] including a title page that showed the 'amateurs' hurling the contents of a chamber pot at a monument to Brown (*41*). The tailpiece was even more scurrilous (*42*), depicting two women swooning in a flower garden on encountering the god of gardens – Pan – in the form of a clipped yew with a 'huge and terrible *Priapus*'.[60] This was a direct criticism of Payne Knight, whom Matthews described as favouring formal French gardens, and a reference to Payne Knight's interest in ancient phallic cults; he had published *The*

40

The picturesque view of the Wye from Belmont is similar to that from Moccas Court, further upriver

Worship of Priapus through the Society of Dilletanti in 1786. It is likely that Repton gave advice on the landscaping at Belmont, as the site appears in Peacock's *Polite Repository* for February 1794. Furthermore, there are three drawings for estate buildings inscribed 'Dr Matthews' in the Notebook of Repton's son's, George Stanley.[61]

David Whitehead has written extensively on Belmont and charts in some detail the landscaping that was carried out there up to Matthews' death in 1827, but Repton does not refer to the site in any of his books, so his input must remain unproven.[62] George Romney's portrait shows Matthews in the pose of a connoisseur with an open book in his hand and an architectural drawing for the house propped up on the table next to him.[63] This suggests that he saw himself as a gentleman improver intimately involved with the development of the house and its landscape. He might have employed George Parkyns, who included a design for the park at Belmont, in his *Six designs for improving and embellishing grounds* of 1793. Parkyns' plan number 5 for Belmont includes a 'Root-House', a banqueting

41 Only eleven years after Brown's death, John Matthews caricatured the contemporary criticism of him in this scurillous engraving. *Hereford City Library*

42 Matthews' parody of Payne Knight's *The Landscape* was accompanied by this illustration, which is inscribed: 'The God of Gardens thou shalt stand,/To fright improvers from the land,/A huge and terrible Priapus'. *Hereford City Library*

43 The Palladian villa at Belmont has been subsumed by an extension in *Nightmare Abbey* Gothic

room, a 'Temple of Harmony' and a 'Temple of the Doric Order'.[64] Significantly, a root house mentioned in 1827 has since disappeared.[65] So too has a grotto that was recorded in 1795 as having a view out to the east over the Wye.[66] This must have been contemporary with another hermitage-cum-grotto overlooking the Wye at **Courtfield**, Welsh Bicknor, which was seen in 1799 by one of the writers on the Wye, Charles Heath:

> On the North side of the house and on an eminence in the park, stands a high parapet wall, with gothick-shaped arches, which when viewed from the river has the appearance of a ruin....A small room adjoins behind called the Hermit's Cell, in which was placed a figure of an old man, with a flowing beard, kneeling, his hands in the attitude of prayer.[67]

The ghost of Matthews' late-Palladian-style building is still just discernible, but subsumed within a nightmarish Victorian Gothic remodelling (*43*). Its garden front has a three-storey semicircular bay like that at Moccas for views down to the Wye. Sadly, the house is now shut up, pending a long-promised restoration, its *porte cochère* a parking lot for golf buggies, while Matthews' landscape is contoured with fairways and putting greens.

Even with Matthews' public support, Repton felt the need to establish his credentials as a credible professional and to distance himself from the controversy in order to gain Hereford's confidence and secure the commission at **Sufton Court**. The Red Book preface is a piece of studied self aggrandisement combined with his usual obsequious forelock touching:

> I have little leisure to enter the lists with Mr. Price or Mr. Knight, and must therefore decline a public controversy which in the hands of the latter gentlemen is become indecently personal; but it is hardly possible to deliver my sentiments on the improvement of any place, especially of one in Herefordshire, without feeling that my opinions may be misrepresented, misunderstood and perhaps disputed, that I shall therefore take the liberty in the course of the following pages to allude to the new system so far as it bears any relation to the immediate object of this small volume. I have made it a general practice not only to deliver my opinion in writing, but also to assign reasons for that opinion and I am in a particular manner called upon to defend those reasons with due caution, as liable to be canvassed with severity in the near neighbourhood of my antagonists: it is however no small circumstance of triumph to me, that I am still consulted even in the enemy's quarters; and for that good opinion of my professional skill which induced you to call in my advice, I must beg leave to express my thanks.

After all that, Hereford did appoint Repton, but his work at Sufton consisted of pruning the existing plantations and clumps rather than a major re-shaping of the small park. Indeed, almost all the comments made in the key to the map concern either taking out trees to provide better views, or introducing plantations and some single trees to hide features, such as 'a ruined barn, which is a bad object from the Hereford approach'. What is interesting about the map, and particularly appropriate in Herefordshire, is the retention of the three large orchards and other field boundaries (*44*). There is no sense here that the whole estate should be opened out into a wide park landscape.

All the emphasis in Repton's text is on views out towards the south and west. It may be that he was in too much of a hurry to propose anything more considered, for his visit to Sufton was 'made in two days of excessive rainy weather', with 'no assistance from previous knowledge of the spot, or from any accurate survey of the premises'.[68] So his improvements in the park were to be effected 'by the axe rather than the spade', in defiance of Payne Knight who 'lays down a general rule for improvement, "to plant largely and cut down sparingly", but this is the over cautious advice of a timorous inexperience'.[69] To emphasise this Repton includes a sketch of the approach to the house with an existing line of trees, which he proposes removing and replacing with artfully sited clumps (*45 & 46*). One panoramic view from the house of the Black Mountains, the city of Hereford, 'the Hill of the Bishop's ear' and a near neighbour's house is to be enhanced in the foreground with single trees dramatising the Lugg. A carriage drive through plantations is proposed, also the removal of hedgerows to make a plain lawn and the introduction of a classical temple. While some of Repton's planting seems to have been carried out at Sufton, the temple remained a paper dream.

As a final dig at Payne Knight, Repton includes a section specifically on 'Landscape Gardening' and argues against his own skill as an artist in an attempt to define the difference between the artist and the gardener:

> I do not profess to be a *Landscape painter* so far from it, the gaudy sketches with which I have found it necessary to elucidate my opinions, are a strong proof that I do not profess to copy the works of great painters....but [it] is in the general *composition* of landscapes that the painter and gardener will feel the difference betwixt their respective Arts: and tho' each may assist the other occasionally yet I should no more advise the Landscape Gardener in laying out the scenery of a place to affect the confined field of vision, or the careless

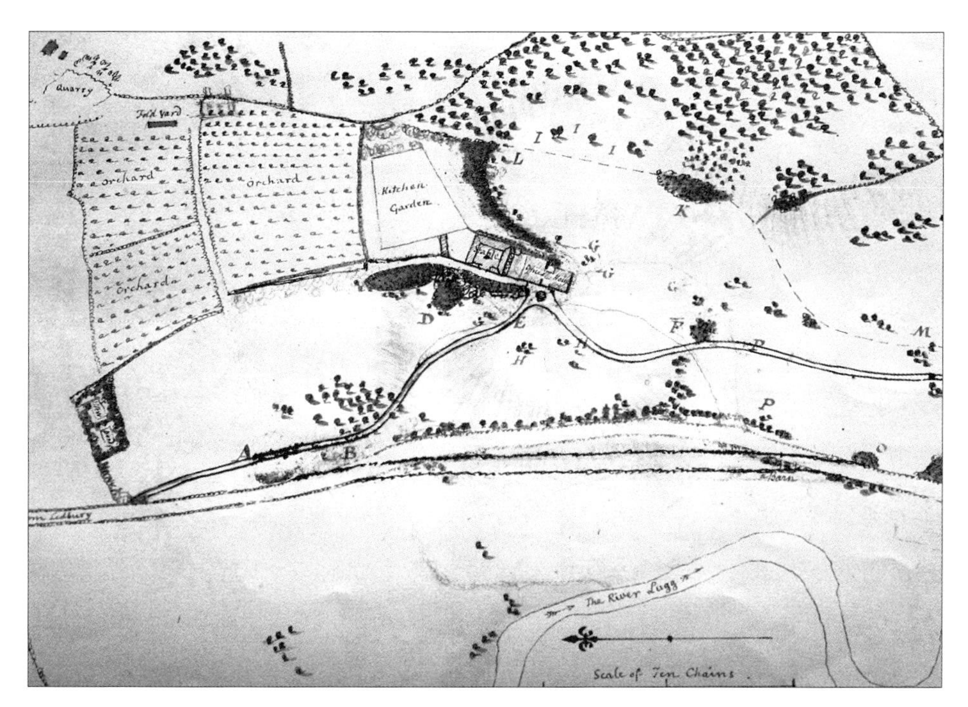

44 The retention of fields and orchards on Repton's plan for Sufton reveals his minimal intervention on the site. *Facsimile, private collection*

> graces of a Claude or a Poussin, than I should recommend to a Landscape painter the quincunx or formal rows of the kitchen garden.[70]

It was, of course, exactly those 'careless graces', which Price and Payne Knight perceived in the works of the great seventeenth-century landscape painters – Salvator Rosa and Jacob van Ruisdael – as well as Claude and Poussin, that they were most anxious to effect in their own landscape compositions on the ground. As Payne Knight was to put it in his poem:

> Hence let us learn, in real scenes, to trace
> The tints of beauty, and the forms of grace;
> To lop redundant parts, the coarse refine,
> Open the crowded, and the scanty join.[71]

This was echoed by Price in his *Essay on the Picturesque* when he wrote, in a mock serious manner, that a man 'full of enthusiasm for this new art, [of

45 The unimproved view of Sufton Court shows a line of trees that blocks out views to and from the house. *Facsimile, private collection*

46 The park at Sufton Court as improved by Repton; much of the planting survives today. *Facsimile, private collection*

modern gardening] and with little veneration for that of painting', would be shocked to see the trees in a Claude painting, 'some with their stems half concealed by bushes and thickets; others standing alone, but by means of those thickets, or of detached trees, connected with other groups of various sizes and shapes'.[72] He would, argued Price, demand: 'all this rubbish must be totally cleared away, the ground made every where quite smooth and level, and each group left upon the grass perfectly distinct and separate'.[73] This last might easily have been a precise description of Repton's tree planting and management at *Sufton*.

Gilpin's 1782 book on the Wye must have been a significant influence on Price, encouraging 'a new object of pursuit; that of examining the face of a country *by the rules of picturesque beauty*; opening the sources of those pleasures which are derived from the comparison'.[74] But a paper, which was read to the Society of Antiquaries in June 1782, and later published in *Archaeologia* in 1785, must have also had an impact, particularly as it had been written by Price's maternal uncle, Daines Barrington, who was a judge, an antiquary and a naturalist.[75] The paper was entitled '*On the Progress of Gardening*', and took the form of a letter from Barrington to the Antiquaries' Secretary, the Revd Mr Norris.[76] After a fairly predictable trawl through the history of writing on gardens and the practice of gardening from Babylon to Spenser's *Faerie Queene*, Barrington ends with an apostrophe to William Kent who was to 'realize these beautiful descriptions [in Spenser], for which he was peculiarly adapted by being a painter; as the true test of perfection in a modern garden is, that a landscape painter would choose it for a composition'.[77] Not surprisingly, he finds Brown's landscapes lacking that painterly approach:

> KENT hath been succeeded by Brown, who hath undoubtedly great merit in laying out pleasure grounds, but I conceive that in some of his plans I see rather traces of the gardener of Old Stowe, than of Poussin or Claude Lorraine. I could wish therefore that Gainsborough gave the design, and that Brown executed.[78]

Interestingly, Gainsborough was a frequent visitor to Foxley, the Price family home, and his success as a professional artist was due in no small measure to the patronage of Uvedale's father, Robert Price, particularly after Gainsborough had moved to Bath.[79] During this period Uvedale Price 'made frequent discursions with him into the country' and must, therefore, have impressed the young man.[80]

That Herefordshire in general, and the Wye in particular, are now seen to have been the birthplace of the Picturesque movement must be due to an early appreciation of the river by the celebrated 'Man of Ross', John Kyrle, immortalised by Alexander Pope in his poem *On the Use of Riches*. Pope had been introduced to the historical figure of Kyrle by his publisher Jacob Tonson, who had retired to his orchards and vines at The Hazel, just outside Ledbury. Pope's motive for writing about Kyrle was 'first to distinguish real and solid worth from showish or plausible expence, and virtue fro' vanity; and secondly, to humble the pride of greater men, by an opposition of one so obscure and so distant from the sphere of publick glory'.[81] Kyrle left three examples of his beneficence to Ross: his own garden behind his house on the market place, **The Prospect** and the cliff-top walk to Lower Cleeve.[82] While his timber-framed house survives, facing the Market House, just one enclosure is left of his garden, the rest being subsumed within later building and a car-park. Although the garden itself has been radically replanted with lively box parterres, what purports to be **Kyrle's Summerhouse** survives (*colour 27*), though the present structure could not have been built before his death in 1724. The Gothick-arched windows and patterned pavement in the porch, which depicts a swan made of animal teeth, are closer in style and atmosphere to the Regency. Sadly, the winding path to the Summerhouse and 'three little grotto arches' noted by Nikolaus Pevsner in 1963 have disappeared.[83] What does survive is the arched substructure of what might have been Kyrle's original summerhouse, in the car-park behind the garden, towards the parish church; the gravelled area might have been a bowling green. This location is close to that recorded by Charles Heath, who published an *Excursion down the Wye from Ross to Monmouth* in 1799 and wrote:

> On the South side of the church is laid down, through the estate which belonged to Mr Kyrle, a neat gravel path, which still retains the name of the person who formed it: and runs parallel with the course of the Wye. Towards the middle it is carried nearer to the edge of a rocky eminence, partially clothed with underwood, and

> shaded with beech and other timber in a thriving state. The trees planted by Mr Kyrle, which had grown to a very fine and large size, have since his death been cut down. At the extremity of this Walk is placed a SUMMERHOUSE which affords an agreeable retreat, as well as a pleasing view of the river and country. Over the door is a landscape, from the side of which issues, out of the clouds, a man's hand (a whimsical idea), the fore-finger pointing to a wood opposite. A Latin inscription (now defaced) was added underneath, claiming the visitor's attention to the hand which planted it. This painting was affixed by Mr. Newman, at that time a Surgeon in Ross, who rented the Summer House of the proprietor. The building is now going to decay, and is not open to public inspection.[84]

Heath then moves on to describe the Prospect, a square sector of level ground next to the Royal Hotel and St Mary's parish church, 'from whence you enjoy a charming view of the country and particularly the river, which meanders, both above and below the bridge, thro' meadows of the richest verdure. In the centre of this field was a FOUNTAIN, which supplied the near inhabitants with water...On the West side of the close stands a very handsome SUN DIAL, on which Mr Kyrle's Arms are engraved....On the North and South sides are handsome gateways, both of which were also surmounted with his Arms...under them is carved the year in which they were erected, 1700'.[85] One of the gateways survives intact (*47*), while gate piers into the churchyard, which are decorated with scrolly volutes, look to be of the same period.

In addition to his good works around the town, Kyrle also planted rows of elms on the east and west sides of the churchyard, and he may have been responsible for similar planting at Hill Court when the house was being rebuilt by Richard and Joseph Clarke in 1700.[86] A nineteenth-century historian, the Revd Charles Robinson, suggested that a 'noble avenue of Elm trees of equal antiquity [to the house]....were perhaps planted by the hand of "the Man of Ross", and the same hand is said, with less probability, to have designed the mansion'.[87] While his authorship of the house has been dismissed, his friendship with the two Clarke brothers may have resulted in the layout of the walled formal gardens, the gateways and gate piers of which were originally aligned to frame views of Goodrich Castle. Mature planting has now obscured these vistas but, given Kyrle's interest in and appreciation of contrived views in the landscape, they may have been of his making.

After all this obsession with views of, and from, the Wye, it is somewhat of an anticlimax to come to **Foxley** at Mansel Lacy, the estate of one of the arch Picturesque aesthetes, because it has no views of the river, the Wye being over two-and-half miles to the south-west and separated visually from it by Garnons Hill. Price's writings on the Picturesque approach to landscape were more potent than his actual gardening and estate management at Foxley, the aesthetic elements of which had been achieved long before Price inherited as a minor in 1764 and finally came of age in 1768. This is not to diminish his considerable impact at Foxley in terms of the expansion of the estate and its agricultural improvement, but the minds behind the laying out of rides to take in contrived views were Uvedale's grandfather Uvedale Tomkyns Price, and his father, Robert Price. Father and son had laid down the structure of a Picturesque landscape before Robert's untimely death aged 44 in 1761, and Uvedale Tomkyns' in 1764, aged 79. Indeed, it was probably Robert, a keen artist who knew William Hogarth and patronised Gainsborough, whose 'naturalistic' method of landscape drawing and gardening was to exert a lasting influence on Foxley.[88]

Foxley is set in a rich wooded valley between Mansel Lacy to the south-east and Yarsop to the north-west, while Yazor is due west, on the other side of Nash Wood. By 1735 both Uvedale Price and his father, Robert 'Baron' Price had completed the house and its formal gardens, while trees and coppice woods had been planted in the wider landscape. The key garden building of this period was the Ragged Castle, set on its mound in Nash Wood, due south of the house. This extraordinary building has eluded precise dating, though a crenellated rainwater head on the structure

47

One of two surviving gateways built in 1700 at John Kyrle's Prospect above the Wye in Ross. Should a town that relies on riverine tourism make more of such an historically important site?

is inscribed 'C 1740'. It is not mentioned by Uvedale Tomkyns Price in a memorandum dated 1735, but it might have been built at some point between 1714, when Anne Price wrote to her aunt Lady Anne Coventry that 'Mr Price is Resolved to have a Summer House on the top' of the mount, and 1744, when Robert Price made a wash drawing of it.[89] Major David Davenport, who restored it in 1975 in memory of his father, believes that it was 'Built Circa 1740 by ROBERT PRICE'.[90] The stylistic combination of round-arched classical openings on the ground floor and the sturdy Gothick battlemented parapet above seem to fit that dating. The building appears to be four-square on approach, but as it is circled it reveals itself to be triangular in form (*48*), consciously planned to take in views back to the house and out south and north-west. Oddly, when Bishop Pococke visited Foxley in September 1756, he mentioned the hill, not the tower, but was impressed by the views:

48

Robert Price's Ragged Castle at Foxley, built about 1740, proves that he was attuned to the picturesque possibilities of the estate long before Uvedale Price took over after 1768

From this place [Weobley] I went two miles to Mr Price's, one of our party to the glaciers in Savoy, and married to Lord Barrington's sister. The house is in a bottom on one side of the vale, which is form'd by a chain of hills in form of a circus, and covered with wood. He is practising a rideing all round the inside and outside of the hills, which within is at least six miles, and making sheep walks down from the wood, and corn fields are to be in the middle. From the house there are winding walks through woods of fine young oaks, up to the top of a little hill, which commands a view of the country to the south-east and north-east, and of the city of Hereford. The same view (except of Hereford) is seen on the south side of the hills which I have mentioned, as well as the Skiret Vaur and Blarens, over Abergavenny; also of Radnorshire, and a great way farther into Wales. The north side commands as far as the north part of Worcestershire, and the north-east a view of the opening

> between the hills and of the two Butts in that vale, through which opening Hereford is seen from some height about Shobden. Altogether the greatest variety of prospects I ever saw without going two miles from the house.[91]

The expedition mentioned by Pococke took place in June 1741 on Robert Price's Grand Tour; Price married Sarah Barrington in 1746 and lived at Foxley from then on, while his father lived mainly in Bath. Any landscape improvements between 1746 and 1761 are, therefore, likely to have been supervised by Price, including the 6-mile 'rideing' throughout the estate. He continued the planting regime instigated by his father and, together with a Grand Tour companion, Benjamin Stillingfleet, who moved to a cottage on the estate in 1746, investigated the theories of Linnaeus and went on tours to sketch from nature and examine the local flora. This joint enterprise resulted in experiments in planting grasses for agricultural feed. Stillingfleet wrote in 1757 that Price's 'walks or rather drives, for they will admit of wheel-carriages, will take in compass of 6 or 7 miles diversify'd with different prospects'.[92] Charles Watkins and Ben Cowell have described precisely the routes of Price's ridings, which can be traced on the 1891 Ordnance Survey map (*49*). They began north-west of the house and led up through Darkhill Wood to the Cold Bath, the footings of which still survive, on to Ladylift Clump – a stand of Scots pines – and thence to the head of the valley through Walks Wood and Shukes Bank below Burton Hill. Then they crossed open land before entering into Bache Wood, north-east of the house, continuing along the contours of the valley side through Pole Wood, then out onto open land again before entering Merryhill Wood, east of Mansel Lacy.

What then did Uvedale Price (*colour 28*) achieve at Foxley, after his return from his own Grand Tour in 1768, in a landscape that had already been perfected for both productive and aesthetic purposes? The answer has to be very little. The 1770s saw a remodelling of the house at the same time as Payne Knight was building **Downton Castle**, near Ludlow, on the Herefordshire border with Shropshire, and Price appointed James Cranston as his head gardener. Surveys of the estate were undertaken in 1770 and 1774 and Price continued to exchange land and buy new parcels to expand his land holdings but, as we have seen, the main improvements of these years were the demolition of the formal gardens around the house and the construction of a walled kitchen garden. However, within his own social circle he was considered a garden and horticultural expert, someone who could advise on planting as well as design, and his expertise in land management found expression in a paper entitled 'On the Bad Effects of Stripping and Cropping Trees' published in 1786 in Arthur Young's *Annals of Agriculture*.[93] As EW Brayley and John Britton were to put it in 1805: 'The beautiful woods of Foxley were chiefly planted by the late Mr Price; but the improvements made both in the woods and grounds by the present possessor, most eminently display his superior knowledge in the difficult science of landscape gardening'.[94]

If Uvedale Price did little more than manage the estate he had inherited, this was not the case at Downton, where Richard Payne Knight was to build a new house and lay out a Picturesque circuit around the Teme Gorge in the valley below; and it was Price's friendship with Payne Knight that was to produce the *Essay on the Picturesque* which led to the controversy with Repton.[95] Price acknowledged his debt to his friend in the preface:

> This unfinished work (and such I fear it is in every respect) I did not intend publishing till it was more complete, and till I had endeavoured, at least, to render it more worthy the public inspection. I have, however, been induced to send it into the world earlier than I wished, from the general curiosity which my friend Mr. Knight's poem has awakened on the subject.[96]

Price attacked Brown's aesthetic by elevating Edmund Burke's theories of the Sublime and the Beautiful and adding a further category of picturesque scenery. This last was characterised by 'intricacy in the disposition, and variety in the forms, the tints and the lights and shadows of objects...the

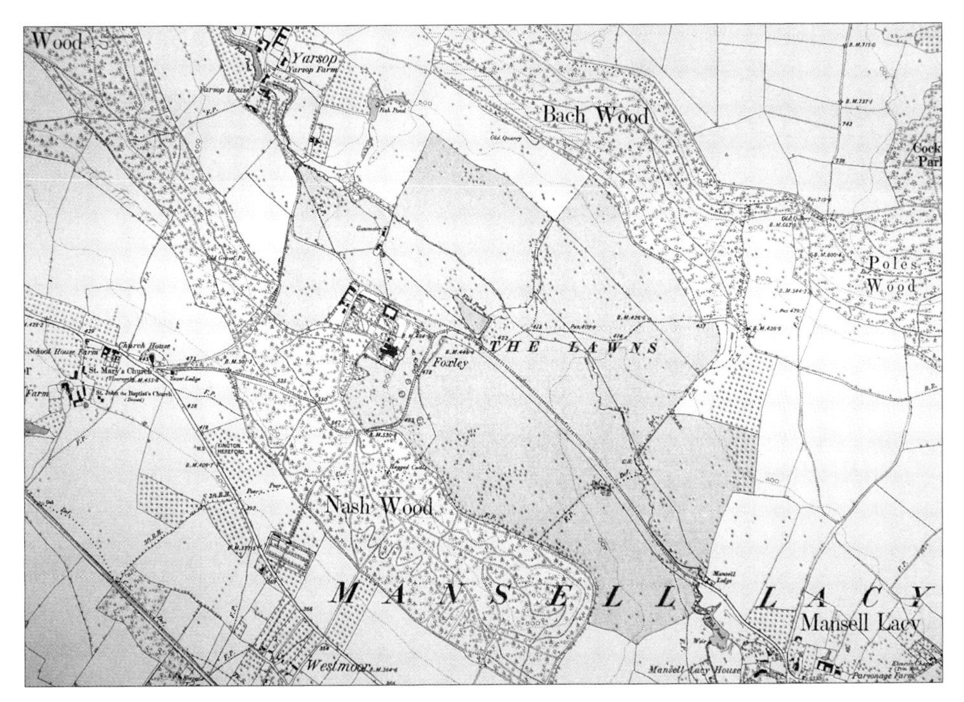

49 Sections of the network of ridings and walks that Robert Price created in the woods and valleys around Foxley are recorded on this Ordnance Survey map.
Reproduced by permission of Herefordshire Record Office

two opposite qualities of roughness, and of sudden variation, joined to that of irregularity, [these] are the most efficient causes of the picturesque'.[97] Hence Payne Knight's delight in the stormy scenes and rough Nature as depicted by Rosa and Ruisdael:

> Not more, where great Salvator's mountains rise,
> And hide their craggy summits in the skies;
> While tow'ring clouds in whirling eddies roll,
> And bursting thunders seem to shake the pole;
> Than in the ivy'd cottage of Ostade,
> Waterloe's copse, or Rysdael's low cascade.[98]

All Payne Knight had to do was transpose these effects from paintings to his Teme-side valley at Downton and he would create a perfect Picturesque landscape.[99] To do this he was aided by the artist Thomas Hearne, who had produced two watercolours, one of an improved scene and one where the planting had been allowed to go unchecked, which were engraved for Payne Knight's *The Landscape*. While Payne Knight's landscape survives relatively intact today, many of the structures have either disappeared or are in a ruinous state, so Hearne's watercolours, made between 1784 and 1786, are a precious record of what was achieved at Downton.[100]

Interestingly, given Payne Knight's avowed distaste for Brown's smooth lawns and contoured slopes, the James Sherriff study of the new castle (*50*) on his survey shows it to have been set in a meticulously manicured landscape, with the only hint of rugged Nature confined to the Teme gorge below it, where tree roots writhe.[101] This was noted by an early visitor, Richard Colt Hoare of Stourhead, when he visited Downton in 1799: 'The want of trees near it [the Castle] has rather a naked appearance at present, but this objection will be removed when those now planted are grown up. The view immediately opposite the house is also rather naked and appears the more so from the uncommon richness of that on each side, but particularly that to the east'.[102] Today the house at least looks far more picturesque with its later overlay of oriel windows, loggias, bastion tower and castellated terrace walls (*colour 29*). A contemporary survey, also by Sherriff, records the house in its bald landscape with the circuit walk that Payne Knight laid out running parallel to the river from the Castle Bridge and back up to the Castle; the Forge Bridge, another picturesque incident, is further upstream. While this map shows the Picturesque walk in some detail, it is no preparation for the Burkean excitement of actually walking the terrain and experiencing the Sublime effects of the Gorge. Here, artistic licence excepted, the Hearne watercolours are particularly helpful in elucidating the various viewing stations and landscape features; they also give a better idea of the rugged nature of the walk and the way in which views from the river back towards the Castle high above produced a perfect composition. As Payne Knight was to write some ten years later in *The Landscape*:

> Bless'd to is he, who, 'midst his tufted trees,

50 James Sherriff surveyed Richard Payne Knight's Downton estate in 1780, setting the Castle in an open landscape that appears remarkably Brownian.
Reproduced by permission of Herefordshire Record Office

> Some ruin'd castle's lofty towers sees;
> Imbosom'd high upon the mountain's brow,
> Or nodding o'er the stream that glides below.[103]

Payne Knight's circuit begins at the Castle, where a snaking walk through trees leads to the Castle Bridge across the Teme. From here there are views up and downstream, one of which by Hearne shows just the kind of 'rubbish' – rocks, tree roots and creeping vegetation – in the foreground that Price thought appropriate for an unkempt, unimproved scene (*51*). Further upstream another Hearne view (*colour 30*) focuses on a rocky cascade worthy of Ruisdael in which there are the branches of a blasted tree, while the banks are ragged with bullrushes. This echoes Price's description of Claude's waters which, unlike 'a piece of made water, or of an improved river', such as those devised by Brown and Repton, have banks that are 'perfectly savage; parts of them covered with trees and bushes that hang over the water; and near the edge of it tussucks of rushes, large stones, and stumps'.[104] Following Burke's *Philosophical*

Enquiry of 1757, Payne Knight constructed his paths so close to the water's edge, and sometimes so high above the Gorge, that the circuit is genuinely terrifying and, therefore, inducive of the Sublime. As Burke put it: 'Whatever is fitted in any sort to excite the ideas of pain, and danger, that is to say, whatever is in any sort terrible, or is conversant about terrible objects, or operates in a manner analogous to terror, is a source of the *sublime*; that is, it is productive of the strongest emotion which the mind is capable of feeling'.[105] Another Hearne watercolour (*52*), where the pathway almost falls away into the river, while rocky crags tower on the opposite bank, gives a good impression of the walk in its prime.[106]

The first picturesque incident to be encountered on the circuit was the Hermit's Cell (*53*), which is essentially a cave cut into the rock face and lit from above by another opening. Hearne took a view of the next cave, the entrance to a short tunnel, from below Pool's Farm on the opposite side of the river. His sketch depicts two horses, their riders having dismounted to take in the view across the river. The gentleman is securing the horses, while his female companion sits on a wooden seat under an oak tree. From The Hermit's Cell the path winds along the Teme, sometimes open to the river, at other points walled off from it and threaded through the Switchback Tunnel to alter the sound of the water as it rushes by, adding another frisson of danger. Today the route is heavily overgrown, though much restoration work on the paths has been done by Natural England.[107] In the 1780s the vegetation was much sparser at certain points, to give that variety sought by Payne Knight and, as Hearne shows in another painting, where the pathway crosses open grassland. Further along the southern section of the circuit the visitor comes across a ruined building surrounded by crashing weirs and a deeply channelled leat. This is Hay Mill, the subject of two Hearne watercolours: one before its alteration, with the Teme racing alongside over a rocky cascade (*colour 31*), the other a much more tranquil scene after the addition of a canted bay to the Mill. Stepping out perilously onto a promontory, kitted out with a hard hat and stout walking boots, to get a photograph of the mill race and the river

51 Thomas Hearne included the Castle Bridge in three different watercolours of Downton, which he painted between 1784 and 1786. The foreground has the rough vegetation he so admired. *Private collection*

52 This Hearne watercolour of the Downton walks along the Teme includes open areas that have now been lost to the expanding woods. *Private collection*

53 It has been suggested that Payne Knight's Grand Tour visit of 1777 to caves in Sicily may have inspired his Hermit's Cell at Downton

54 Access to the sublime thrills of Downton's landscape, as here at the Mill, is limited to specialist groups; in Payne Knight's day visitors were more frequent

alongside was one of the scariest and, it has to be said, sublime moments of a memorable tour (54).

Thereafter, the river relaxes to glide quietly under Bow Bridge, which spans the water from the bedrock by the bank; Hearne's view shows it to have had an Alpine-style wooden handrail originally. On the northern side of the river the walk climbs high up above the Teme. It reaches a climax in the Cold Bath – or it once climaxed there, as there is little left above ground to denote the building. But the substructure survives slung out above the drop. A drawing of the ground plan shows how the building functioned as a complex of interconnected oval spaces, which comprised the cold bath itself, a dressing room, and a root house.[108] A watercolour by William Owen (55) shows the three elements clearly, entered through a gate under a cromlech-like archway. A section of fine squared masonry from the external wall is still visible at the site today, while the cavernous interior, in its partly ruinous state, sends a chill through the body at the thought of naked male bathing in such a darkly cavernous eyrie – the homosocial Sublime. Anna Seward saw it in 1787, soon after it had been built and gave an evocative description:

> In the highest elevation of the rocks, the master of this Eden has formed a rustic grotto and cold-bath, with very exquisite taste. We penetrate the recesses of these rocks by a narrow winding passage, which conducts us into their centre, where they form a rotunda, filled with water, except a mossy bank about a yard wide, which encircles the bath. Its water is of the most perfect clearness, though of shadowy gloom; and the scanty light, admitted from above, is yet sufficient to shew to advantage the moss, the shells, and fossils, which cover the sides, and the beautiful little marble Naiad, who lies reclined, and bending over the brink, with pendant tresses, and a pensive sweetness in her countenance, that well becomes the magic seclusion of that watery con-cave.[109]

To walk from this numinously atmospheric place back to the Castle and then on to **Stonebrook Cottage**, set in a dell beside the lane through

55 William Owen's painting depicts a studious gentleman, possibly Payne Knight himself, reading under the archway to the Cold Bath at Downton. Behind the Bath were a Dressing Room and a Root House. *Courtauld Institute of Art, London. Private collection*

the village, is to move from the starkly elemental to the flowery kitsch. The one reeks of youthful exuberance while, according to Payne Knight himself, the other smacks of genteel retirement. Indeed, in a letter he wrote in August 1809 to Lord Aberdeen, Payne Knight saw his vernacular retreat as his 'Sulky', a place in which to skulk around while enjoying the leisure that later life brings:

> It is too soon for you to think of a Sulky – when a man enters his 60th year, as I am about to do, he has a right to live for himself; but before, he ought to live for Society. The dreggs of life then left are not worth bestowing; and all that can be hoped is that one may not become tiresome to oneself as well as to others. From this last and greatest evil I am however hitherto free, having past the four months that I have been in my Hermitage in as perfect Happiness as my Nature is capable of – wandering thro' my romantic woods,

56 At Stonebrook Cottage, along the lane from his Castle, Payne Knight enjoyed in miniature the same natural features of rocks, woods, lawns and water that he had experienced in his walks along the Teme gorge

> planning and executing Improvements every morning, and enjoying my old books in undisturb'd tranquillity every Evening.[110]

Ever the dilettante, Payne Knight was working on a Greek translation of Homer when he was staying in his country cottage. To mark this endeavour he added a Greek inscription to the cottage as if to proclaim his erudition and labour, even in retirement:

> In the architrave of the former [sitting room] I have inscribed the following line [rendered in normal text as KALLISTON ENTHA KTEMATON SCHOLE TUCHOI], which I have made out of a maxim of Plato's [translated as 'may there be leisure here, the finest of possessions'], with what success critics may decide. It expresses my meaning very exactly. The whole of what is marked *Lawn* in the plan is not more than a Rood and all that the Rocks would allow to be tilled was lately a Cottager's Garden, so that it is very fertile and the trees

> grow in the rocks most luxuriantly....The Creepers & Mosses, with which I have enrich'd it very abundantly, will soon mellow it.[111]

The cottage survives (*56*), its valley garden threaded by a small rivulet, but the inscription above the bay window is now badly weathered and almost illegible. In the space of twenty years or so, Payne Knight had moved from the savage Picturesque to the emergent Gardenesque, the fussy, bourgeois style that Repton, his arch-enemy, was at that very moment perfecting for his *nouveau riche* clients.[112] With advances in technology, particularly the development of greenhouse environments for rearing exotics, the Gardenesque was to encourage formality around the house and an interconnection between drawing rooms and glasshouses. Suddenly pleasure grounds were taking on a completely new guise, that of flowery formality, edging into a more manicured and predictable wider landscape of flowering bushes and specimen trees. Savage landscapes were out; flower gardens were in.

6

Regency eclecticism and the post-Picturesque

Hope End · Haffield · Eastnor Castle · Croft Castle · Goodrich Court

AT FIRST GLANCE THE CHARMING LITTLE MARKET TOWN OF LEDBURY, which nestles under the southern end of the Malverns ridge, appears to have little to connect it with the 1934 film *The Barretts of Wimpole Street*, starring Norma Shearer as Elizabeth and Charles Lawton, in a tyrannical portrayal, as her father, Edward Barrett Moulton-Barrett. However, every July, Ledbury's poetry festival celebrates the town's links with three famous poets, William Langland, John Masefield and Elizabeth Barrett Browning. Elizabeth Barrett recalled her childhood home in Herefordshire in a letter written to RH Horne on 5 October 1843:

> We lived at Hope End, a few miles from Malvern, in a retirement scarcely broken to me except by books and my own thoughts, and it is a beautiful country, and was a retirement happy in many ways, although the very peace of it troubles the heart as it looks back. There I had my fits of Pope, and Byron, and Coleridge, and read Greek as hard under the trees as some of your Oxonians in the Bodleian; gathered visions from Plato and the dramatists, and ate and drank Greek and made my head ache with it. Do you know the Malvern Hills? The hills of Pier's Plowman's Visions? They seem to me my native hills; for, although I was born in the county of Durham, I was an infant when I went first into their neighbourhood, and lived there until I had passed twenty by several years. Beautiful, beautiful hills they are![1]

Hope End, just north of Ledbury towards Coddington, was Elizabeth Barrett's home from 1810, when she was a young child, up until 1832; her father seems to have bought the property in 1809. The family was forced to sell up due to financial pressures, as Edward Barrett's fortune had declined rapidly following the abolition of slavery, a collapse in the price of sugar and a legal case brought against him in Jamaica in which he lost much of his inheritance. He died in 1857 and is buried in the parish church of St Michael and All Angels in Ledbury. Hope End and its garden (*colour 32*) feature in Elizabeth Barrett's poetry, her father having christened her in 1812 'the Poet Laureat of Hope End' in recognition of 'some lines of virtue which I had pen[n]ed with great care'.[2] Her 1844 *The Lost Bower* is set in the wood above the garden at Hope End:

> Green the land is where my daily
> Steps in jocund childhood played...
> Dimpled close with hill and valley,
> Dappled very close with shade;
> Summer-snow of apple blossoms,
> running up from glade to glade.[3]

The grounds also inspired several descriptive passages in her 1856 novel-poem *Aurora Leigh*, the first book of which is set in Florence and in England, where Aurora goes to live with her aunt in Leigh Hall, the family's ancestral home. Aurora's bedroom, 'as green as any privet-hedge a bird/Might choose to build in', gave a view through the leaves of a lime tree of

> the lawn,
> Which, after sweeping broadly round the house,
> Went trickling through the shrubberies in a stream
> Of tender turf, and wore and lost itself
> Among the acacias, over which, you saw
> The irregular line of elms by the deep lane
> Which stopt the grounds and dammed the overflow
> Of arbutus and laurel.[4]

Much later, Barrett's husband Robert recalled in the preface to an 1887 edition of his wife's works that her father 'had a fine taste for landscape gardening, planted considerably, loved trees...and for their sake discontinued keeping deer in the park'.[5] All of which suggests that the Barretts had fashioned the extensive landscaped grounds around the strangely exotic Moorish house overlooking a deep-delved valley. Only the stable block survives, the house having been dynamited in the 1870s.[6]

There is, however, some doubt as to the authorship of the grounds and the possible influence of Humphry Repton at Hope End before Elizabeth Barrett's father purchased the estate in 1809 from Sir Henry Vane Tempest. As we have seen, many of the sites of Repton's commissions were illustrated in Peacock's *Polite Repository*, an almanac-cum-diary, as miniature scenic engravings.[7] Peacock's competitor was *The Royal Repository*, whose 1796 diary carried an engraving of the house at Hope End, preceding the Moorish fantasy, which was built after 1810. Repton is known to have remained loyal to Peacock, but the *Royal Repository* of 1796 has views of a series of sites with which Repton was associated. It is possible, therefore, that he may have advised the Tempests, or that he might have returned to Hope End once Edward Barrett had purchased the estate. Interestingly, he was trying to obtain a commission, without success, at nearby Eastnor Castle in about 1810.[8]

The eccentric styling of the house might also be another clue to his involvement. Its Hindu-Moorish character resembles elements of Sezincote in Gloucestershire, where Repton is known to have laid out the Thornery, a rill garden, after 1804,[9] and also the Brighton Pavilion, unexecuted designs for which he produced in 1806. The appearance of the earlier Hope End in the *Royal Repository* came just a year after Thomas and William Daniell had begun to publish in parts their views of *Oriental Scenery*, which had such an impact on Regency exoticism; Thomas Daniell was also involved in the creation of the gardens at Sezincote. On the other hand, Barrett's Hope End is similar to a contemporary house at Coleorton, Leicestershire, designed for Sir George Beaumont by George

Dance junior, and built between 1804 and 1808; Dance had first experimented with the style in the late 1770s at the Guildhall in London. Uvedale Price is the Herefordshire link with Coleorton. Beaumont was a frequent correspondent with Price, who invited him to Foxley to see his new house as it was being built, and loaned him his gardener, Cranston, to stake out planting positions in the grounds.[10] Price was on friendly terms with Elizabeth Barrett, but did not begin to correspond with her until June 1826, long after her father had rebuilt Hope End and tended to the landscaping.

The surviving pleasure grounds around the former stable block, set within its wooded valley, must be the result of an overlay on the existing eighteenth-century landscape by John Claudius Loudon, who recorded in the 1822 volume of his *Encyclopaedia of Gardening*: 'Hope End, near Ledbury: J. Baret, Esq. The house and grounds recently improved from our designs; the latter highly romantic by nature, and well wooded'.[11] It would seem that Loudon had been associated with the site as early as 1812, when he referred to Hope End in his *Observations on Laying-out Farms in the Scottish Style*.[12] The house was completed in 1815, so Loudon's reshaping must date from between 1815 and 1822, when a guide was published, giving an account of what had been achieved: 'In front of the house are some fine pieces of water, and on the banks, a variety of fine shrubs and evergreens. From the windows on one side of the house, is a very large projection of rock, which the taste of the owner has highly ornamented, with a fine collection of plants. There is a subterraneous passage, from the house, leading to the garden'.[13] And later, long after the Barretts had left Hope End and it was on the market again, a description from the sale catalogue mentions Loudon again and lists both features and trees:

> beautiful lawn and pleasure grounds laid out with singular taste by Loudon; and planted with the choicest specimens of Abies, Cedar, Cupressus, Perciperus, Pencisthuja, Wellingtonia Gigantea, and other rare Trees and Shrubs; Beautifully Undulated Park, studded with stately forest trees, of large growth, and ornamental clumps; A

57 The moss-covered plinths set around the Chinoiserie entrance to the Grotto-Cold Bath at Hope End may have produced the effect of statuary rising out of the water

> fine sheet of water, fed by pure springs, stocked with the most rare Aquatic Plants, well stored with Carp, Tench, Perch & other Fish. Fernery; Ladies' Flower Garden and Shrubbery, of great extent, with extensive walks and drives.[14]

This is essentially what survives at Hope End today: the bizarre remnant of an exotic country house set in a secret valley of great woods, undulating lawns and a small, tree-shaded lake, but with two other features not mentioned by contemporaries which must, however, date from the Regency. These are the Quarry Garden, threaded with steps and now planted with modern exotics,[15] and a curious Grotto-cum-Cold Bath. This last is reached down a flight of fern-licked steps, ending in a sunken courtyard before an ogee-arched entrance of Chinese tilt giving onto the enclosed Bath (57). The walls of the courtyard are of Regency brickwork, whereas the façade of the Bath is covered in stone and topped with a balustrade. The archway is the only oriental touch in a landscape of otherwise typical early nineteenth-century planting and ornamentation. The fernery mentioned in the sale particulars might well have been the triangular-shaped covered areas either side of the stable court Gateway that are now awash with moisture-loving plants.

One last Loudon contribution to the estate is the Lower Lodge, facing the Malverns ridge, which is decorated with ogee-arched, latticed windows and fancy bargeboards; it was originally thatched. This is similar to many illustrated in his *Encylopaedia*, but there again it is close to both Nash and Repton's work, and also to a watercolour design for Panson Cottage, on the south side of the Wye in the Hereford suburbs, possibly by Repton or his son George Stanley.

Loudon may also have given advice to William Gordon of **Haffield**, three miles south of Ledbury, when he was reconstructing the house between 1817 and 1818 to designs by Sir Robert Smirke. Gordon was taking the opportunity to engage Smirke, who was working for Earl Somers at nearby Eastnor Castle. The possible Loudon connection is through the Haffield Head Gardener, David Beaton, who was also a Scot and knew Loudon well enough to review his paper on the *Amaryllidaceae* family in the *Gardener's Magazine* for 1836.[16] Beaton had arrived at Haffield in 1829 and went on to establish his reputation through the thriving horticultural press. He had already published an account of Haffield in the 1836 issue of the same magazine. The core of his piece concerned Jacob Tonson's vineyard and plantations at the Hazle-Haffield estate, but it also included a 'Notice of the Improvements lately made, and now in Progress, at that Place'.[17] After Smirke had completed the house 'the grounds were planted from 1820 to 1823, chiefly with forest trees on dry shallow soil'.[18] These were typical for their period: larches, Scots pines, spruce and silver firs. But, interestingly, in the lower part of the grounds, where it had been wet, alders, willows and black Italian poplars were introduced. Loudon, who was working at Hope End, might have had some input at Haffield, but a letter of 5 November 1820 from Uvedale Price to Sir George Beaumont suggests otherwise. After lamenting the destruction, by Gordon's uncle, of old yews and pollarded oaks at Haffield, 'the yews for gateposts, the pollards for firewood', Price remarked that Gordon 'means to employ Gilpin', by which he was referring to William Sawrey Gilpin.[19]

Whatever the truth, the austerely elegant house, dramatised by a Greek Doric porch and a Doric loggia giving views out to May Hill, is set within a typical Regency landscape of sweeping lawns planted with specimen trees. There are, however, two notable features not discussed by

58 The tunnel to the Walled Garden at Haffield is more than just a means of avoiding the lane. Its curving design is intended to lead visitors from darkness to burst out into the light with maximum drama

Beaton: a Quarry Garden set in a rock face opposite the entrance front, and a walk leading to a serpentine tunnel under the lane which gives access to the Walled Garden. Loudon was of the view that any entrance to a walled garden should be from the south, so that the first view was of the most impressive northern walls with their glasshouses, frames and pits. The Tunnel (*58*) fits these requirements and debouches into the garden between ivy-clad rocks and two mature yews in a picturesque composition of which Gilpin would have approved. The walls of the Tunnel are lined with chocolate-coloured breccia stone that was mined on the estate and is something of a geological curiosity.[20]

While the pleasure grounds at Haffield are humanly scaled and conform to the prevailing fashion for shrubs, specimen trees and horticultural experimentation in hothouses, the landscape around **Eastnor** is on a much grander scale, as befits a revived medieval castle. As we have seen, the old house of Castle Ditch was almost completely submerged under the new lake that was dug to flatter and reflect the somewhat pedestrian garden front of Smirke's new Eastnor Castle, an uneasy hybrid of Early English and Norman styles.[21] Viewed from the lake to the south-east, Eastnor is truly Tennysonian in its romance, but this medieval vision is essentially superficial, the result of the soaring towers at its four corners (*59*). The approach to the Castle is perhaps more architecturally rewarding, with the drive sweeping across lawns studded with great cedars, yews and laurels to cross the grassy moat through a barbican lodge and climax at the *porte cochère*. This is overshadowed by twin towers linked by a strainer arch, a device that is mirrored at Payne Knight's Downton Castle and derived from Warwick Castle. While the evergreen foliage of the planting provides a suitably Gothic gloom, there is no suggestion here that either Smirke or his patron, Earl Somers, intended to create pleasure grounds that were, like the Castle, a conscious attempt at medievalising. Perhaps we should not expect at Eastnor the kind of landscape setting that Thomas Love Peacock satirised in his contemporary novel, *Nightmare Abbey*, where Scythrop's 'venerable family-mansion, in a highly picturesque state of semi-dilapidation' had a terrace, 'which was called the garden, though nothing grew on it but ivy, and a few amphibious weeds'.[22]

The same air of stagey Gothicism is apparent in the Curtain Wall (*60*) on the approach to **Croft Castle** at the end of the Beech Avenue. Both entrance and avenue are said to date from around 1810, and the Wall is close in style to work by John Nash, who was in the county at this time.[23]

59 Robert Smirke's weak garden front of Eastnor Castle is saved by the drama of its corner towers and central keep. The lake has all but submerged Castle Ditch, the earlier house on the estate

60 Family ties to Owain Glyndwr made the Regency's passion for castellated garden buildings all the more convincing at Croft Castle

Of more relevance to the site's garden history is the Fish Pool Valley to the north-east of the Castle, which was landscaped in Picturesque style in the early nineteenth century. As early as about 1799, the stream running through the valley had been dammed by a series of sluices and weirs to create an artificial chain of pools; this is shown on an estate demesne map of the period.[24] Thereafter, perhaps under the influence of Uvedale Price's writings, and certainly in accord with the published work of William Gilpin, Thomas Johnes II planted the valley sides thickly with ash, oak, willow and poplar, together with evergreens, to produce that rough effect so desirous of aficionados of the Picturesque.

The finger of parkland to the south-west was reached until the mid-twentieth century by a carriage drive carried by the now demolished Gothick Bridge. The Bridge, for which no known image has been traced, was demolished by the County Council Highways Department some time between 1947 and 1958. Its sandstone rubble piers survive, as do the lower parts of two round towers just at the point where the public footpath crosses Lucton Lane. On the western side of the lane the footpath skirts a large serpentine earthwork that mirrors the line of an adjacent quarry.

After the Gothick scene-setting of Croft's Curtain Wall and Bridge, and the somewhat ponderous façades of Smirke's Eastnor, **Goodrich Court**, just south of Ross-on-Wye, achieved the heights of the architectural Sublime. Set on a high plateau above a bend in the river, the house rose like a towered and turreted vision of the Middle Ages. As an 1838 tourist guide recorded, its owner's intention was to 'make such building as best suited the character of the scenery, and was also peculiarly adapted for the reception of one of the most celebrated collections of Armour in Europe, to cast bold shadows by various projections and thus produce a picturesque effect'.[25] Its creator was Samuel Rush Meyrick, who appears, wildly caricatured, as Mr Chainmail, in Thomas Love Peacock's *Crotchet Castle*. Meyrick was a serious antiquary and collector of armour, who published a book in 1824 entitled: *A Critical Enquiry into Antient Armour*, which was praised by Sir Walter Scott, then busy with his series of medieval romantic novels.[26] Peacock portrayed him as

> A good-looking young gentleman....with very antiquated tastes. He is fond of old poetry, and is something of a poet himself. He is deep in monkish literature and holds that the best state of society was that of the twelfth century, when nothing was going forward but fighting, feasting, and praying, which he says are the three great purposes for which man was made. ....He lives within two or three miles, and has a large hall, adorned with rusty pikes, shields, helmets, swords, and tattered banners, and furnished with yew-tree chairs, and two long, old, worm-eaten oak tables, where he dines with all his household, after the fashion of his favourite age.[27]

It is not surprising then, that when he began to construct a new house in 1828 near Goodrich Castle, whose surviving ruins date principally from the thirteenth century, Meyrick chose to commission a design, as he put it, 'in the style of Edward 2nd'.[28] He had been trying since 1823 to purchase the Castle ruins and convert them into a country house. The Meyricks' London town house in Upper Cadogan Square had become too small for their collection of armour and Herefordshire was chosen as a suitable place for their new home by Meyrick and his son Llewellyn, because they believed that they were descended from the owners of Meyrick Court in the Golden Valley. It is likely that Scott encouraged Meyrick to abandon his plan to convert the Castle on grounds of architectural preservation and conservation. Meyrick wrote to Scott in December 1824 that he 'need not dread demolition [of the Castle], for unless I could make it fit to live in without the slightest alteration, even cutting an additional window, I would forbear and build my residence within view'.[29] Such strict architectural propriety might have been exercised by the fictional Mr Chainmail, but was beyond Meyrick, who promptly commissioned Edward Blore to design a new house, within view of the Castle, as Scott had suggested.

As well as employing Blore, who had worked for Scott at Abbotsford,

Meyrick also engaged the antiquary and arboriculturalist, Sir Henry Steuart, whom Scott referred to as having 'wonderful power, certainly over the vegetable world, and has made his trees dance about as merrily as ever did Orpheus'.[30] At Goodrich Court, Llewellyn Meyrick, who took the lead in laying out the grounds, employed Steuart's new scientific techniques for relocating mature trees.[31] In his 1828 book, *The Planter's Guide*, Steuart boasted that his method for moving trees worked on a scale that was capable of creating an '*entire* Park, and advancing a planting scheme by forty years'.[32] To accompany his text, Steuart included an engraving of his tree-moving machine (*61*). This was just the artifice that Meyrick and his son required to site their new country mansion on a headland adjacent to a historic castle and, at the same time, create a convincing approach to a historic museum of armour. In January 1831 Llewellyn wrote of his success in moving trees 'two miles or more and has placed a couple of yews near the building, which being thirty feet high give the place completely the air of antiquity.'[33] In the winter and spring of 1831-32 he was planting more trees, although some were inexplicably vandalised in the March.[34] Trees were planted below the terraces to form impressive walks down towards the Wye, and even the lawns played their part in this historical pastiche. The grassed area beneath the east front, aligned on Goodrich Castle, became the 'tilt ground', which would have provided an ideal place for mustering the entourage of twenty-six javelin men, two mounted trumpeters and 200 or more supporters that Meyrick brought together to escort him to the Hereford Assizes when he served as the county's high sheriff in 1834.[35] Llewellyn Meyrick died in 1837, having completed the landscaping around the house. Meyrick died in 1848, leaving the Court and his armoury to a cousin, Colonel Augustus Meyrick. The armour was dispersed by auction in 1868 and the house was put on the market in the following year. The 1869 sale particulars are an important record of what father and son had completed before their deaths, particularly as the grounds were eventually to be remodelled by Thomas Mawson in the Edwardian period. Not only do the particulars provide a

61 Llewellyn Meyrick transplanted large trees at Goodrich, possibly using a contraption similar to this from Henry Steuart's *The Planter's Guide* of 1828. *University of Bristol Library, Special Collections*

description of the grounds, but accompanying engravings show an undulating parkland dressed with specimen trees and a view from the plateau overlooking the Wye in the valley below (*62*). A ground plan of the house, offices and terraces marks the tilt ground on the east and four geometrical parterres of shrub trees at the south-east corner; this must be the 'Italian Gardens' mentioned in the narrative. A view of the 'Terrace Front' is dramatised by this formal area of grass plats, shrubs and standard roses. Later on in the century, when sale particulars were drawn up again in 1884, the 'Italian Garden' was still in place, but it was reshaped after 1888 when Harold Moffat pulled down the adjacent stable and service quadrangle.[36] It is likely that the Yew Walk, leading down to the Wye, was planted after 1868 and before 1884. The Edwardian remodelling of the Italian Garden will be reserved for a later chapter.

All that is left now of Meyrick's vision of medieval England is the tall gatehouse Lodge on the A40, modelled by Meyrick on a gatehouse he saw in Frankfurt in July 1823, and the be-pinnacled Hostelrie Hotel in

62 A vantage point above the Wye, such as this shown in the 1884 sale particulars of Goodrich Court, was one of the most prized possessions in any Herefordshire landscape. *Reproduced by permission of Herefordshire Record Office*

Goodrich village. In its day, however, Goodrich Court was heralded as having 'superadded renown and elegance to the natural charms of this picturesque and highly adorned locale', and Meyrick was commended for opening it to 'every respectable and well-clothed individual' on each day of the week except Sunday.[37] In his 1845 guide to the Court, Charles Nash foresaw the advent of a new class of tourist, the 'intelligent artisans of our manufacturing towns', who would take advantage of the 'gigantic powers of steam locomotion....to embrace the opportunity of reaching the Court by lines of Railways running close to it'.[38] It is to the Victorian gardens of the affluent employers of these 'intelligent artisans' that we must now turn.

7

Pines, parterres and a Pulhamite rockery – Victorian excess

Eastnor Castle · Bryngwyn · Broxwood Court · Garnstone Castle
Belmont · Rotherwas · Stoke Edith · Downton Castle · Newport House
Shobdon Court · Brockhampton House · Whitbourne Hall · Treago Castle
Bredenbury Court · Wyastone Leys · Lincoln Hill House · Holmer Park
Buckfield Keep · 46 Etnam Street Leominster · Grange Court

THE ROUNDED SILHOUETTE OF OAK TREES IS SO FAMILIAR IN THE COUNTY that they have been dismissed as 'Herefordshire weeds'. So, when John, 2nd Earl Somers, planted young Atlantic cedar trees on the slopes around **Eastnor Castle** in 1845, he was breaking with the natural character of the place. He was also turning against Humphry Repton's 'disgust at seeing modern Gothic buildings, however well designed, surrounded by firs and Lombardy poplars'.[1] The Earl had gathered the seed for his cedars at Téniet-el-Hâad in modern-day Algeria, and the experiments in germination that followed at Eastnor would help to fuel the Victorian delight derived from the display of such horticultural skill and the assembly of plant collections. Miles Hadfield, a modern-day arboriculturist and adopted son of Herefordshire, has written: 'It is generally accepted that this was the first introduction of this tree in Britain'.[2] With the Earl's planting, particularly of deodar and Lebanon cedars, between his succession to the title in 1852 and his death in 1883, Eastnor was building up 'one of the most magnificent collections of cedars in the British Isles'.[3]

Combined with its vast lake, the cedars create a sympathetic setting for Smirke's Castle; one that is far more appropriate than the herbaceous flower borders and fountain added when the terraces beneath the garden front were enlarged in the 1870s. A few of the original Victorian conifers still crowd in along the main approach that rises from the village of Eastnor to the north-west of the Castle. A champion Blue cedar (*Cedrus altantica* Glauca Group) stands to the west of the main approach, partnering a champion specimen of dragon spruce (*Picea asperata*) to the east. To the south of the Castle the conifers on Summerhouse Hill include an impressively large Santa Lucia fir (*Abies bracteata*), identified by Hadfield as coming from the first batch of seed imported into this country in 1853 and planted out in the 1860s. It is now reputed to be the second tallest in the country.[4] A modern, municipal-looking covered seat now tops Summerhouse Hill, amongst a stand of gnarled old Monterey pine (*Pinus radiata*) and Western yellow pine (*Pinus ponderosa*). This was once the site of the Castle Ditch summerhouse. However, while these single specimen trees are impressive, they were only the highlights in the planting style being developed at Eastnor. They provided punctuation marks amongst single species clumps that were very different from the single-specimen catalogue planting of the traditional Victorian pinetum. The Eastnor style was reflected in the estate's cash accounts where, in 1868, the 3rd Earl paid for consignments of 40 Italian (stone) pines and 100 deodar cedars, as well as single specimens of Giant Fir (*Picea grandis*) and Noble Fir (*Picea nobilis*).[5]

William Coleman was then Head Gardener, and the survival of his cash book for the years 1860 to 1868 reveals the part played by Veitch & Son in supplying conifers and shrubs at a time when that nursery's plant-hunters were exploiting the flora of Japan for the first time for the British market. This was geographically balanced by the 3rd Earl's membership of a group known as the Oregon Association and his financial support for Robert Browne's plant-hunting expedition to British Columbia between 1863 and 1865.[6] In this way, new tree species were brought to Eastnor from across the globe; many prospered and reached impressive proportions. In 1878 the *Gardeners' Chronicle* was reporting admiringly that Coleman had nurtured a Wellingtonia cutting to nearly forty feet in only seventeen years,[7] and ten years later *The Garden* suggested that many more specimens were 'assuming the proportions of those of their native forests'.[8] In the twentieth century many of the Eastnor conifers reached maturity and the collection entered a period of decline, but James Hervey-Bathurst has reversed this with a new fifteen-year maintenance programme overseen by Tim Stuart-Smith.

An impressive stand of Victorian Wellingtonias can be seen in the valley just outside the village of Much Birch. They line the approach to **Bryngwyn**, an unloved Victorian country house built between 1868 and 1870. Its architect was Frederick Roderick Kempson and the client was James Rankin; the following year the same architect was appointed to design Hereford's new library, with Rankin as the leading benefactor. At Bryngwyn, Kempson's combination of brilliant red terracotta and dull grey composite stone in both the house and the balustrade of the raised garden terrace were singularly unsuccessful (*63*). One can understand why the *Gardeners' Chronicle* concentrated on the surviving walls of 'old Bryngwyn', dressed with jasmine, *Chaenomeles speciosa*, sweet briar, and ivies, which included *Hedera helix* 'Palmata', 'an indifferent climber, but with large leaves – a handsome variety for ruins'.[9] That scene was made all the more picturesque by an encircling 'sort of trellis, formed of Larch poles...carried round the house with excellent effect, the poles being completely hidden by Ivy which hangs in luxuriant festoons, amid which the eye detects the ruin behind'.[10] A lawn had also been laid out in one of the principal rooms and the walls 'hung with creepers and planted with Ferns'.[11]

The conservatory at the rear of Kempson's house has been compromised by the addition of domestic-scaled 1960s windows. They make the Victorian encouragement to '*Prudentia et Virtute*' carved above the doorways appear futile. The same sentiment was repeated on Rankin's headstone on his death in 1915, but it is the Wellingtonias that he planted in 1874 that provide his most intimate memorial. His father, Robert, had purchased the Bryngwyn estate for him in 1865, thanks to a fortune made importing timber from North America. In 1812 Robert had been despatched by his employer, Pollok, Gilmour & Co, to Miramichi in New

63 An unkempt terrace devoid of flowerbeds and a defaced Conservatory are the only reminders of floral riches at Bryngwyn that were once compared to Kew

Brunswick to establish an important new trading post for the company. At the time, the firm was one of the largest importers of timber into Britain, operating mainly through the ports of Liverpool and Glasgow. In 1857, when James was fifteen, his father took the family on a tour of North America and Canada. It was most likely this trip that inspired him to plant his Wellingtonias thickly in Herefordshire.[12]

In 1884, subscribers to the three volumes of Edward Ravenscroft's study of evergreen trees hardy in this country could eventually place their copies of his delayed *Pinetum Britannicum* on their library shelves. Among them were two Herefordshire landowners, Stephen Robinson of The Moor, near Hay-on-Wye, and Richard Snead-Cox of **Broxwood Court**, near Weobley. The Moor was demolished in 1952, a few years after becoming the unlikely subject of a high profile occupation by squatters. A lodge and a Gothic tower survive beside the A438, two miles outside Hay-on-Wye, but many parkland trees have been felled, removing any evidence of whether Robinson's interest in conifers extended to his estate. Broxwood Court has faired comparatively better and, although the house was demolished in 1955, its listed landscape survives around a modern house set out on the original footprint.

Unlike Rankin at Bryngwyn, Snead-Cox of Broxwood had not seen the newly fashionable exotic conifers growing in their natural habitat. However, by taking the advice of the leading landscape gardener of the second half of the nineteenth century, and giving expression to his own Catholic faith, he came remarkably close to emulating the scene from nature that Ravenscroft had chosen for his frontispiece: a grove of deodar cedars near a waterfall at Narchar. But, this is to move beyond the arrival in the county in 1832 of William Andrews Nesfield.

In July 1832 Nesfield was sketching the river Wye as it winds through Hereford and, even though he may have launched his career as a landscape gardener the previous year, there is nothing to indicate that this first visit to the county produced paid employment.[13] He may have been studying Herefordshire's famously picturesque scenery, although strong evidence of Anthony Salvin's family's presence in the county – Salvin was his brother-in-law – suggests that it might also have been a social visit, with the added prospect of potential introductions to a new circle of clients.[14] The first evidence of a paid commission comes in the 1840s, when Nesfield gave advice to Captain Daniel Peploe of **Garnstone Castle**, a towered and castellated house at Weobley designed by John Nash. Here Nesfield argued strongly for the opening up of views, particularly from the approach and the house.[15] His radical proposals for tree felling even extended to the cedar of Lebanon in the flower garden. He thought it was essential if he was to dispel the sensation that 'the whole place is overloaded with Foliage'.[16] Nesfield concluded his recommendations by suggesting that a new parterre would improve the flower garden, which was 'at present....an anomaly, inasmuch as it is a heterogeneous mass, altogether devoid of Artistical and Architectural design – No house of any pretension is complete without its line of circumvallation and Parterre ...thus the peculiarities of the artificial would enhance the flowing lines of Nature and Vice Versa.'[17]

Garnstone Castle was demolished in the late 1950s and the park is now in decline. However, the surviving Nash-style castellated lodge guarding the entrance to a mature avenue of Wellingtonias suggests that some of Nesfield's ideas were accepted, and that even more radical action was taken in replanting much of the approach. Furthermore, Nesfield's recommendation for a parterre also appears to have been implemented in a 'Dutch Garden' of topiary set around a central fountain and a grander 'Italian Garden', where an assortment of geometric flowerbeds enlivened a long arcaded walk.[18] It is possible that the naming of these gardens as Dutch and Italian post-dated Nesfield's work at Garnstone. These nationalistic style stereotypes, along with 'French' and 'English' gardens, were often invoked in horticultural literature in the 1810s and 1820s. But by the middle of the century they had become so vague and confused that 'Italian Garden' was used to describe any formal design. The naming of flower gardens as Dutch and Italian saw something of a renaissance in the 1880s and 1890s, but there was little to distinguish them other than a mild association with Dutch horticulture and topiary.[19]

The Garnstone commission appears to have inspired confidence in another prospective client, Peploe's close friend and neighbour, Snead-Cox. On 23 March 1858 Snead-Cox was invested as the county's High Sherriff, in a lavish ceremony devised by the antiquary Samuel Rush Meyrick of Goodrich Court. Snead-Cox recorded the event in his journal: 'A very fine day – I went to Mass [as he did every day unless occupied by 'struggles' with a testing religious text] and about Noon I started in state with my Retinue of twenty two javelin men & two trumpeters – and attended by Mr Lambe as Under Sheriff'.[20] Seven of his javelin men came from the Broxwood area and five from the local militia, in which he served. Such a prominent position in the county required a new house, and two days later he dined with his Bristol architect, Charles Frances Hansom, presumably selected because of his experience as a church architect. The following week, on 7 April, Snead-Cox 'drew a plan – Mr Nesfield the Landscape Gardener arrived to look at the proposed site of a House – I went out with him to the spot but what with the rain, &c, & apple trees we could see next to nothing – In the evening we looked at the Plans'.[21] The following day they had more success and Nesfield fixed the site for the house so that the dining room and drawing room would face south, offering distant views to the Welsh hills, whilst the adjacent library would occupy the prime position, with yet more southerly views, and the advantage of the morning sun from the east.

Snead-Cox took a close interest in the design and construction of the new pleasure grounds. He called on Nesfield from his London house to collect plans, and throughout 1858 and the early months of 1859, together with his wife Marie Teresa and some visiting friends, he constructed a wood-and-paper model of the new house and its terraces. However, on 25 March 1859 Snead-Cox recorded Nesfield's name for the last time in his journal when his gardener, Davison, was busy at Broxwood planting trees 'after Nesfield's design'.[22] In the following months Snead-Cox worked alongside Davison, helping him to lay out drives, put up continuous fencing and write labels for trees.

The foundation stone for the new house was laid on 2 July 1861, the feast of the visitation of Our Lady. The site was decorated with arches festooned with flowers and banners sporting encouraging religious-sounding inscriptions: 'It is founded in Faith', 'Success to Broxwood' and 'May it stand as a Rock'. The assembled crowd of friends and well-wishers included six members of the Salvin family, each of whom would have delighted in the gardens that were taking shape about them. A surviving plan from April 1858 shows Nesfield's proposal for a long straight terrace walk running from east to west to link the un-walled kitchen garden with the new house.[23] It was to run beneath the principal rooms, past a new evergreen hedge and narrow parterre, the detailed design of which had yet to be completed. However, photographs from the 1890s focus on a different feature. The easterly end of Nesfield's long straight walk fanned out into a goosefoot of three paths interspersed with flowerbeds (*64*). The central path disappeared sharply down a flight of steps to emerge at the

64

A nineteenth-century photograph of the grounds at Broxwood Court records WA Nesfield's goosefoot of the path and his geometrical flowerbeds. *Private collection*

entrance to St John's Avenue, which was almost half a mile of conifers stretching out to the edge of the park. A modern fountain has now replaced the goosefoot, but the avenue survives. The section nearest the house was planted with deodar cedars, some of which have recently been replaced. They were followed by six Wellingtonias, three on each side, and finally a line of Scots pine. Snead-Cox's journal, rather than the 1858 plan, confirms that Nesfield designed this avenue.[24] Shirley Evans has noted that he also planted a deodar cedar avenue at Keele Hall, Staffordshire, in 1852.[25]

Snead-Cox seems to have been confident enough to add his own ideas to Nesfield's original design. In October 1861 he planned a Yew Walk, which was eventually planted in March 1864. It survives as a series of apsidal bays in a yew hedge to the south-east of the house. The couple also embellished their new garden with symbols of their Catholic faith. In

65 The miniature Chapel, just off St Michael's Walk at Broxwood, has stained glass commemorating family marriages conducted between 1700 and 1804

1861 the 'hut', known as St Joseph's Hermitage, was erected. It stands on a short walk leading south from the main avenue and is encircled by an appropriately austere wooden verandah with a simple wooden seat. However, inside there is no sign of a religious statue of St Joseph carved specially for a niche. This place of devotion and contemplation also doubled as a welcome resting place for friends touring the garden. Such excursions were taken very seriously, as on the occasion when Snead-Cox tutored an unnamed guest in the library, using his copy of *Pinetum Britannicum*, before going out and 'exhibiting' the pines in the garden.[26] In 1874 urgent instructions were issued for the construction of a second religious garden building, a brick and slate Chapel (*65*) that enlivens St Michael's Walk as it cuts across the avenue just west of the Hermitage. Snead-Cox had been seriously injured in a fall from his horse, and the chapel was presumably built in preparation for his anticipated death. However, he recovered and went on to live until 1899, leaving the Chapel to be decorated with stained glass in celebration of happier events, including family weddings.

Snead-Cox's faith inevitably shaped his social circle as well as his garden, and it also appears to have linked Nesfield's future clients at **Belmont** and **Rotherwas**. Snead-Cox noted in his journal a visit to Broxwood by Francis Wegg-Prosser, the new owner of Belmont House. Prosser had recently converted to Catholicism and in the 1860s would commission Edward Welby Pugin to remodel with questionable effect the austere classical villa that was now his home. Snead-Cox's journal is the only evidence that dates Nesfield's involvement at Belmont. Prosser arrived by train at Broxwood, accompanied by the landscape gardener, on 12 October 1858. There Prosser persuaded Snead-Cox to 'forego' Nesfield's attention for two days and so delay marking the trees that were to be removed from the site of the new house.[27] This presumably allowed Nesfield to return to Belmont, where he could give timely advice in the midst of so many architectural improvements, although there is no evidence to prove precisely what he suggested.[28] The same is true of Rotherwas. The Catholic Charles de la Barre Bodenham had inherited the estate in 1865, embarking on a similar pattern of patronage and engaging EW Pugin to work on his family chapel. He also contacted Nesfield and his son, Arthur Markham, some time during the 1860s, although there is nothing to suggest that this approach came to anything. However, failure to get this scheme off the ground would not stand in the way of Nesfield's rising reputation in the county.

Nesfield's largest and longest commission was for the widowed Lady Emily Foley of **Stoke Edith**. It began in 1853 and continued until 1860. It was sandwiched between two nationally important commissions: the first for the Duke of Westminster at Crewe Hall, Cheshire, and the second a controversial design for the new Horticultural Society garden, which formed part of Prince Albert's vision for a new centre of culture in South Kensington, London. Stoke Edith gave Nesfield an opportunity to reveal the breadth of his skills and the depth of his talent. As a gifted artist, his colour sense enabled him to advise on both the interior decoration of the house and the design of his new parterres.[29] He demonstrated a sound, if unexciting, working knowledge of plants, drawing up detailed planting lists, and it seems that he even sourced some plants direct from the Veitch nursery.[30] He also offered detailed horticultural advice to support the implementation of his designs,[31] sourced statuary and decorative items direct from the manufacturers,[32] and demonstrated patience and tact in the management of a cautious client.

At the heart of the scheme were two new parterres deliberately placed to foreground the views from the principal rooms on the south and west fronts. As at Broxwood they were to be connected by a straight terrace walk, but this time it was to be 288 feet in length. The southern parterre, described by Nesfield as the 'great compartment', was a *parterre de broderie* set out on an existing slope to ensure best visibility from the reception rooms.[33] The design was assembled using a selection of curlicues, arabesques and scallop-shapes almost certainly taken from the scrapbook of parterre designs that Nesfield had compiled.[34] These were largely drawn from seventeenth-century French sources, including André le Nôtre and Alexandre Le Blond. A letter from Nesfield to Lady Emily confirmed this revivalist preference and his rejection of the 'vile manner of the last 100 years (based upon no principle at all)' of English gardening when compared to 'the genuine manner of two Centuries ago' and 'the fundamental laws of Art according to the *old Masters* [which] should at one glance, be apparent to an enlivened mind'.[35]

His colour scheme for the south parterre was sophisticated and considered: 'The darkest & most sober colours should be in the North beds to advance the more positive colours at the South end'.[36] The scallop-shaped bed at the farthest end was to be made 'prismatic by means of light colours, yet gradating at the south ends from darker, shading to very pale & by way of enhancing the dark introduce white spots of verbena'. Generally he sought '*gradations* of *one* colour in the same bed', even specifying how white would move through 'yellowish white' to 'bright bluey white' and on to 'real white' (*colour 33*). He also chose the plants carefully so that their form reinforced the design, pointing out that those near the house 'should be as low as possible and pegged', and that 'foliated beds must have particularly low flowers or their form will be confused'.[37] When, in 1855, he was approached about variations to an agreed planting scheme for this parterre, he did not challenge the suggestion that dwarf dahlias should replace roses, but he could not agree that rhododendrons replaced Portuguese laurel because they were 'not dark enough for a background and grow ragged & uneven – formality being most desirable in the Compartment'.[38] The estate steward's record of the planting costs of the south parterre confirms that Nesfield's recommendations were followed exactly. In the opening months of 1854 dwarf box, laurels for hedging, standard roses, laurestinus, and rhododendrons were planted along with *Araucaria imbricata* and Swedish junipers.[39] However, the planting was not a total success. Three years later Lady Emily was complaining to Nesfield that the box was all dead, killed by lead leaching out of a blue mineral, which was, no doubt, the Derbyshire Blue John that he had incorporated into the design.[40]

Today the south parterre survives as the footprint of the estate's pheasant pen which, as a result, slopes at a surprisingly steep angle towards the platform of the lost house and the remnants of the long terrace walk. All trace of the planting, the statuary and the armillary sphere that Nesfield placed so carefully at its centre have gone. There is also little evidence on site of the location of his western parterre. It was planted at some distance from the drawing room, where existing evergreens crowded the site. Such a situation called for a simpler, bolder design and Nesfield opted for a long narrow bed, using a favourite guilloche pattern bisected by a narrow central path. Further from the house the walk was lined with standard roses, each set in its own circular bed. The guilloche-patterned bed was balanced by another oblong of four arabesques on the south side of the terrace walk.

Throughout the commission Nesfield slowly persuaded his client to accept the removal of some much-loved trees and shrubs. His letters are peppered with evidence of his gradual approach. In September 1855, writing of the 'solitary beech on the hill' he explained 'the said Beech (which happens to be a very common place object) not only ruins the compact & good group of trees behind it, but by *scale* of comparison, it seriously injures the grandeur & breadth of the beautiful wooded distance'.[41] In the same letter he also turned his attention to a pair of arbutus that would interfere with the line of the western parterre. He favoured more drastic treatment than his client would permit and so began a long slow campaign to reduce the trees in this area. Along the way he feigned sympathy when nature intervened to his advantage, declaring that

> the poor Arbutus (left of the House) was doomed. Altho both plants were splendid, yet their position is very questionable now that the whole garden has been so completely revolutionised hence if the remaining individual were to disappear, I confess it would be a great relief – but till now I have never had courage thus to own my feelings, in consequence of having already dealt severely tho deservedly with other plants.[42]

In 1858 he was still agitating to reduce the evergreens around the same parterre, noting: 'With reference to your operations westward I feel confident they are right altho' I grant I had not the courage to prescribe such a dose after my dreadful *slaughter* in other places'.[43] A year later his successful campaign to thin out this part of the garden was drawing to a close as he acknowledged, 'I have always felt that the whole of the ground in front of Ding. Rm. was insipid & wanted some degree of play of lines to keep pace in a subordinate manner with the other dressings – I shall be glad to hear when all the condemned trees are down feeling that after the operation a few scattered groups, single trees and thorns will loosen the *tight* lines & do wonders in several places'.[44] In the corner where his two parterres met, Nesfield wanted to manage carefully the transition between Art and Nature by creating two amoebic-shaped beds around some existing shrubs.[45] They also helped to channel views out from the house into the park. In establishing a vista towards the village of Tarrington he sought to create 'an interminable or rather a mysterious ending of the Park', although such subtle effects could only be achieved by his attendance on site: 'this matter...is very difficult to deal with & ought to be well studied on the spot with a powerful telescope'.[46]

Nesfield continued to attract more Herefordshire clients during the 1860s and 1870s, although these later commissions were somewhat predictable when compared to his work at Stoke Edith. At **Downton Castle** he worked for Thomas Andrew Knight's grandson, Andrew Rouse Boughton Knight. In 1861 they called in the architect, S Poutney Smith, to make alterations to the Castle and begin work on the new church of St Giles, immediately to the west. By June of the following year a reporter for the *Journal of Horticulture and Cottage Gardener* was informing readers that the Downton gardener, John Gribbin, was 'now executing plans of embroidery and other works under Mr Nesfield'.[47] His new parterre and adjacent T-shaped pool with apsidal ends extended the garden below the Castle in the direction of the new church spire. An opening in the enclosing semicircular yew hedge focused the view on another flowerbed, decorated with a stone urn with the spire rising beyond, and, while there is no evidence to take Nesfield's involvement beyond this flowerbed, the planting of a Wellingtonia avenue, The Lady's Walk (*66*), also framing the church spire, could have been undertaken on his instructions. The Downton *parterre de broderie* included two griffins and was laid out using minerals and flowers. This was a combination that attracted much press criticism when Nesfield used it at the same time in his South Kensington gardens for the Royal Horticultural Society.[48]

On Downton's south front a new terrace wall with appropriate military-looking bastions, turrets and loopholes was constructed, while within this space Nesfield laid out another characteristically arrow-straight terrace walk. Irish yews, *Yucca gloriosa*, *Rhododendron myrtifolium* and standard Portuguese laurels also enriched stone-edged raised beds. A sundial that was 'to be introduced' at the centre bastion of the terrace in 1862, is presumably the Scottish-revivalist-style dial that has been relocated nearer the T-shaped pool.[49] The pool itself has suffered by having

66 A ninteenth-century postcard showing WA Nesfield's scrolling parterre and hedges, firmly aligned on The Lady's Walk, which leads to St Giles. *Collection of the late Dr Nigel Temple*

its round-edged stone moulding replaced by an uncompromising concrete rim. All the flowerbeds that Nesfield cut into the lawns and his parterre have gone, although a network of shallow steps connecting lost formal walks to the south-west of the Castle, together with standard clipped shrubs that have grown free, hint at his planting further afield.

Concurrent with Downton was another Herefordshire commission that had further metropolitan parallels. At **Newport House**, three miles south-east of Kington, Nesfield introduced a large circular stone vase or tazza, supported by four crouching lions (*colour 34*). It originally sat on the first of two shallow terraces beneath the south-east front of the house. Beyond this, in an echo of his design at Downton, a clipped yew hedge inscribed another semicircle, punctured by an allée forty metres long, centred on the nearby lake. Today the stone tazza has been moved to this point next to the water. Ringed by a gravel walk and a circle of bedding plants, it copies the siting of its Austin & Seeley-manufactured twins on the Broad Walk in London's Regent's Park. Nesfield created this London scheme with the help of his son, Arthur Markham, between 1860 and

1863. His Newport House design was developed for James Watt Gibson, the grandson of James Watt, some time during the same decade.[50]

By the time Nesfield reached his last Herefordshire commission at Shobdon Court, his son Arthur Markham was taking the lead in the family business. During the 1850s Lord Bateman had brought in the architect Alexander Milne to give his home a typical Victorian remodelling including, to the south of the house, an extraordinary elevated terrace 200 yards long and 20 feet high.[51] This was to provide an ideal vantage point from which to view a flower garden, so it is not surprising that, in the following decade, the Nesfields were often working at **Shobdon**. Between 1867 and 1870 Arthur Markham was drawing unspecified plans for the family, with whom he remained in correspondence for a further two years.[52] An 1877 article in the *Journal of Horticulture* described his work there, but attributed the scheme to his father.[53] Seven acres of garden now surrounded the house. To the north and west were lawns and shrubberies. To the east a flower garden shaped like a Maltese Cross had at its centre a fountain, while to the south a more conventional Nesfield design featured a round-headed parterre bordered by a terrace walk striking out in a straight line from the midpoint towards the lake (*67*). It was a conflation of the outline of Stoke Edith's 'great compartment' and the central terrace walk focused on a distant view, as at Downton and Newport House, but heavy geometric blocks of flowers replaced the elaborate swirling excitement of Nesfield's earlier *parterre de broderie*. Even though it demanded less manpower to maintain, this uninspiring design has not survived.

Similar gardens by other designers at **Brockhampton House** and **Whitbourne Hall**, near Bromyard, have faired better. These two properties are located on opposite sides of a small valley to the east of Bromyard, but in many respects they make surprising neighbours. The Brockhampton estate and its Georgian house were given to the National Trust in the 1940s, while Whitbourne Hall remained in the same family until 1980, when it was bought by the intensely democratic Whitbourne Hall Community Ltd. They converted all but the largest reception rooms in this

67 This early photograph is a rare record of WA Nesfield's parterre at Shobdon Court, which recalled his Great Compartment at Stoke Edith. *Reproduced by permission of English Heritage. NMR*

huge Victorian house into units suited to modern family life. In 2010 Whitbourne featured in Channel 4's television programme *Country House Rescue*, when the presenter, Ruth Watson, cajoled the residents into entering the holiday market by establishing facilities for 'glamping' (posh camping) in the grounds in order to boost income for maintaining the Hall and its gardens.[54]

In stark contrast, the public never visits Brockhampton House. The National Trust's tenant guards his privacy as best he can, given that his gardens are adjacent to the parkland which the Trust is so keen to promote to its paying visitors. One of the parkland paths gives views across to a nineteenth-century rockery and a formal parterre recreated in 1996 to an original design drawn by Alexander Roos in 1865. Roos was an interior decorator, architect and landscape designer who came to this country from Italy around 1832 and whose career is gradually being rediscovered.[55] He frequently found work in Scotland under the influence of his Scottish-based, Bristol-born mentor, Onesiphorous Tyndall Bruce. It is unclear how he came to work for John Habington Barneby at Brockhampton, in what appears to be his only Herefordshire commission, although he is known to have worked in two of the neighbouring counties: at Hadzor Hall, Worcestershire, in the 1830s and at Southam, Gloucestershire, in 1844. Roos established a reputation as a designer of floral and mineral parterres, and the more geometric flower gardens that became popular from the late 1850s.[56] The flower garden below the house, with its two rectangular parterres of clipped evergreens surrounded by wide gravel walks, would appear to reflect his style. However, the existence of another plan by William Broderick Thomas casts some doubt on the extent of Roos' work here. This undated plan, which may well have been prepared the year before Roos arrived, depicts an identical network of paths, except that the parterres are no longer separated by a central walk with steps, but remain as a single expanse of open turf. All the other hard landscape features drawn by Thomas and by Roos were identical, including the semicircular bastion of lawn below the parterres, surrounded by another wide gravel walk, and the roundabout-like junction of the paths just to the south of the house. It would seem, therefore, that Roos was responsible for the parterres and the steps and walk that divided them, but that the other features were by Thomas, another Victorian landscape gardener whose career is only slowly being uncovered.[58]

One further question hangs over this recreated Victorian parterre. A usually reliable observer of country houses, Mrs Francis Baldwin Childe of Kyre Park, Worcestershire, sketched the garden in October 1895, when the billowing planting was unrestrained by hedges.[59] There was also no sign of the 'standard evergreens' Roos specified to line the parallel walks above and below the parterres. The present clipped hedges might, therefore, be a curious mix of interpretation and omission of Roos' plan, but as such they illustrate the conundrums that face anyone recreating a historic garden.

There is, however, more certainty about the origins of the parterre that survives at Whitbourne Hall. This was a new estate, developed in the 1860s. Its creator, Edward Bickerton Evans, used a fortune made from the

30 Thomas Hearne's 1786 view of the Teme Gorge shows his developing interest in Picturesque aesthetics; it might easily have been painted by Jacob van Ruisdael. *Private collection*

31 In 1787 the poetess Anna Seward enjoyed a picnic at Downton's 'Otaheitean' Mill. Hearne's view shows the Mill before its alteration; it is now a ruin. ***Private collection***

32 Moorish pinnacles and towers around the former stables are all that survives of Hope End, but its Regency landscape is well preserved

Stoke Edith Park

N° V. Arrangement of Colours for Beds.

All Plants nearest the House should be as low as possible & pegged – Those for the subdivision at the North end of Compartment may be as high as the most dwarf Geraniums –

The foliated beds must have particularly low flowers or their forms will be confused –

The endeavour should be to make gradations of one colour in the same bed, if long, as for Example, the South Scroll, where the deepest scarlet commences at the Circle A & blends imperceptibly towards B into orangy red & thence towards C into salmon red –

At D the gradation is from deep yellow to very brilliant pale yellow at E & so on throughout in the purples, blues &c – The darkest & most sober colours should be in the North beds to advance the more positive Colours at the South end –

The foliated Beds N°s 1. 2. 3 should gradate in colour from light rose No 1 to the deepest rose or maroon N° 3 –

The flank foliated Beds N° 4 should contain the deepest blue possible –

The Scallop to be prismatic by means of light colours, yet gradating at the South ends from darker, shading to very pale & by way of enhancing the dark introduce white spots of Verbena –

N° 5. Yellowish white such as Mignionette
6. very bright bluey white
7. Real white
8 Pale blue –

W.A. Nesfield
Oct. 54

Proposed additions to Embroidery & coloured Alleys –

33

William Andrews Nesfield brought a professional eye for colour to the Stoke Edith parterre, providing detailed design notes and intricate sketches that could be followed by the head gardener.
Private collection

34 This tazza, manufactured by the firm of Austin & Seeley, was once at the heart of an 1860s terraced design by WA Nesfield at Newport House

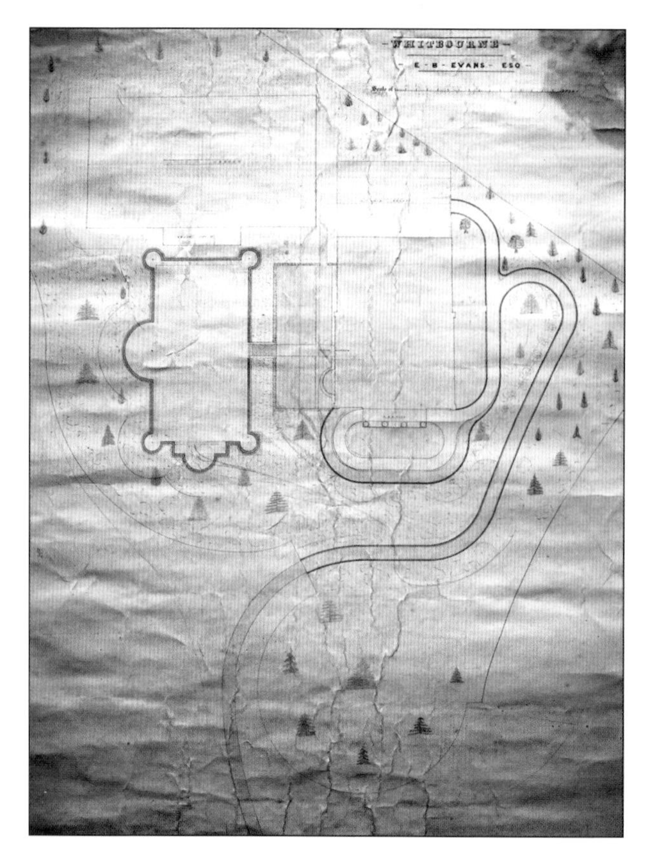

35

This undated design for Whitbourne Hall, attributed here to William Barron, shows an empty, hedged enclosure that now contains the Italian Garden and a fine selection of conifers. *Private collection*

36

The steeply battered walls, Italianate arches and exuberant array of windows at Whitbourne's Worcester Lodge are prime examples of Victorian 'rogue architecture'

37 The flower parterre at Treago Castle, shown in this 1837 watercolour, is now centred by a modern pool decorated with a sculpture of a girl holding a bear's paw – a pun on the family name of Mynors. *Private collection*

38 The decaying ironwork of a greenhouse for exotics marks the entrance to Buckfield Keep's romantic Pulhamite fernery and dripping well

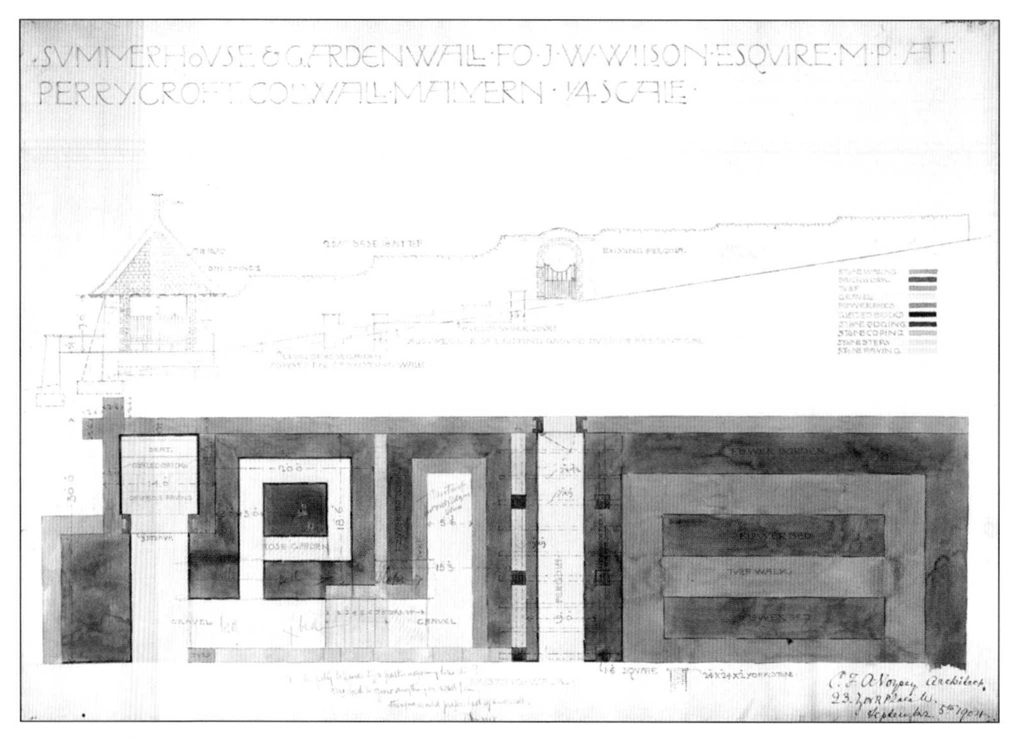

39 Pencilled notes on CFA Voysey's 1904 garden plan for Perrycroft request that the gravel path and beds be reversed so that climbers can be set against the wall; this has since been implemented. *RIBA Library Drawings & Archives Collections*

40 Voysey's arched gateway at Perrycroft was designed to sit at the end of a pre-existing pergola. It looks far better today, surrounded by Gillian Archer's free planting of the borders and the wall

41 The Summerhouse at Goodrich Court may have been designed by E Guy Dawber, who often worked in concert with Thomas Mawson

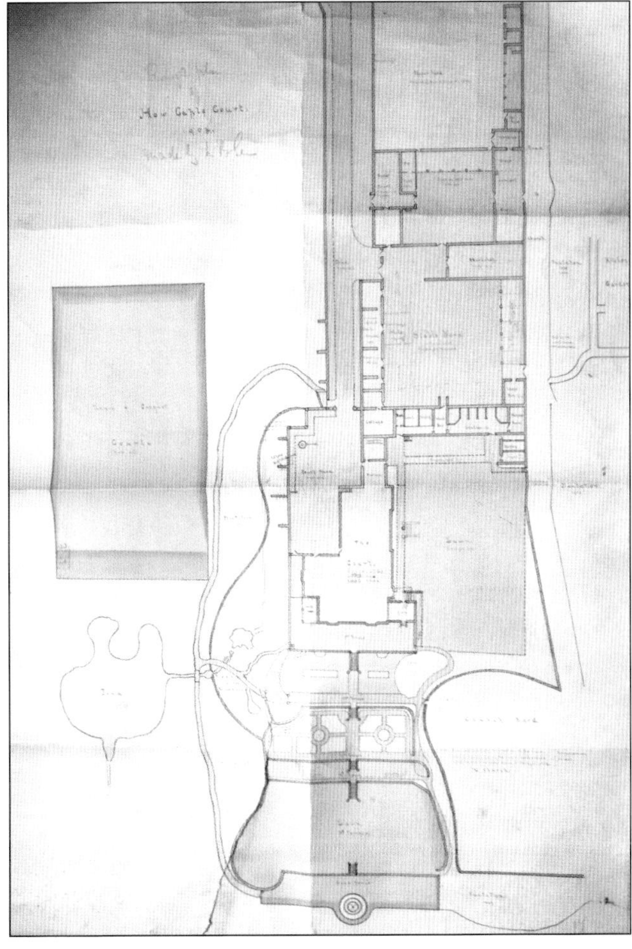

42 Lennox Bertram Lee drew his own plan in 1904 for the continuing improvements to the garden at How Caple Court. The rockery adjacent to the terraces dates from 1887, but was rebuilt by Lee in 1903. *Private collection*

43 The beds of the Sunken Garden on the fifth terrace at How Caple were laid out to a design by Arthur Clayton. The architect of the Gazebo remains a mystery, though LB Lee must have have a hand in it

44 This present day view of one of the terraces at How Caple mirrors almost exactly a 1910 photograph of Edith Lee, who is sitting on the *scola* that terminates the paved walk

distillation of vinegar to buy up small parcels of land and engage the architect E W Elmslie to design a vast classical mansion. Professional advice was also sought from a very early date, probably during 1860, for the plan of the new pleasure grounds. An undated, unsigned design (*colour 35*) was to wrap around an early footprint of the Hall; it was subsequently amended in pencil to reflect architectural changes, including the addition of a large bow window to the drawing room and the extension of the huge portico from four to six columns. The plan marks the approach from the

68 The carefully maintained parterre in the Italian Garden at Whitbourne Hall is the centrepiece of one of the best surviving examples of Victorian landscaping in the county

south-west, which ran below the north-east front, then branched off to the service wing before curving back to the portico in what must have been something of an anti-climax. The hedged outline of the geometric Italian Garden is shown where it continues to flourish, with its crisply-clipped, curving yew parterre (*68*). The anonymous designer also took great care in placing a collection of conifers along the approach and over the slopes beneath the Hall, with each specimen drawn so as to distinguish its size, habit and the tone of its foliage.

Evans was another Victorian passionate about trees, particularly conifers. They were well represented in the horticultural section of his library, which included Henry Steuart's *The Planter's Guide* of 1828, Augustus Mongredien's 1870 *Trees and Shrubs for English Plantations* and George Gordon's *The Pinetum* of 1880.[60] He received several gifts of conifers from William Henry Barneby of Bredenbury Court, whose elder brother lived at Brockhampton House.[61] Evans also bought trees from John Hitchman, a doctor and tree enthusiast who planted an arboretum in Leamington Spa, Warwickshire, from Wood & Co of Worcester, and, most famously, from William Barron's nursery at Elvaston, Derbyshire. Barron was Head Gardener to the Earl of Harrington at Elvaston Castle, where he created several formal gardens enclosed by hedges and topiary similar to the Italian Garden at Whitbourne. These had been well publicised in the *Gardener's Chronicle* in 1851 and in Edward Adveno Brooke's *The Gardens of England*, which appeared the following year. Barron also went into print with his own little manual entitled *The British Winter Garden*, which appeared in 1852, as well as offering a design service from the nursery he founded the year before. His 1855 plan for Aqualate Hall, Staffordshire, with its hedged but empty enclosed garden, and the individual depiction of the different conifers species to be used, suggests that the Whitbourne plan should be attributed to him.[62] Photographs from the end of the nineteenth-century showing the heart-shaped curves of a mature yew parterre within the Italian Garden would also suggest that this dates from Barron's time. Indeed, the Italian Garden appears to be a rare example of a surviving nineteenth-century parterre and the best-preserved Victorian formal garden to survive in the county, despite its recent alteration when gravel replaced turf and a simple fountain was added as a reminder of lost flower beds.

Once the pleasure grounds were planted and construction of the Hall was complete, Evans needed to announce his new estate to the world. He did this with two new lodges, one of which is the beautiful and ebullient Worcester Lodge (*colour 36*). The commissioning of the London-based 'rogue architect', Robert Lewis Roumieu, would be surprising if it were not for that architect's success in designing a prominent London vinegar warehouse that Nikolaus Pevsner has dismissed as 'utterly undisciplined and crazy'.[63] Between 1869 and 1871, Roumieu designed and oversaw the construction of both the Italianate Worcester Lodge and the bridge taking its drive over the Whitbourne Brook.[64] The combination of roughly-hewn stone, smooth ashlar and polychrome for the Lodge, together with the individual design of every window and the battered walls, which give a reassuringly solid appearance to visitors, but which gave architect and client some difficulty when contriving the splay of the gates, is thrilling.[65] A cleverly angled, covered flight of steps also climbs the bank opposite the Lodge, to keep pedestrians and carriages apart, although the dividing wall in the elegantly elongated Lodge entrance appears redundant if, as seems likely, it was intended to separate the supervision of arriving and departing carriages. The part-brick Tedstone Lodge is a less confident essay in the Italianate style and, although there is no archival evidence to link it to Roumieu, it must, on stylistic grounds alone, be to his design.

Roumieu was next retained by Evans to add a massive Conservatory and Fernery to the south-west front of the house. He covered Elmslie's kitchen courtyard with a giant glass and iron-domed roof, blending the classical Greek architecture of the Hall with Italianate details from the Worcester Lodge, such as the elongated porch archway. The Conservatory had been abandoned by 1909, as heating costs outstripped the family purse, and it now stands as an elegant glassless ruin on the lawn above the Italian Garden, while the more manageably sized Fernery forms a conservatory to the Gardener's House that is filled with the heavy scent of lilies in the summer.

Another typical Victorian flower garden once enlivened the square terrace beneath the towers of the fifteenth-century fortified house, **Treago Castle**.[66] Located in border country just north of Monmouth, Treago has remained in the hands of the same family since it was built, and the current generation, Sir Richard and Lady Fiona Mynors, now open the grounds occasionally to interested groups. A twentieth-century octagonal pool centres the elevated platform that was once the south-facing flower garden. When Jane Perceval painted the scene in 1875, flowerbeds of assorted geometric shapes were bordered by miniature clipped hedges and paths, which were seemingly constructed from hoggin or local red sandstone (*colour 37*). The straight terrace walk that she painted disappearing from view is no longer there, but it would have connected to the four steeply-tiered mid-Victorian terraces that rise to the west of the house.

A few remnants of steps from much shallower garden terraces, together with an occasional untamed golden yew, survive at **Bredenbury Court**, six miles north-west of Bromyard. These are the vestiges of the gardens laid out by Ernest Milner around 1876 for William Henry Barneby and his wife Susan, a member of the Elwes family from Colesbourne in Gloucestershire.[67] Milner began his career as an apprentice to Joseph Paxton at Chatsworth, Derbyshire, before studying at the *Jardin des Plantes* in Paris in 1841. On his return to England he worked again for Paxton before launching his solo career as a landscape gardener in the mid-1850s. By the time he came to Bredenbury he had completed a sequence of private and public commissions, establishing a reputation at the top of his profession alongside Robert Marnock.[68]

It is difficult to define the precise extent of Milner's work at Bredenbury, although the sale particulars for 1898 refer to his 'pretty flower garden, with geometrical beds [that] adjoins the house'.[69] A photograph from the same year (*69*) shows gardeners tending a typical bedding display laid out here in crescent-shaped and circular beds on a lawn beneath the house. This connected with a long straight terrace walk that struck out towards the road and was bordered by banks of laurel with 'nooks' for ferns and a rustic summerhouse. The terrace walk was still in place on the map accompanying the 1924 sale particulars, but these placed much less emphasis on the grounds than their equivalent had done 26 years earlier, so it seems that Milner's flower garden had already disappeared. Today

69 Stone steps and changes in level are the only evidence today at Bredenbury Court of Edward Milner's short-lived flower garden. *Reproduced by permission of Herefordshire Record Office*

the terrace promenade has also gone, leaving a large, blank lawn edged with trees and only the decaying steps and a forlorn collection of urns that once connected it with the flower garden.

Milner is also known to have laid out shrubberies around the Court, which were dotted with rhododendrons and cut through with winding walks. Again there were no references to these in 1924, when only the 'fine selection of ornamental trees' drew any real enthusiasm.[70] An early photograph, taken before Barneby demolished the church that until 1876 stood immediately next to the Court, shows young conifers already growing in the pleasure grounds.[71] Another undated, but roughly contemporary, photograph shows them being planted around the lake in the park. Whether the conifers were introduced under Milner's direction, or on Barneby's own initiative, is unclear, although Barneby's several gifts of conifers to Whitbourne Hall mentioned earlier show that he had been taken in by this craze. This could only have been fuelled by the extensive travels he undertook in North America in the 1880s.[72]

The county's tradition of building picturesque lookouts above the Wye was reinterpreted by the Victorians at The Leys, now renamed **Wyastone Leys**, near Monmouth, and at Lincoln Hill House on the south-western edge of Ross-on-Wye. In the summer of 1884 members of the Woolhope Club climbed Doward Hill heading for the summit, an ancient hill fort and an iron tower 'of easy ascent...[that] affords very fine views on all sides'.[73] Revd Webb, the curate at nearby Ganarew from 1851, could not join the party, but wrote to Club members describing the frequent excavation of bones in the vicinity by Richard Blakemore, the builder of the tower, who also dug out 'caves' to enhance his new deer park. Today the scene resembles a moonscape following major restoration by the Woodland Trust to clear trees and introduce free-roaming cattle to control the vegetation. This also allowed the archaeological investigation that rediscovered Blakemore's park.[74]

When the grounds of the stuccoed **Lincoln Hill House** were divided in the twentieth century the extraordinary 100-feet long sandstone ramp that terminates in a three-storey battlemented tower became marooned in the garden of the 1930s Arbour Hill House. The ramp imitates a curtain wall and the wooden posts and iron chain that formed its handrail now dangle free in front of the blind arrow slits. Bertie Cumerford has converted the tower into an immaculately ordered garden tool store with an artist's studio and sitting room above. It seems to have been constructed for Ferdinand Beeston, a Bristol trader in tea and timber, who came to Ross-on-Wye around 1850.[75] In the 1830s he built a less ambitious castellated lookout at the entrance to the Bristol Channel just outside Clevedon, that was used by local sugar dealers to watch for returning ships. The economic advantage gained from early knowledge that a valuable cargo was to arrive safely in port had fuelled a tradition of lookouts including an observation point in Thomas Goldney's famous eighteenth-century Clifton garden, which is now in the care of the University of Bristol. When Beeston moved to

Herefordshire he seems to have given up commerce, applying his experience in lookout construction to embellishing the scenery along the Wye. The views from the ramparts across the Wye valley, described in 1883,[76] are now obscured by grey commercial warehouses and a thick line of alder trees. More trees have crowded out the view of Goodrich Castle, although the distinctive outline of Coppet Hill remains.

A surprising expression of Victorian revivalism took place in the grounds of a new suburban villa on the outskirts of Hereford in the 1860s. **Holmer Park** was constructed in the fashionable Italianate style for a successful local tradesman, Charles Watkins.[77] At the same time, in 1862, the decision was taken to demolish the city's late-sixteenth-century timber-framed Market Hall. Three of the columns and two pairs of spandrels from the Hall came as architectural salvage to Holmer Park, where they were recycled into what would now be described as a summerhouse, but in 1921 functioned as an 'Old Carved Oak Aviary'.[78] Like many Victorian villas, Holmer Park has lost its parkland to the encroaching city suburbs, and much of what remains of the pleasure grounds has been lost to car parking for the clients of the spa and health club which has been set up in the house.

A second suburban villa, on the outskirts of Leominster, shelters the county's only example of rockwork by the successful and prolific firm of James Pulham & Son. **Buckfield Keep** was constructed in 1863 for Josiah and Phoebe Newman, who added in 1872 a charming Pulhamite complex consisting of a 'Fernery of Rock all round, and a Corridor; Dropping Well and Streamlet from it, and path over to look down over all from above'.[79] Part of the Rockery, described by Pulham as the 'Corridor', was enclosed beneath a glass roof which extended out from a small glasshouse (*colour 38*). While Pulham seems to have included steps at the opposite end of the Rockery to provide overhead views of the complex, the ring of ornamental gratings set into the ground following the line of this section of horseshoe-shaped rockwork suggests that the entire structure was originally glazed over. Water may have been supplied from the mysterious set of galvanised

70 Henry Newman poses proudly in the grounds of his Leominster garden among his prized collection of succulents. *Leominster Museum*

tanks in the roof space of the adjacent service building. Today the Rockery and Glasshouse, together with a nearby Conservatory, make up one of the most romantic and intimate Pulhamite creations in the country, although quite how long it will survive is a matter for concern. Decay is setting in, as the imitation rock facing deteriorates, revealing the supporting brick structure beneath.

Josiah Newman's unusual choice of a rockery and dripping well for Buckfield Keep, when others in the county were preoccupied with parterres and pine trees, must have been due to the influence of his brother Edward, a fern expert. In 1840 Edward Newman published the first edition of his successful *History of British Ferns*, and the following year became editor of *The Phytologist*, a position he held until 1854.[80] Pulhamite was the ideal medium for displaying ferns, and several late nineteenth-century photographs include friends or family self-consciously posed to show off the ferns flourishing at Buckfield Keep.

71

Helen and Theodore Neild enjoyed the twin Victorian manias for excess and competition in their garden at The Grange.
Leominster Museum

A third member of the Newman family, Ernest and Josiah's youngest brother, Henry, was simultaneously establishing his own garden, having inherited the family home at **46 Etnam Street, Leominster**. Here he assembled an enviable collection of succulents, including a group of the prehistoric-looking stapelias that were rated 'for many years the best in England'.[81] He was photographed proudly seated in front of his glasshouse (*70*) surrounded by his collection and in 1908, even his obituary in the *Leominster News* chose to remember him standing next to the towering flowering spike of one of his echiums.[82] His daughter Helen followed her father's gardening example, posing for a similar photograph with her husband, Theodore Neild, admiring her own flowering echium (71). In a strange twist that calls to mind Holmer Park, this photograph was taken outside the Neild's home, **Grange Court**, which had been constructed in 1859 from reassembled portions of Leominster's timber-framed Market Hall. The couple bought Grange Court from the Hampton Court estate in the opening decade of the twentieth century, but as products of the Victorian age they continued to garden with a taste for excess and oddity. Henry Newman's home in Etnam Street has been demolished and replaced by social housing, while Grange Court now stands in the centre of Leominster's public park, where it is being restored as a cultural and heritage centre. Buckfield Keep is, therefore, the only surviving example of the Newman family's gardening tradition.

8

Puritan dawn to Hawaiian sunset – the Edwardians

Perrycroft · Goodrich Court · How Caple Court · Brand Lodge
Gatley Park · Michaelchurch Court · Broadfield Court · Donnington Hall
Burton Court · Brinsop Court · Winforton House
Dinmore Manor · Birley Court

THE MALVERNS RIDGE IS A HAPPY HUNTING GROUND FOR EARLY WORKS by that most puritan of Edwardian architects, Charles Francis Annesley Voysey. His first country house commission was Walnut Tree Farm, at Castlemorton on the east side in Worcestershire, which has been renamed Bannut Tree House, 'bannut' being Worcestershire dialect for a walnut.[1] There is also a pair of lodges linked by a Voysey archway of 1901 at that most secretive house of the earls Beauchamp, Madresfield Court, just along the road. Strung out along the eastern contours there are two small cottages by him in the Great Malvern suburbs,[2] while in 1919 Voysey designed the war memorial at Malvern Wells. Walnut Tree Farm was a rare Voysey variation on the local timber-framed vernacular, his mature style being a combination of white harled walls with heavy buttresses, buttressed chimneystacks, sloping roofs with overhanging eaves, and small-paned windows, often jettied out on the first floor as oriels or set within bays to catch the sun. His elevations are enlivened by doors placed asymmetrically to serve the internal planning, and settles or seats within nooks for sheltered views out to the grounds, or simply to offer privacy for quiet contemplation. All of these signature design features are present at **Perrycroft**, on the Herefordshire side of the hills at Colwall. This was

72 CFA Voysey's Perrycroft has projecting windows and recessed niches with garden seats to take in views of the British Camp on the Malverns. Gillian Archer's recent planting around the house anchors it sympathetically to the land

Voysey's first major country house commission of 1893-5 for the MP John William Wilson, a Liberal politician from a Quaker family, whose father founded a Birmingham chemical company.[3] It may be that Wilson knew the owner of Walnut Tree Farm, RH Cazalet, but the two commissions have a definite link in the local builder, W Porter of Malvern, who was responsible for constructing both houses.[4]

Voysey's houses are linear in their internal planning, and Perrycroft is no exception, with the main reception rooms facing south-west to take advantage of the sun (*72*). At the western end of the main block he sited a drawing room, which has bay windows facing west down the garden and out to the more informal area with the end of the Malverns ridge as its backdrop. What is curious about several writers who have discussed Perrycroft, especially Wendy Hitchmough in an excellent book on the architect, is that none seems to have noticed why Voysey sited his house on a level platform at right-angles to the hills. Hitchmough writes: 'Perrycroft was not without its faults. Despite its L-shaped plan, Voysey made no attempt to tuck the house into the hillside or, through craggy contours and local materials, to blend it into the landscape in true Arts and Crafts tradition'.[5] Voysey's service rooms – kitchen, butler's pantry, scullery and stores – were cleverly laid out in the short stroke of the L, parallel to the road, while his main range, as we have seen earlier, was effectively a viewing wing on both floors aligned squarely on the British Camp. Perrycroft responded, therefore, to the locality in a direct way and, perhaps more indirectly, in the Worcestershire timber-framed vernacular features of corbelled-out, jettied windows on the upper floor. True, his houses usually deploy the white roughcast facing to brick walls more characteristic of the Lake District or Scotland, but this was a conscious attempt to throw off historical styles and, by reducing houses to their bare essentials in ornament, an effort to keep costs at a minimum.

The rational and geometric layout of the interior of a Voysey house is often extended out into the grounds, particularly where, on the rare occasions when he was asked to provide them, there are designed gardens. Significantly, almost all his houses were commissioned and completed before he turned to the surroundings. This was the case at Walnut Tree Farm and at Lowicks, near Frensham in Surrey, which predates Perrycroft by a year; Voysey added a summerhouse to the tea lawn there as late as 1911.[6] At Perrycroft, Voysey was asked back to design stables in 1903, a year later for the Summerhouse and in 1908 to design the coachman's cottage.[7] Although his garden designs were typical of the Arts & Crafts movement in that they were architectural extensions of the parent house, Voysey was no plantsman and his drawings rarely specify particular species. His plan for the 'Summerhouse and Garden Wall' at Perrycroft (*colour 39*), which is dated 5 September 1904, nine years after the house was completed, marks out the area parallel with the western boundary wall in sections inscribed: 'Flower Bed', 'Flower Border' and 'Turf Walk'.[8] Not surprisingly, the plan gives clear details of all the architectural structures – ramped wall, summerhouse, pergola and arched gateway – together with the materials to be used in their construction. Much of the scheme survives on site and has been recently replanted by Gillian Archer. She has retained the formal structure but softened it with relaxed planting both here and closer to the house in the sunken garden under the drawing room windows. There, swathes of planting cascade over the rectangular enclosure, which is centred by a terracotta birdbath framed by a box hedge that was introduced in 2010. The earthy quality of the piece, which has a Liberty's air suggestive of Archibald Knox that is perfectly in keeping with Voysey's

73 Voysey's Summerhouse at Perrycroft invites visitors into the garden, but its position at the foot of the steeply-sloping site provides contemplative seclusion rather than wide vistas

house, combines with the russet palette of planting here later in the year. Archer has also been working with the plants she has inherited in the wild area below the house platform, following advice, particularly about mowing regimes, in Christopher Lloyd's *The Well-Tempered Garden*.

Voysey's Summerhouse (73), whose specifications included a glazed brick interior, Delabole slates on the floor, oak shingles to the roof and an oak finial, still commands an internal view up the garden, focusing on steps that lead up to the top terrace on the south-west front of the house.

It was originally flanked by an ascending sequence of a rose garden, a gravel walk, a pergola, which appears from the plan to have been an existing feature but given new brick piers, and a raised area of flowerbeds and turf walks. The pergola, now gone, was aligned on the Arched Gateway (*colour 40*) in the wall, whose black paint has now been stripped and replaced by a light Brunswick Green that Voysey is known to have used. A contemporary journal article on his work noted this idiosyncrasy: 'That Mr. Voysey is fond of green painted wood-work, or of green-coloured furniture, one has heard urged against him'.[9] The black gloss paintwork on the joinery of the main house has also been repainted in this more sympathetic colour, one that complements the newly-trained climbers on the south wall and provides a link between house and garden. This almost subliminal connection is nowhere more apparent than in Voysey's rainwater heads, which feature vases of flowers. As Voysey was to write in one of his articles on furniture, which could stand for his approach to all craftsmanship, including architecture and garden design, the craftsman should ask of his creation:

> Is it true – is it all it pretends to be? Does it express qualities and feelings consistent with its owner and its surroundings? Is it faithful work? And for love's sake ask, Is it proportioned, coloured, and disposed as the natural beauties in creation? Are its lines and masses graceful and pleasing? Do any of its parts quarrel? Does it express sobriety, restraint and purity'.[10]

Perrycroft, with its garden, is a perfect expression of all those qualities.

While Voysey's Summerhouse is archetypally of the Arts & Crafts period, with its emphasis on natural materials and its conscious lack of a historicist styling, the slightly earlier Summerhouse in the Italian Garden at **Goodrich Court** is unashamedly revivalist: a hybrid of Tudor and Jacobean detail (*colour 41*). As such it must have been a perfect complement to the formal garden laid out to the south-west of Meyrick's Gothic

Revival house. An early photograph of the Summerhouse seen through the gates suggests that the Italian Garden was remodelled before the Summerhouse was built.[11] The lost gateway was dated 1889, while the gable of the Summerhouse carries the later date of 1900 and the initials HMC for Harold Moffatt. It is not known who designed the Summerhouse, or who sculpted the figure that once rose from a gadrooned plinth in the centre of the garden. It has now been replaced by a piece of spiky modern metalwork: 'Spring', by John Henry White. However, Moffatt is known to have commissioned E Guy Dawber, a prolific Edwardian architect, at Hamptworth Lodge, Downton, Wiltshire, in 1910.[12] Dawber had also been working in Herefordshire earlier, at Bredenbury Court in 1902.[13] Whoever may have been responsible, the landscape architect Thomas Mawson was certainly engaged in 1907 to embellish the Italian Garden by adding a double-flight staircase up to the raised terrace on the eastern boundary.[14] This still survives intact, though choked in undergrowth.

Voysey and Mawson were two major players in the Edwardian period, often providing houses and landscaped gardens for the newly rich who were looking for small country estates as summer retreats from the pressures of city life. One of these self-made men was Lennox Bertram Lee, a wealthy textile industrialist from Manchester, who by 1899 had taken the family business into the Calico Printers Association, an amalgamation of forty-six textile and printing firms. He became CPA's chairman, spending most of his working week in Manchester, but at weekends preferring to retreat to his Herefordshire estate of **How Caple**, sited near a huge bend in the Wye north of Ross, rather than engaging in public life in the city. Lee had bought the How Caple estate in 1901, and thereafter, with his wife Edith Gertrude, threw himself into country life: building and gardening. Instead of relying on a recognised professional like Voysey or Mawson, Lee seems to have preferred to act as his own architect and garden designer, but he was undoubtedly a gifted amateur and his Water Garden, as it was first known, is the county's most atmospheric and wonderfully decadent horticultural space. Whereas nothing about the formal enclosure at Goodrich even remotely suggested Italy, the Italian Garden at How Caple could have been used effectively as an illustration for an Edwardian edition of Boccaccio's *Decameron*, or for the backdrop of a contemporary painting by Frederic, Lord Leighton. As early as 1900, Lee had already begun a scrapbook inscribed: 'Album of Illustrated houses (for ideas)', in which he gathered photographs, mainly from *Country Life*, but also from *The Connoisseur* and other similar magazines. The Album documents features he would assemble in the house and the formal gardens, including pergolas, massive stone piers, terraces, sunken gardens, rills, sundials and dry-stone walls studded with plants. All made their way into the gardens that he created to the south of the Court.

The best way to approach How Caple is from the B4224, where a lane branches off at Crossway and heads due west for the village. On the left a huge wall rears up, above which a bizarre copper-roofed pavilion is just visible. Lee set up this sheltered seat at the end of a paved terrace parallel to the wall after he had moved to the house from the Court. It is the perfect preparation for Lee's homespun architecture around the grounds close to the main house, but not the great Italian Garden in the valley below. Before the Court and its environs is explored the church is worth a visit, for Lee and his wife Edith are buried in the churchyard below a gleaming white Renaissance-style tomb chest, and in St Andrew & St Mary there is a matchless sequence of early twentieth-century stained glass windows by AJ Davies of the Bromsgrove Guild and James Powell & Sons of Whitefriars. This includes two blazing war memorial windows to Lee's brother, Noel, and his son Noel Esmond Lee, and to Lennox Cleland Lee, all of whom were killed in the Great War.

There is a particularly rich archive at How Caple, which includes garden plans, architectural drawings and, most importantly for dating, a range of photographs of the Court and its gardens. One of the earliest pieces of architectural evidence that Lee was directing the works himself is a timber-framed gateway, like a lychgate with a wildly upswept roof, which connects the service courtyard to the main driveway. This has the date 1909 and the initials LBL. From this point the main house in seen through the gatehouse, another more traditional addition in timber-framed Herefordshire vernacular set on red sandstone piers. Beyond that rises a pagoda-like roof of a garden building sited for views down into the dell below the house. This is close in style to a 1902 drawing in the archives for a pigeon cote. While the architectural embellishments to the existing house were obviously enjoyable distractions for Lee, he prepared a detailed plan for the formal gardens to the south, which overlook the Wye. The close proximity of the river is shown in an early photograph,

74 The county's garden makers continued to be drawn to the Wye in the twentieth century. This photograph of the terraces at How Caple Court was taken from an aeroplane in 1933. *Private collection*

taken from an aeroplane in 1933 (74). Lee's coloured drawing is inscribed: 'Rough plan of How Caple Court 1904 made by LB Lee'. It shows the terraces with their enclosures, and the grass tennis and croquet courts and pond in the dell to the west (*colour 42*).

These elements are all present in the photographic sequence contained in the 1905 and 1910 albums, which show the development of the terraces as they were altered and architectural features added.[15] There

75 Lennox Bertram Lee used small planting troughs in many of his garden walls. This first attempt at laying out the fifth terrace at How Caple was quickly reworked.
Private collection

is a particularly evocative 1910 shot of Edith in a jaunty straw hat, sitting on the Pompeian-style *scola* seat on the fourth terrace, and another of her on the steps to the second terrace, alongside which is a rockery. Another 1910 photograph of the Sunken Garden below depicts the enclosure as an open grass area with hardly any architectural elements (75). Today it is a paved area punctuated by yews and decorated with urns and statuary (*colour 43*). Arthur Clayton, an architect and surveyor of Adlington in Cheshire, drew out the geometric design for the planters and central pool for Lee.[16] The terraces survive intact with their garden furnishings (*colour 44*) and the addition of copper planters – no doubt another legacy of Lee's manufacturing business – plus a gazebo and statuary.

However, the great excitement of How Caple is what Lee contrived in the Dell Garden below the house. His 1904 plan shows the tennis and croquet courts, which were later given a covered pavilion for spectators, and the pond. By 1910 this had been encircled by a pergola of randomly stacked stone piers like menhirs, which sweeps around the watery enclo-

76 Lee already had an indoor racquet court and a grass tennis court at How Caple when he added this classically-inspired ampitheatre in the 1930s as a grandstand for a new hard-surfaced court

sure and became known as the Rose Garden. The yew-shadowed walk under the rose-entwined pergola, more Victorian than Edwardian in feeling, is no preparation for the next garden incident, which is another *scola* seat backed by Doric columns and flanked by terracotta vases (*76*). Beached in its present isolation in open greensward it is hard to judge how the feature first functioned. Fortunately, a 1937 photograph of the hard tennis court reveals it to have been a viewing station for the sport; the columns once supported a wooden structure for climbers. This extraordinary element, coupled with the blockish stone seat on the terrace slope, is strikingly reminiscent of Sir Arthur Evans' reconstruction of the palace at Knossos on Crete. Significantly, this and the great Water Garden beyond were both constructed at exactly the same time that Evans was recreating the Minoan complex.

The Water Garden, so called in the early photographs, but named both the Sunken Florentine Garden and the Italian Garden in the promotional literature, is now in sad but breathtaking decay. By 1924 the cruciform rill

77 Lee collected photographs of pergolas, rill gardens and loggias in an album before embarking on his own Water Garden at How Caple. This 1930 photograph shows it in its prime. *Private collection*

and the Doric Summerhouse had been constructed, but there were few vases and the enclosing pergola had only just been planted with climbers. By 1930 the paved courtyard had been filled with urns and planters, flowerbeds had been planted parallel to the canals and wooden posts set up for climbing roses (77). The effect was decidedly stony, but atmospherically Mediterranean. Today stone plinths stand forlorn, their fine furnishings long gone, the pergola is collapsing in places, box hedges have replaced the flowerbeds, and the Summerhouse is completely engulfed in summer by rampant growth (*colour 45*). Located out here in rural Herefordshire, How Caple is a hidden secret, yet its Water Garden is one of the most significant early twentieth-century designs in the entire country.[17] The grounds are regularly open to the public, and it is to be hoped that the revenue from visitors and weddings might aid its restoration.

With the Italian Garden we have strayed out of the Edwardian period and into the 1920s, but the grounds of How Caple took more than twenty years to develop and should be seen in their entirety, reflecting the particular taste of the man who achieved them. After the Florentine vistas of that paved courtyard, the remaining gardens of the Edwardian period are somewhat desultory, the county rarely attracting wealthy manufacturers like Lee until the Manchester businessman, Richard Hollins Murray, who invented the reflecting lens used for cats-eyes on roads, bought the Knights Hospitaller property of Dinmore Manor. However, his extraordinary Cloister Garden was not created until the mid-1930s. Furthermore, the county is resolutely Georgian and Victorian in its stock of country houses; there are few seventeenth-century manor houses, as there are in Dorset, for example, which would have encouraged owners with new money to create architectural gardens around them. So, while Herefordshire has two Edwardian layouts of significance, its other gardens of this pre-Great War period are disappointing, even when important architects such as Henry Avray Tipping, Clough Williams-Ellis and Ernest Newton were commissioned.

The creation of Jubilee Drive at Colwall on the west side of the Malverns in 1887 opened up that slope for building plots and, as we have seen, J W Wilson took advantage of one of these to build Perrycroft. The close proximity of Jenny Lind's cottage at nearby Wynd's Point also made the area desirable socially. Wilson's near neighbour, further south, was a Miss Holland, probably of the Holland Martins of Colwall and Overbury in Worcestershire. Leadwork on the canted bay to the rear of the house has the initials: 'JH' set within a floral wreath of thistles. Ernest Newton, who had been employed at Overbury, designed **Brand Lodge** in 1910 on the site of an existing property that already had a planned landscape.[18] Newton had been assistant to Richard Norman Shaw and was conversant, therefore, with the current fashion for architectural gardens to act as extensions to the parent house. At Brand Lodge the main garden area is set directly below the house, which is built parallel to the hillside, rather than at right-angles like Perrycroft. There is a small tank garden with raised walls to the south elevation, where a canted bay provides access from the house, while to the west there are terraces linked by sturdy stone steps and retaining walls, which end in an elliptical area of crazy paving. The panels of Pisces and Libra, set in the walls, connect with Newton's impressive zodiac chimneypiece inside the house. Finally, also set within the rubble-stone walls there is a sculpture of Ceres, holding wheat sheaves and wielding a sickle.

Whether or not Gertrude Jekyll had any input in the gardens at **Gatley Park**, Leinthall Earls, south-west of Ludlow, which were laid out after J D Coleridge had rebuilt the house in 1907 is unclear. He extended the 1630 brick core with a range overlooking a steeply-wooded valley; terraces were set below it, the second of which terminates in an open, rustic Pergola. The north-west lawn has a substantial yew hedge, which has been cut into embattled form. On the low terrace walls there are several terracotta pots, which are stamped with Jekyll's seal. Looking out from this top terrace across the valley a cylindrical building like a windmill without its sails can just be seen. This is the Gatley Park Folly, designed by Raymond Erith for Mrs Victor Willis and built between 1961 and 1964, acting like an eye-catcher in the very best tradition of eighteenth-century garden buildings.[19]

Of less significance and uncertain date are the gardens at **Michaelchurch Court** and **Broadfield Court**, while those at **Donnington Hall** are dated to around 1909. At Michaelchurch, near the south-west border with Wales, the attention strays initially from the gardens and is taken with the plasterwork decoration in the front porch, which is modelled with grapes, a Tudor rose and a green man, and carries the date 1602. The walling, the steps up to the porch, the large rectangular pool with scalloped ends and a further pool in the Rose Garden must be Edwardian, but possibly laid out on existing seventeenth-century terracing. There is an open grass area that might once have been used for tennis and croquet and, further out, a romantically wooded stream garden developed from a tributary of the Escley Brook. South-east of Leominster, Broadfield Court, now a modern vineyard, has another pool garden enclosed by yew hedging and a paved rose garden centred by a cider press.

These are likely to date from the ownership of the Burchall family, who were active at Broadfield until the 1930s. The gardens at Donnington Hall also have a cider press flanked by conical yews and a series of D-shaped stone planters set on the terraces. The main sunken lawned area to the east of the house has two cruciform pools overlooked by a delightful Loggia set within one of the earlier timber-framed service ranges. The owner responsible, who rebuilt the house, was Admiral Sir Arthur Dalrymple Fanshawe; his architect was Gilbert F M Ogilvy, who may also have laid out the gardens. When the property was sold in 1926 the particulars mentioned the lily pools, a flower garden, herbaceous beds, a rose garden and a tennis lawn.[20]

The grounds of **Burton Court** at Eardisland, due west of Leominster, and Brinsop Court, east of Mansel Lacy, are of more consequence, but only because they were possibly laid out by two important Edwardian architects: Clough Williams-Ellis and Henry Avray Tipping. At Burton, the eighteenth-century house, which was remodelled by F R Kempson in 1865 and again by Williams-Ellis in about 1913, masks a fourteenth-century hall. John Brewster, the famous apothecary, lived here in the seventeenth century and built up an impressive library, including a collection of gardening books. But the only garden of any note on the site is the enclosure below the house (*colour 46*) with its great ramped yew hedges sheltering an area of grass in which beds have been cut; there is also the stone stump of a sundial. Dating is again imprecise, though Williams-Ellis is known to have added his wonderfully playful and eclectic entrance porch, which would not look out of place in Portmeirion, for P L Clowes, while the date 1911 is carved on the terrace wall facing the Yew Garden. The present owners, together with Simon Dorrell, are restoring the garden with a medical and herbal theme.

Brinsop Court comes close to Lower Brockhampton House as vying for the title of the most picturesque site in the county. It is a palimpsest of chronological periods and mixed materials – brick, timber-framing and sandstone – set within a wide and flowery moat (*colour 47*). Tipping, the architectural writer and trained architect, who would remodel the house after 1910, wrote the first article on the Court in *Country Life* on 22 May 1909. At that time the house was owned by Mr Dearman Evans and let as a tenanted farm. Tipping wrote eloquently of the potential for restoration and regeneration:

> Although some reparation, of a careful, knowledgeable and restrained kind, would be welcome and would add to the interest and value of Brinsop Court as an ancient monument, yet it is, as it stands, so entirely enjoyable, free from discordant notes, so completely picturesque, that it arouses a strong feeling that no change is desirable and that most change would be unfortunate. The simple yet sufficient manner of its present upkeep is, in its utilitarian and homely character, more in accord with the ways of a small old-world country house, surrounded by the various offices needed for a self-supporting mode of existence, than would be the large pleasure gardens and universal smartness which now mark a rich man's house. At the same time, it must be admitted that the delightful south side of the moat, with a little strip of gardenable ground between the water and the long line of building broken by three tall chimney shafts, is, in its present condition, a neglected opportunity.

Fortunately, Hubert Astley bought the Court in 1910, and Tipping was given the opportunity to 'preside over the remodelling'.[21] He had signed off his article with the obvious expectation of this new commission: 'This [neglected opportunity], however, is under consideration, and will be remedied in due course, together with other matters claiming attention on the property'.

As well as architectural works in the house itself, Tipping concentrated on the inner courtyard and that strip of land he had identified as in need of gardening.[22] The homely muddle of the courtyard, illustrated in H Timmins' 1892 *Nooks and Corners of Herefordshire*,[23] was transformed into an elegant paved area of rectangular beds punctuated by trees in tubs and

78 Steps, stone vases and a repaired stone seat seen in the distance may be part of H Avray Tipping's remodelling of the grounds at Brinsop Court

centred by a columnar stone basin. The beds survive, mostly planted with roses, but the basin has gone, to be replaced by statues of two marble cherubs on stone plinths. One of these is present in a 1921 watercolour by Gwen Dorrien-Smith, so they must be part of the original layout devised by Tipping.[24] In the outer environs, Tipping divided the moat with a sturdy stone bridge and constructed a pergola to make an area for Astley's flamingos: he was a keen ornithologist. This has since gone, but the causeway on which it was built survives, while another Dorrien-Smith watercolour shows its extent, together with three of the flamingos.[25] Finally, to the south, Tipping designed a dry-stone wall to support a long herbaceous border with more flowers planted within the wall, and moon steps down to a tennis lawn. Another straight flight of steps at the western end has tall stone vases, while close by is a high-backed stone seat, both of which might be original garden furnishings (*78*). Two pyramidal-roofed pavilions to the rear of the house are probably also by Tipping, though their function is not clear. In the 1920s Tipping also designed a tennis pavilion and a dog kennel at Weston Hall, Weston-under-Penyard in the grounds of the Jacobean house. Its gardens have been recently recreated and will feature in the last chapter of this study.

There are similar vestiges of a formal Arts & Crafts-style garden around **Winforton House**, south-west of Eardisley, but it dates from as late as the 1920s, when the house and gardens were remodeled in 1922-23 by Michael Waterhouse for the physicist, Sir Thomas Ralph Merton. The RIBA holds 58 drawings by Waterhouse for Winforton, which show how much of his scheme was carried out. The low, walled enclosure to the west of the house ties in with Waterhouse's plan to demolish the coal house but retain lower portions of two walls to create an enclosed, rectangular Herb Garden. To the south, the pyramidal-roofed Summerhouse that connects the former kitchen garden and the large lawned area is sited exactly where Waterhouse intended.[26] The 1923 drawing for this specifies: 'Full size fish for wind-vane...cut from copper sheet'.[27] This survives as a reference to Merton's fishing rights on the Wye. There is, however, no sign on the site of the over-ambitious 'Combined tennis court and skating rink in reinforced concrete' that Waterhouse designed in August of the same year.[28]

Fortunately, Richard Hollins Murray wrote his own guidebook to the house and gardens at **Dinmore Manor** and the whole complex survives there as a record to his extraordinary achievement and that of local architects, Bettington & Son. Sadly, for this present study we were not allowed access, so what follows is an account based upon mirrors: that guidebook, an excellent *Country Life* article by Clive Aslet on the architecture and another on the planting by Noel Kingsbury.[29] These give a clear insight into the last flourish of true Arts & Crafts practice in the county.

The house and the adjacent Commandery, which traces its origins back to the Knights Hospitaller of St John, is hidden away up a drive from the Hereford to Leominster road, which winds through a valley with hanging woods on either side for over a mile. Electronically-controlled entry gates bar the way and virtually nothing can be seen of either house or garden. So, to take up Aslet's first sight of the house on his visit:

> You only realize the breathtaking character of the site on the other side of this range [on the north side], where there is a broad terrace of lawn. From here, on a clear day, you can enjoy a spectacular panorama over a great, wide plain of unspoilt farming country for 40 miles, as far as the Malvern Hills. The terrace looks out over the landscape like a stage, and there is a sense of theatre about the buildings, too – even the medieval chapel, which stands isolated in the middle of the lawn.[30]

The main garden elements skirt the terrace and the cloisters that Hollins Murray added to the existing house between 1932 and 1936. There is another viewing terrace along the parapet above the cloisters between the octagonal tower and a further octagonal structure used as a summer-house. Within this southern arm of the Cloisters is a remarkable Grotto (*colour 48*), which visitors once viewed through a non-reflecting window. Aslet is in raptures: 'it consists of the expected dank rockwork and pools, but with, at the back, a stained-glass window of palm trees against a tropical sunset. The brilliant colours reflect in the pool. Suddenly we are whisked out of the world of the Hospitallers and into that of Hawaii or, more appropriate to the '30s, the South of France'.[31] Hollins Murray's account of what he had achieved in the Cloisters is more prosaic:

> From this court on the western side is a room with a large Gothic-shaped window which has been glazed with coloured glass depicting an Eastern landscape, the horizon of the window having been measured to coincide with the true horizon beyond. A grotto effect has been reproduced, the roof being formed with concrete passed small pools are within, and the effect of the reflection of the window on the lower pool is very pleasing....Eventually the water passes under the Cloisters into the pools of the Rock Garden.[32]

Although Hollins Murray's account of the reconstruction of Dinmore gives details of both the artists and the craftsmen who collaborated with him, he does not describe the gardens or their planting. Fortunately, Noel Kingsbury visited the garden and plant centre at Dinmore when it was open and has given a good account of the site. Essentially, the area beneath the Cloisters was planted up as a Japanese garden, with maples interspersed with yews and cypresses to give vertical accents, and the rocks threaded through with 'varieties of bergenia, peony and the blue-flowered *Brunnera macrophylla*' early in the year, while 'hemerocallis, crocosmia and the yellow *Phlomis russeliana*' predominated in August.[33] This 1920s creation recalls the vestigial Japanese-style garden at **Birley Court**, south of Leominster, which was created at some point between 1906 and 1913, and also the overgrown area at the top of the terrace at Treago Castle, which has Japanese elements and appropriate planting. While these two are minor experiments in the style, Hollins Murray's exotic creation brings to mind another contemporary garden, achieved by Sir Frank Crisp at Friar Park in Henley-on-Thames which, like Dinmore, was smothered in mottoes and symbolic statuary, and still has exotic underground spaces lit by water-reflecting stained glass.[34] Significantly, both favoured Japanese-style rock and water gardens enriched with maples and, in Friar Park's case, under later informed and sympathetic owners, the whole grounds have became a spectacular arboretum for maple varieties.[35]

9

Exotics, daffodils, eclectic garden buildings and a pioneering plantsman

Hergest Croft · Sutton Court · Kinsham Court · Hellens · Luntley Court
Hill Court · Elton Hall · Gatley Park · Dillon's Orchard · The Vern

AFICIONADOS OF 1970S POP MUSIC WILL BE AWARE OF MIKE OLDFIELD'S first album, *Tubular Bells*, an orchestral piece, which sways rhythmically with an insistently repetitive refrain. After its sensational reception Oldfield found it hard to deal with his unexpected celebrity status and retreated to Herefordshire to concentrate on a follow-up. This was released in 1974 and entitled Hergest Ridge, after the hill to the east of Kington in the north-west of the county, close to the Welsh border, where he was living at the time. Not quite as well known, but nevertheless remarkable, is a garden on the lower slopes of the Ridge, just outside Kington. Access to it is via the Ridgebourne Road, which phases into the Offa's Dyke Path as it continues across the hilltop on its way to Gladestry in Wales. The lane passes a stuccoed Regency villa – Ridgebourne – and then leads to a red brick, tile-hung Arts & Crafts house, which looks like a refugee from Surrey. This is **Hergest Croft**, pronounced locally 'Harguest'. From the gardens of both Ridgebourne and Hergest panoramic views extend across the valley of the River Arrow and focus on the Black Mountains. The grounds of Ridgebourne are private, but those around Hergest Croft have greeted visitors ever since the 1920s. A delightfully welcoming honesty box, an interesting display of well-labelled trees and shrubs, and a charmingly homespun tearoom suggest that this is a garden where visitors are actively encouraged rather than merely tolerated.

A centenary plaque on the tea room verandah celebrates the three generations of the Banks family who have gardened with knowledge and passion at Hergest Croft: William Hartland and Dorothy Alford Banks, Dick, Jane & Rosamund Banks and, finally, Lawrence and Elizabeth Banks, who passed the garden on to their son Edward in 2009. The continuity was marked in 1967 when Lawrence's birth was celebrated by the planting of a Greek Fir (*Abies cephalonica*) in the orchard, the same tree that had been planted in the south-east corner of the Kitchen Garden by Richard William Banks a century earlier, in 1867, to mark the birth of his son, W H Banks.[1] In 2010 Elizabeth Banks, a professional landscape architect, became the first woman President of the Royal Horticultural Society. The head gardeners are also remembered at the entrance to the garden from the lane by a rank of three slim *Quercus robur* 'Cupressoides', planted to commemorate George Bamfield (1895-1918), George James (1924-1957) and William 'Bill' Cowdell (1957-1976). The current Head Gardener, Stephen Lloyd, who arrived in 1980, has yet to be so dignified.[2]

Hergest Croft is a collection with particular strengths in plants gathered from western China and the Himalayas, the national collections of Acers, Betula and Zelkova, and several champion trees. However, its value and fame as a collection does not detract from its beauty as a garden. It stands apart from rival collections at Bedgebury Pinetum in Kent and Westonbirt Arboretum in Gloucestershire by retaining a house at its heart and owners who care for it as a garden.

William and Dorothy Banks created the bones of the large garden that extends to some seventy acres (79). The first rockery was seemingly inspired by an 1894 photographic excursion to Kew. In 1900 the conifer avenue was nicknamed the 'avenue of crates' among family members because of the heavy timber frames protecting the young trees. This still extends westwards from the house, although it has lost its impact as an avenue. The single species clumps of exotics that frame the views southwards from the Lawn across the park came later and, after the First World War, William began the serious development of Park Wood, half a mile

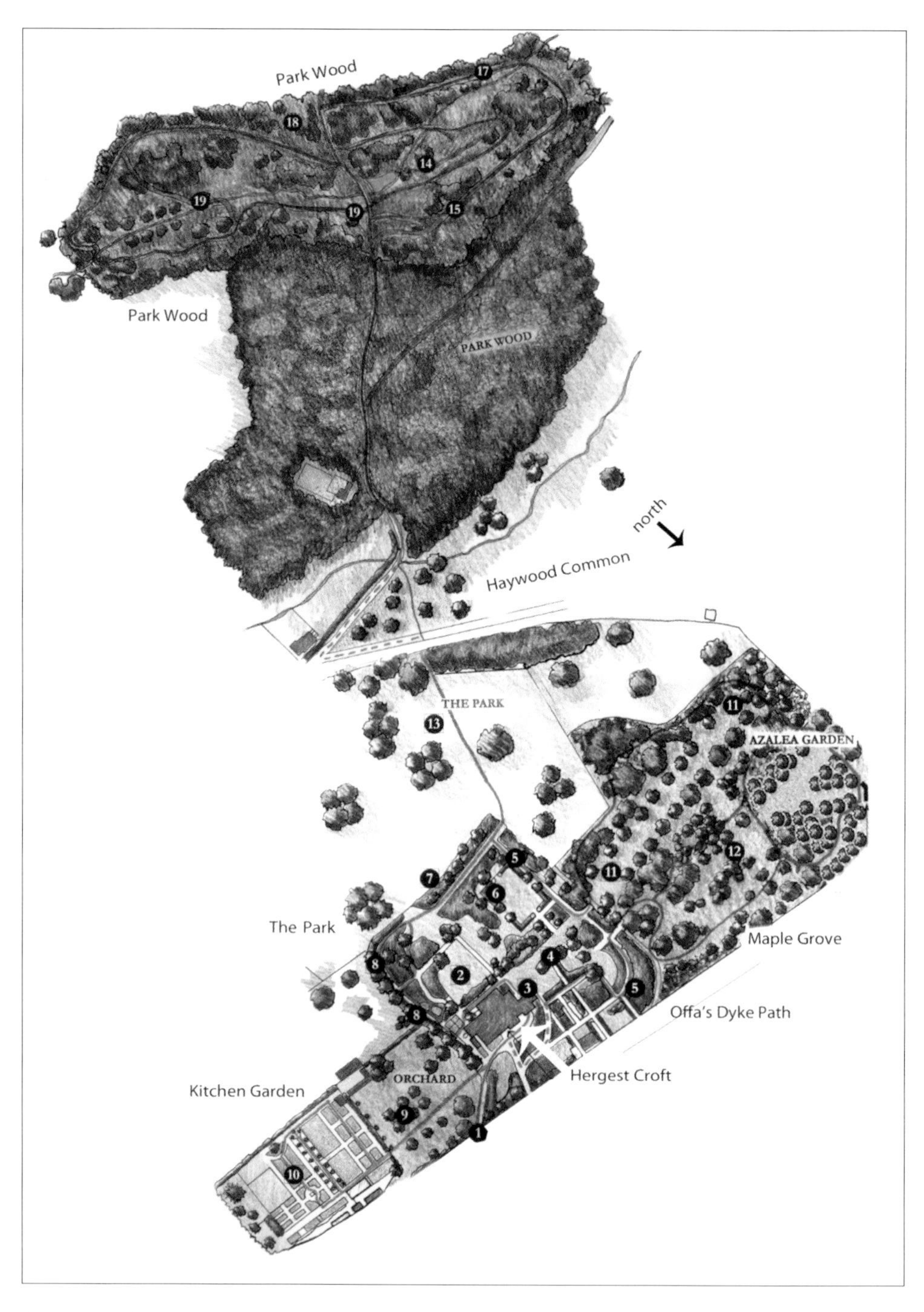

79 Formal gardens, parkland and a woodland garden combine to make Hergest Croft one of the county's most beautiful horticultural sites. *Kind permission of Lawrence Banks*

45 A view of the most atmospheric garden enclosure in Herefordshire, made all the more numinously evocative by its suffocating vegetation

46 The scalloped yew hedges at Burton Court accord perfectly with the spirited improvements to the house carried out immediately before the Great War by Clough Williams-Ellis

47 Hubert Astley, who bought Brinsop Court in 1910, was a keen ornithologist. In his time flamingos strode along a pergola and rare teal and black-necked swans swam in the moat. H Avray Tipping's new bridge across the water can be seen in the distance

48 A Hawaiian sunset enlivens the more traditionally-styled 1920s Grotto in the Cloisters at Dinmore Manor. Sadly, the garden is now strictly private. © *Country Life*

49 Hergest Croft's National Collection of acers adds vibrant autumnal colour to the planting, seen here from beneath a magnificent cut-leaved beech

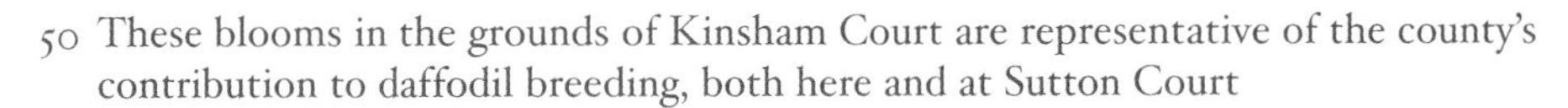

50 These blooms in the grounds of Kinsham Court are representative of the county's contribution to daffodil breeding, both here and at Sutton Court

51 This delightful Moorish-Gothick Summerhouse is one of a number of eclectic buildings added to the grounds at Hill Court. Views out from it across the ha-ha have been marred by polytunnels, which have changed the face of agriculture in the fruit-growing regions of the county

52 Visual humour enriches the grounds of Elton Hall, as here on the entrance front with its imitation palm tree, made originally for Edward James' Surrealism-inspired Monkton House in Sussex

53

Elton Hall celebrates Herefordshire's horticultural history in these murals to Thomas Andrew Knight.
The RHS Knight Medal was awarded in his honour for edible fruits and ornamental stove or greenhouse plants

54 Pebblework, statuary and a traditional stone cider press have been combined in this architectural centrepiece to the immaculate borders at Fawley Court

55 The sandstone of southern Herefordshire has directed Peter Clay's planting palette of blood red and purples at Brockhampton Cottage

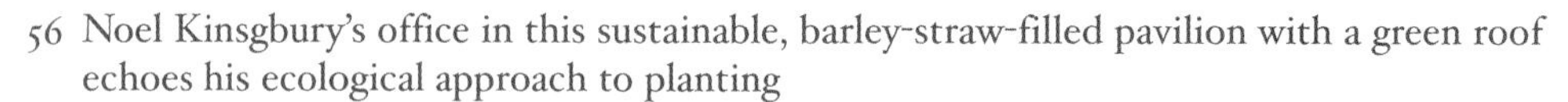

56 Noel Kinsgbury's office in this sustainable, barley-straw-filled pavilion with a green roof echoes his ecological approach to planting

57 In the Walled Garden at Abbey Dore Court, Charis Ward mixes elegant *Buddleia alternifolia* with vivid *Gladiolus communis* subsp. *byzantinus* and blowsy peonies

58 Simon Dorrell advises those planning to visit Bryan's Ground that the fleeting display of *Iris siberica* 'Papillon' in the orchard usually reaches perfection on 21 May. They are preceded by the springtime blooms of *Anemone blanda*

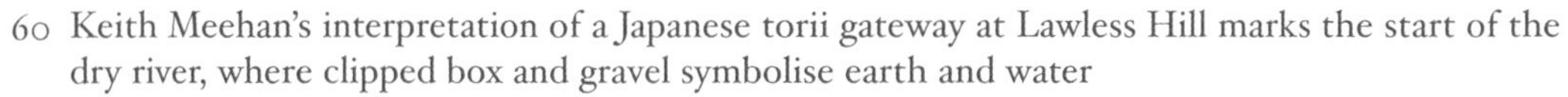

59 At Sir Roy Strong's The Laskett, Britannia's trident and holly topiary provide vertical accents in the relaxed planting of feverfew, foxgloves, lychnis, hostas and *Verbena bonariensis* in the Serpentine

60 Keith Meehan's interpretation of a Japanese torii gateway at Lawless Hill marks the start of the dry river, where clipped box and gravel symbolise earth and water

80 An early photograph of Dorothy Banks sitting under the pergola at Hergest Croft shows how much the grounds have matured since the 1890s. *Kind permission of Lawrence Banks*

away from the house. This is a rare use of a Herefordshire oak wood as the backdrop for a cascade of vivid rhododendrons by the generation that followed the planters of the greatest Cornish gardens. WH Banks was a close friend of Charles Coltman Rogers of nearby Stanage Park who, in turn, was the son-in-law of JC Williams of Caerhays, with its famous plant collection. Lawrence Banks has charted many ways in which William's approach at Hergest Croft also reflected the views and advice of William

Robinson.[3] Early photographs in the Banks Family Archive, such as that of Dorothy sitting beneath the Pergola bordered by Spanish irises (*80*), record its somewhat barren feel, but it does bring to mind an Alfred Parsons engraving for Robinson's *English Flower Garden*. William and Dorothy purchased plants from many of the sources used by the famous Cornish gardens, particularly from the Veitch Nursery before it closed in 1913, and nurtured successfully many of the new introductions by Ernest 'Chinese' Wilson. These included the *Clematis montana* var. *wilsonii*, which is the sole surviving example from Wilson's original introduction of this popular garden plant. It climbs above the ornamental gates bought from the 1924-5 British Empire Exhibition at Wembley, and hence known as the Wembley Gates, to which the local blacksmith added side panels and William and Dorothy's initials. Another of Wilson's introductions is *Acer henryi* that is planted alongside the appropriately named Chinese Path in Park Wood.

The next generation exercised excellent stewardship over the collection, calling in Bruce Jackson from Kew to advise on its maintenance. He was co-author with William Dallimore of the standard reference guide on conifers, *A Handbook of Coniferae*, and also advised on the arboretum at Westonbirt in Gloucestershire. Lawrence and Elizabeth Banks' own collecting expeditions continued to enhance the collection from the 1980s so that they are now enlivened with the red autumn foliage of *Acer micranthum*, which has been positioned at the wicket gate into the garden from the car park. They have also acquired many more new plants from other modern-day plant hunters and plantsmen, including Roy Lancaster and James Russell.

Two open grass areas dominate the grounds: the sunken Lawn in front of the house, which was originally used for tennis, and the yew-hedged Croquet Lawn to the west. These are bordered on the east by the Old Rockery and the Slate Garden, while further west are the Azalea Garden and the Maple Grove. The Orchard and the Kitchen Garden are sited to the east outside the main pleasure grounds. Mature trees, including the cut-leaved beech tree, *Fagus sylvatica* 'Aspleniifolia' (*colour 49*), originating in Europe and planted here in 1930, dominate the Lawn. There is also a

Pinus sylvestris Aurea Group, planted in 1910, and an *Acer palmatum* 'Sango-kaku' introduced to the garden in 1930. The Rockery has a 'Dripping Well', which has been restored, and once had a miniature version of the Matterhorn (*81*), like the one at Sir Frank Crisp's Friar Park in Oxfordshire, which has been lost.[4] Today the Rockery has been enriched by a new formal Slate Garden designed by Elizabeth Banks, with a slate cone sculpture by Joe Smith at its centre.

As the surviving grounds at Hergest Croft prove, the Banks family were wonderfully eclectic in their tastes, whereas the Backhouse dynasty spent much of their time and wealth focused on breeding daffodils. The Backhouses were Quaker bankers from County Durham, the family fortune having been made in the eighteenth century by James and his sons Jonathan and James.[5] William Backhouse, great-grandson of James senior, was the first to begin rearing daffodils at St John's Hall, Wolsingham, County Durham, in 1856. He may well have begun earlier, while living in Darlington, where it is thought he made the acquaintance of Edward Leeds of Manchester. Leeds and Backhouse were the 'originators of the first commercially available stocks of hybrid daffodils'.[6] More than 200 named daffodil cultivars are credited to William Backhouse, who died in 1869. After his death, three of his sons carried on his work: Charles James, Henry and Robert Ormston. In 1886 the youngest, Robert Ormston, moved down to **Sutton Court**, close to the River Lugg, north of Hereford, and became a prolific breeder. He had married Sarah Elizabeth Dodgson in 1884 and together they became famous breeders, Mrs RO Backhouse exhibiting regularly at the RHS Westminster show.[7] She was most famous for her 'red-cupped, white-perianthed daffodils: 'Ladybird', 'Red Planet' and 'Hades', the latter having a cherry-red cup.....and many other valuable red and white narcissi'.[8] Two years after her death in 1923, Robert Ormston produced the first pink-cupped, white-perianthed daffodil, which he named 'Mrs RO Backhouse'.[9] While some of William Backhouse's cultivars can still be found in the grounds of St John's Hall today, there are only a few desultory lines of flowers in the field in front

81

Despite the loss of the Matterhorn, the Hergest Croft Rockery is an important survival of a typical Victorian garden feature. *Kind permission of Lawrence Banks*

of Sutton Court, a somewhat blank-faced brick house.[10]

The Lugg connects Sutton to another daffodil site in the county, at **Kinsham Court**, which is perched perilously above the river, west of Aymestrey, close to the Welsh border. A literary mystery surrounds Kinsham, which was originally the dower house to Brampton Bryan and supposedly where Byron continued his affair with Lady Oxford of nearby Eywood Park. Byron met her in 1812 when she was forty and he was twenty-four, on the rebound from his tempestuous affair with Lady Caroline Lamb. The local legend, supported by David Whitehead, is that Byron wrote the first two cantos of *Childe Harold* at Kinsham in 1809, under a cedar tree in the grounds, of which there is only a stump left today.[11] However, these cantos had been published by March 1812, while the first hint that Byron was in the neighbourhood, at Eywood rather than at Kinsham, is when he stayed there from October 1812 to January 1813, returning for a fortnight in March. In a letter to Lady Melbourne of November 1812 he wrote: 'This country is very much to my taste, & I have taken a seat of Ld. Oxford's (Kinsham Court about 5 miles off in a *delightful* situation) for next year.'[12] Certainly, *Childe Harold* was dedicated to 'Ianthe', Lady Oxford's daughter Charlotte, and Byron is reputed to have scratched his signature on one of Kinsham's first-floor windows; a looping script survives on one of the sashes. Although the dingle below the house, through which the Lugg meanders, was locally praised for its scenic beauty, it was in the grounds on the ridge above that Sir John Arkwright began to breed daffodils in 1919.

Arkwright had sold Hampton Court in 1911 and moved to Kinsham Court, which had been formerly owned by his brother-in-law, Francis Lyndon Evelyn. Thereafter, in happy semi-retirement from politics, he devoted himself to rearing daffodil cultivars, as well as writing the remembrance hymn 'The Supreme Sacrifice', for which he is best remembered. The eighteenth-century grounds had been laid out in an informal picturesque manner with the practical support of a walled garden, which survives. In June 1793 the gardener, Byeland Jones, and his men were paid wages of £6.6.1,[13] and on 23 February 1795 Lady Oxford paid Thomas Corbut the cash balance of a guinea 'due to him for forming the Pleasure Grounds & making a Pond in the Stable Yard'.[14] The grounds remained substantially unaltered in the nineteenth century and are shown on the first edition Ordnance Survey map, but there were plans to create a new garden at Kinsham after William Bevan, Arkwright's gardener, returned from the western front in 1918.[15] It may be that the stone-edged, stepped Pool to the rear of the house dates from this period. Elsewhere, especially close to the church and by the recently restored glasshouses, there are drifts of daffodils, some of which are rare species.[16] Arkwright was a member of the Midland Daffodil Society, becoming President in 1937-9.[17] In 1925 he contributed the Society's Arkwright Challenge Cup, 'presented for six varieties of bicolour trumpets judged for the contrast between perianth and trumpet',[18] and in the same year was elected a fellow of the Linnean Society.[19] Surviving blooms at Kinsham, where more than sixty varieties still flower (*colour 50*), reveal his main area of interest.

At first sight the gardens surrounding **Hellens** at Much Marcle, especially around the octagonal brick Dovecote, which is on the cover of this book, appear to be of seventeenth-century date. The Dovecote itself is dated 1641 and displays proudly the initials of Fulke Walwyn and his wife Margaret, who were responsible for the renovation of the house at that period. However, the box parterres around the base of the Dovecote and the Lavender Terrace to the rear of the house date from the twentieth century when Hellens was lived in first by Hilda Pennington-Mellor and later, after her marriage to Axel Munthe, by their sons Viking Peter and Malcolm Grane Munthe.[20] She was related to the Walwyns and also to the Cookes, who had lived at Hellens during the nineteenth century. Her husband Axel Munthe was a 'philanthropist, lover of animals, physician to the Queen of Sweden... and was occasionally known as the Scandinavian Rasputin'.[21] Much restoration work has been done recently by Adam Munthe, Malcolm's son, including the recreation of the gardens and the restoration of the Dovecote.

Apart from the Tudor-style garden around the Dovecote, which was laid out by Mrs Axel Munthe after the Second World War, the grounds at Hellens are wonderfully haphazard, with an air of unkempt insouciance that seems perfectly in keeping with the eccentric family that has lived at the house during the last hundred years. An arched wooden gate in a brick wall welcomes the visitor, who is then presented with a semicircular fountain decorated with stone seahorses, constructed for the 1953 Coronation celebrations at the house.[22] Apparently it was filled with cider for the festivities. Around the back a circular lily pool on the Lavender Terrace is centred by a terracotta statue of Diana with one of her hounds (*82*), while further out in the field beyond is a recent Knot Garden, its design taken from panelling inside the house.

There is another seventeenth-century dovecote at Dilwyn, south-west

82

Not all the sculpture at Hellens is as traditional as Diana or the cranes behind. Modern pieces by sculptors such as Emily Young continue to be added to the collection

of Leominster, just across the village street from **Luntley Court**. Unlike the one at Hellens, which is built of sturdy brickwork, the Luntley Dovecote is timber-framed with a tiled, gabled roof; a date on the Court of 1674 has been taken for its construction. Luntley's significance is two-fold: the Dovecote inspired a recent addition by Simon Dorrell and David Wheeler to their garden at Bryans Ground and, while there is not much of a garden around the skirts of the house, which is now let as a holiday cottage, the landscape architect Geoffrey Jellicoe devised a plan for its remodelling in 1982.[23] The plan was drawn up for Martin Boulton, but was not executed. Jellicoe proposed a new carriage drive ending in a reshaped entrance court and, to the rear of the house, a geometric flower and kitchen garden. The existing lawn was to receive a covered swimming pool and archery ground, and a new tennis court was to be laid out behind the shelterbelt of trees.

Rather more was achieved at **Hill Court** by John Trafford, whose father Guy had married Dorothy Moffatt, heiress of Goodrich Court, thereby uniting the two neighbouring estates. Before Goodrich Court was pulled down, some of its contents were brought to Hill Court in 1946. John Trafford had inherited a mature garden and productive walled Kitchen Garden, so he satisfied himself with adding exotic buildings to the grounds. The commemorative gates on the forecourt, set up in 1933 to John's younger brother Guy, have already been mentioned. Another memorial is the fountain to the side of the house, which was a wedding present from Guy to Dorothy and has an inscription: 'Naples GTD 1908'. Further out, in a tree-shaded yew enclosure with pets' graves, is an urn containing John Trafford's ashes; he died in 1978. On the end of the ha-ha is a delightfully eclectic Moorish-Gothick Summerhouse with an onion dome (*colour 51*), while close to the Walled Garden in the middle of a water-course is a flimsy Chinese Seat. These recall Dicky Bateman's 'Sharawadgi taste', as deployed at Shobdon Court, and have the air of early-1970s Georgian revival, perfectly in keeping with the painted trophies on the Morning Room panelling in the Court, which were contrived by Hugh Robson.[24]

There is a later, but similarly exotic collection of structures at **Elton Hall**, south-west of Ludlow, inspired by the eighteenth-century Gothick detail of the house and its ownership, between 1791 and 1808, by Thomas Andrew Knight, horticulturalist and brother of Richard Payne Knight, who experimented in the garden with fruit trees. James Hepworth began the garden in about 1990 as a sophisticated playground for his two daughters, with its battlemented Tortoise Castle and Sheep's Palace. It has since mushroomed into a folly garden of architectural, horticultural and historical incident. The eclecticism begins at the drive gateway with a Summerhouse rescued from the grounds of Cornwall House, which is just over the Worcestershire border in Tenbury Wells. Next to the main house, fronting an earlier timber-framed range, is a gigantic wood and metal palm tree, bought in 1985 at the sale of effects from Monkton House, Sussex, which was altered in the 1930s for the Surrealist enthusiast Edward James by Kit Nicholson and Hugh Casson with help from Salvador Dali (*colour*

52). Behind the Hall there is a Turkish Tent overlooking the tennis court and several elephants on gatepiers. Other follies encircle a meadow criss-crossed by mown paths, one of which leads via a bridge over the stream to a rustic Hermitage. This has an inscription '*Hic Vivet Genius Loci*', mischievously undermined by the deathly presence inside, laid out on a rustic bed, of a partially covered skeleton and another skull, used as a candle holder, on a side table.

The route back into the pleasure grounds passes a Gothick-arched Conduit from Nostell Priory and a stone statue of a soldier from Alnwick Castle leaning against a tree, then continues to a miniature orchard of appropriately chosen varieties of apple, pear and cherry trees surrounding Knight's Temple, which was erected in 1997 in honour of Thomas Andrew Knight. He bred many successful and improved fruit varieties such as 'Elton Cherry', which was raised at Elton by fertilising the seed of Bigarreau with the pollen of White Hart. The original tree was six years old when Knight sent fruit to the London Horticultural Society in July 1817.[25] The orchard has Cherry 'Black Eagle' and 'Waterloo', apple varieties 'Downton Pippin', 'Bringewood Pippin' and 'Lemon Pippin' and a 'Broom Park' pear. Knight published his *Pomona Herefordiensis* between 1808 and 1811, and in 1811 he was made President of the Horticultural Society. Inside the Temple are painted roundels of an apple, a pear, a cherry and a strawberry, together with imaginary armorial supporters and a portrait of Knight (colour *53*). Caroline Hainsworth painted the murals.

As we have seen, in the 1960s the architect Raymond Erith designed a folly of a more scholarly and cerebral kind for the slope across the valley at **Gatley Park**. During the same period James Russell was brought in by Captain (now Sir) Thomas and Henrietta Dunne at the Park to supervise a replanting of the terraced garden and the environs to the front of the house. His association with Gatley lasted from 1963 until 1984 and is charted in archives deposited at the Borthwick Institute at the University of York.[26] Russell was a pioneering plantsman, who had acquired an encyclopaedic knowledge of plants through rescuing the family nursery at

Sunningdale in Surrey, where important introductions brought by Sir Joseph Hooker from Sikkim and plants sourced by Robert Fortune from Japan were held.[27] When Graham Stuart Thomas was brought in to help run the business, Russell developed the design element and, at his death in 1996, he had designed over 200 gardens in the British Isles, many for clients coming through connections with Eton, as well as gardens in Italy, France, Belgium and Nassau. Russell shared with Thomas a particular passion for roses – in 1955 Russell had co-authored with Sacheverell Sitwell the first part of *Old Garden Roses* – and rhododendrons, which culminated in the publication in 1960 of *Rhododendrons at Sunningdale*. After the sale of the nursery in 1968, Russell moved to North Yorkshire to live on the Castle Howard estate where, together with George Howard, he developed the arboretum and planted rhododendrons and forest plants in Wray Wood. Russell also worked for Lord Hastings at Seaton Delaval, Northumberland and for Sitwell at Renishaw in Derbyshire.

In 1963 Russell provided Henrietta Dunne with detailed planting suggestions for the enclosed forecourt at Gatley Park, which is now being re-designed for the next generation by the Ludlow-based landscape architect Charles Chesshire.[28] In characteristic style Russell's plan was accompanied by a written account of a walk around the garden taken with Henrietta, during which his own planting suggestions were combined with decisions about what should be retained or re-sited and Henrietta's requests for particular favourites to be incorporated. Russell understood plants, horticulture and people. In this respect he merits Henrietta's recollection of him as the 'Tom Stuart-Smith of his day'. Peter Clay, who works closely with Stuart-Smith and whose garden at Brockhampton Cottage will feature in the next chapter, believes that one of Stuart-Smith's greatest strengths is his ability to communicate with his clients.

At Gatley Park, roses dominated Russell's forecourt planting scheme with strong groups of peonies, including 'a rather expensive clump of the white double *Paeonia lactiflora* 'Le Cygne' that he thought 'almost the most beautiful'.[29] The 'bad' wall fruit (this was often the way he described plants he wished to see removed) were to be replaced with a large group of yellow, pineapple-scented *Cytisus battandieri*. He mingled border perennials that remain fashionable today, including delphiniums, phlox, campanulas and agapanthus, with the occasional shrub, such as the golden-leaved *Philadelphus coronarius* 'Aureus' and a silver-leafed pear, *Pyrus salicifolia* 'Pendula'. His colour scheme was soft apricots, yellows and pinks, punctuated with shots of blue and occasional accents of red.

Other ideas for hard landscaping and greater formality included yew hedges clipped to take herms or terms beneath the terraces at the rear of the house and an 'Italian Garden' in the forecourt formed by planting pencil-slim junipers around a formal pool and cascade. Sadly, neither was realised. His 1967 proposal for a 'little wilderness of paths' on the steep slope beneath the rear terraces was scaled back in recognition of the impossible task of removing the bracken that had taken hold there, although the viewing platform he suggested for the newly-constructed Folly had been implemented by August 1967, when Russell again discussed the planting below 'your eyrie'. However, today's pergola-topped platform by the house, which was restored in the 1990s, has a somewhat suburban look about it.

Russell also provided advice for tree planting further afield, including some simple improvements to the village green. A row of red-twigged lime, set 25 feet apart to screen a barn, were to be supplemented by a clump of *Prunus avium* 'Plena' (double wild cherry) and another of *Salix alba* var. *sericea* near the stream, while an achievable regime for improving and maintaining the hedges, which introduced the desired look of control, was preferred over an impractical scheme for regular grass mowing. In 1983 planning permission was granted for the expansion of the limestone quarry to bring it up to the narrow belt of land that screens the approach to the house, and Thomas Dunne called Russell in again to advise on improving the *Leylandii* screen, which had already been planted. Russell was impressed by what had been achieved at Gatley, reassuring

Dunne in March 1984 that the quarry 'will really vanish more or less out of sight in the bowels of the earth as it advances'. For the far side of the quarry, Russell proposed screening, using a mix of 'the more interesting Himalayan conifers', *Picea likiangensis* and *Picea smithiana*, 'one very blue in the foliage and the other extremely graceful', alongside cedars, Scots pine and American acers. These last included *Acer saccharinum*, *Acer rubrum* 'Scanlon' and *Acer rubrum* 'October Glory'.

Miles Hadfield, the arboriculturalist and garden historian, was approached in November 1966 to advise on the magnificent but ageing avenue that frames the steep approach to the house. He noted somewhat prosaically that he 'visited to inspect the remarkable avenue...leading up the valley to the house...suggested planting beech between the present trees but well outside them, so as to form eventually a new, wider avenue. In the meantime as trees fail or become dangerous, they should be removed'.[30] The replanting advice was ignored in favour of Russell's ideas for unusual trees that created a collection that is halfway between parkland and an arboretum. The weeping beech is particularly successful, although it has yet to mature into the 'waterfall of leaves' that Russell envisioned in August 1967.

Miles Hadfield's grandfather had owned the Regency Moraston House at Bridstow, near Ross-on-Wye, and Hadfield lived from the 1960s at **Dillon's Orchard**, at Wellington Heath, close to Ledbury, which he acquired in April 1961; he moved into the bungalow on 13 May 1963.[31] The terrain, an old orchard with 'a number of very decrepit fruit trees on it', was unpromising, so he spent the first year planting daffodils and other bulbs and the next introducing new trees and shrubs. This expedient of planting flowers in the grass to avoid creating smooth lawns was the subject of a 1975 *Country Life* article subtitled 'a planting guide for lawn-haters', which was based entirely on his experience in creating the garden at Dillon's Orchard.[32] Together with blooming bulbs from his previous garden, which he had carefully dug up, bagged and labelled for replanting, Hadfield created, 'year by year, a mass of "fayre boy narcissus" from

Narcissus pallidiflorus, almost always precisely on the middle day of March', and the 'old Pheasant's Eye, with its stiff white petals and small flat cup ringed with crimson' three months later.[33] However, his 'main show', which by 1975 had 'grown into a golden sheet of an old favourite', was the bi-coloured (yellow trumpet, white crown) daffodil, 'Horsfieldii'.[34] Today the garden is cared for by new owners – Jen and Ian MacKie – and is still awash with spring bulbs in a delightfully haphazard layout, with glimpses of lawn here and there.

It seems fitting to end this small selection of the more significant twentieth-century gardens in Herefordshire with one of James Russell's most inspired plantings, especially as he is now becoming recognised as the father of the modern plant-inspired designers, which will be the focus of the last chapter of this book. Our knowledge of **The Vern** at Marden is due entirely to David Whitehead's *Survey of Historic Parks & Gardens in Herefordshire*, without which we would have missed it. The Vern's inclusion in Whitehead's gazetteer is principally for the commissioning by Captain Richard Sayer de Quincey of Percy Cane, who created a formal flower garden and a water garden there. However, while these survive and give much-needed structure to the grounds, the planting as it exists today is mainly due to Russell who, between 1950 and 1964, developed Cane's original design and extended the garden down towards the riverbank.

The name 'The Vern' is shared by a small farmhouse of mellow brick and the handful of properties that cluster around it. The house is at the end of a lane that leads nowhere other than an idyllic spot to make a garden by the River Lugg. This is where De Quincey made his name as the twentieth-century's leading breeder of Herefordshire cattle, became an expert on hummingbirds and created one of the finest plantsman's gardens in Herefordshire. He chose a spot running down to a sweeping curve of the river, just downstream from Hampton Court, which was still sheltered by the long arm of Dinmore Hill. It is well known that De Quincey, a kinsman of Thomas de Quincey, the nineteenth-century author of *Confessions of an Opium Eater*, engaged Cane some time before

1950 to design the bones of this garden. What has hitherto not been recognised is Russell's contribution to the site. Cane had trained as an artist and architect in the early 1900s before launching out as a garden journalist and establishing, in 1919, his own London-based practice as a landscape and garden architect.[35] His career was at its peak in the 1940s and 1950s, with commissions for Falkland Palace in Scotland, Dartington Hall in Devon and Hoare's Bank in London's Fleet Street.

His design for The Vern was subtly simple, leaving an open sweep of lawn running down from the house to the river, while using his favoured medium of stone to create a terrace that extended the garden into the old kitchen garden abutting the house. Here he moved from formality to informality through a clever combination of walls and hedges as the garden moves towards the adjacent pasture. Arthur Hellyer identified the second important characteristic of Cane's style as 'the slightly formalized woodland glade', and it is presumably because the mature wilder areas of The Vern closer to the river have just this feeling that he appeared to be the right designer for the site.[36] In fact, he was responsible for the easy union of the curving stone terrace and the formal lawn, the Sunken Garden (*83*) and the long herbaceous borders, which enclose a straight turf path terminating at the ha-ha ditch and the view of Bodenham church, now obscured by mature trees.

After Cane had completed his work, De Quincey turned to the area that slopes gently down to the river, where he spent a small fortune on shrubs, bulbs and trees. These were sourced mainly by Russell, although it was the scheme for a glazed Winter Garden and Bird House that came closest to fulfilling De Quincey's gloomy prophecy that Russell might well bankrupt him.[37] Russell was allowed an almost free hand by De Quincey, who only occasionally queried the planting lists he drew up following his regular visits to the garden; in November 1952, for example, when De Quincey suggested scaling back from the proposed 900 to 500 *Narcissus cyclamineus*. The client was, however, an ardent collector, no more able to resist a rare or exotic shrub than he could resist adding to his collection of

83 Percy Cane's hard landscaping around The Vern was brought to life by sustained planting advice from James Russell. Many of the rare species in the garden have yet to be identified

'tinsel pictures' by artists such as Richard Wilson, Thomas Lawrence and James Tissot; his fine collection of eighteenth-century English mahogany furniture; or his champion Sealeyham terriers and Hereford cattle.

Under Russell's guidance the glades leading down to a new lake carved out in the wet winter of 1953 became impressive collections of rhododendrons, azaleas, the hybrid azaleadendrons, tree peonies, magnolias, camellias and acers. Most of the plants were supplied direct by the Sunningdale Nurseries, although particularly choice and expensive forms or cultivars of rhododendrons were sourced by Russell from the Rothschild collection at Exbury in Hampshire and JB Stevenson's widow at Tower Court, near Ascot in Berkshire. Stevenson's efforts during the First World War and the decades that followed had saved many rhododendron species introduced into this country at the end of the nineteenth and early part of the twentieth centuries. Russell and De Quincey were particularly taken with Stevenson's spectacular hybrid rhododendron 'Polar

Bear', with its lily-like white trumpet flowers and perfume to match. This was among the first of the plants added to the area that De Quincey called 'Russell's greedy glades'.[38] Unfortunately, this particular specimen has been lost from the garden, along with all trace of the Peony Garden and many of the bulbs, including every one of the 3,000 Crocus plants E P Bowles supplied through Russell from the C G van Tubergen nursery in Holland. The rhododendrons, azaleas, magnolias, bamboos and acers, planted personally by Russell during his regular visits to the garden, have fared much better, although many are still waiting to have their exact identity rediscovered.

Although a domed, eighteenth-century temple that Russell had spotted in Scotland was not transferred to the grounds, he did supervise the construction of a glasshouse-cum-avairy, albeit in a much reduced form from that originally intended. De Quincey first raised the matter in a letter to Russell of 1954. He was 'toying with the idea of putting up [green] houses in the kitchen garden, along that sunny length' for cymbidiums and cypripidiums (orchids), 'tall enough....to take those tender Rhododendrons and Camellias, and things like Mimosa more or less planted about as trees'.[39] This was the collector in him responding to a perceived absence of space in the pleasure grounds that had first struck him in November 1952, when he noted: 'Things have grown so much there doesn't look to be room for anything else, but I am sure we can squeeze in what you have reserved for me'.[40] De Quincey already had an outdoor Aviary Garden and a collection of hummingbirds that he went on to combine with his plans for a new orchid house, despite their markedly different environmental needs. The structure, designed by Strawson & Son of Horley, Surrey, was built in 1958 and survives at The Vern, though most of the cement staging for the orchids has been removed, together with the glass cabinets that segregated the plants from the birds.

After De Quincey's death in 1966, The Vern was sold and, while the gardens were used as the venue for Girl Guide gatherings and an expanding collection of exotic birds, including flamingos, it gradually fell into decline. The house lay empty and the garden untended for eight years until Brian and Chris Evans rescued it in 1983. Chris has cared sensitively for Russell's plantings and carefully expanded and modified Cane's terrace and garden walls. She has even extended the garden to take in the pasture below the ha-ha and the paddock next to the stalls, which were used for the parade of the famous Vern Herd when international visitors came in the 1950s and 1960s. The decaying gates alongside the ha-ha have been retained as a romantic reminder of the prize-winning herds that contributed to De Quincey's paradise of exotics.

10

'Taste Gestapo' versus Establishment – the latest gardens

Ivy Cottage · Brockhampton Court · Fawley Court
Brockhampton Cottage · Grendon Court · Trippleton House
Montpelier Cottage · Lower Hopton Farm · Abbey Dore Court
Lower Hope · Monnington Court · Weston Hall · Hampton Court
Bryan's Ground · The Laskett · Knill Court · Lawless Hill

THE LAST CHAPTER OF THIS BOOK ON A COUNTY WITH FEW GARDENS OF national stature must end on a controversy. This concerns the current reaction against traditional, or more disparagingly termed 'country house style' gardens, and those designed to display plantsmanship, often with little regard for design. In one case, Noel Kingsbury's garden at Montpelier Cottage, these last are often experimental spaces where plants are allowed to find their feet and flourish or to wither. This historic gardens series, particularly in its early volumes, has championed unashamedly hard landscaping and structure, while plants have been allotted a subsidiary importance. This is merely because plants other than some veteran trees rarely survive at historic sites, whereas walls, steps and garden buildings remain to indicate the design intentions of owners and practitioners. However, an overview of the latest gardens in any county has to take into account contemporary developments in design, and Herefordshire is fortunate in this respect. As well as Kingsbury's garden laboratory, there is a heaven of hellebores contrived by Veronica Cross at Lower Hopton Farm. There are also layouts by three generations of the Clay family culminating in Peter Clay's Brockhampton Cottage, and gardens by his friend and collaborator, Tom Stuart-Smith.

In contrast to these plant-inspired gardens, there are other sites where a more traditional approach to hard landscaping takes precedence, as at Simon Dorrell's design for the walled garden at Hampton Court and at his own garden, created in concert with David Wheeler, the plant expert and editor of the garden magazine *Hortus*, at Bryan's Ground. There, if anything, the architectural salvage shades it in a remarkably eclectic layout of sheer exuberance. Some Herefordshire gardens take sculpture as their artistic cue, as at Lower Hope with its nubile bronzes, and Monnington Court, where the garden is more of a sculpture park showcasing the work of its owner, Angela Conner. At one site alone, overlooking the Wye at Sellack, the modernist architecture of the parent house has produced a garden of striking ingenuity and breathtaking beauty. And then there is Sir Roy Strong's The Laskett, the garden of a cultural icon that is now being promoted as a tourist attraction rather than as a private passion to be enjoyed by choice friends. Celebrity attracts enthusiasts as well as detractors, and in making The Laskett, essentially a paean to his and his late wife's academic and cultural achievements, Sir Roy has become a sitting target for the taste brigade.

One of these plant aficionados is Anne Wareham who, together with Charles Hawes, has created an important layout at Veddw House, over the border in Monmouthshire. Wareham's latest book is entitled: *The Bad Tempered Gardener,* so it comes as no surprise that she is a passionate critic of contemporary garden design and writing about gardens. She has remarked that 'people glibly and carelessly refer to gardens as "art". Well, maybe gardens could be art – but not until we get some serious garden criticism'.[1] As this book was nearing completion in October 2011, she delivered a cruelly damming analysis of The Laskett, subtitled: 'Even a dreadful garden will receive warm praise if you open it to the public',[2] to which we shall return in an attempt to offer a more balanced view of the undoubted contribution of Strong and Julia Trevelyan Oman's garden to both the local and national gardens scene. Perhaps we are moving into a stimulating period, like that of the Blomfield-Robinson debate of the late nineteenth-century, where plants vied with architecture for precedence in design. Or possibly it is a question of what the garden photographer, Andrew Lawson, has termed 'the taste Gestapo' versus the garden Establishment, of which Sir Roy most certainly is an influential member.[3]

A loose chronology will help to put the several gardens discussed here into a coherent structure, so it will be useful to begin with Eleanour Sinclair Rohde's herb garden at what is now The Cider Barn, but was then **Ivy Cottage**, in Ewyas Harold, sited on a steep ridge overlooking the River Dore. The homespun cottage, its walls smothered with rambling roses, is set at right-angles to the hillside, from which paths extend along the contours. These are edged with borders of cottage garden plants perfectly in keeping with the rural feel of the place. There is no sign of Rohde's traditional rectangular herb garden with a sundial at its heart but, if one was planted, it is thought to have been on the level area, now covered with grass, in front of the cottage. Rohde's connection with the site is suggested by the survival of a manuscript garden notebook, *Ivy Cottage, Ewyas Harold: Notes on the Herb Garden*, which she wrote in 1935.[4] The bookseller's catalogue offering the manuscript for sale in 2004 records that she was attempting to produce the effect at Ivy Cottage of a 'picture by an old Dutch master' by using pot marigolds and salvia.[5] The garden was to have evergreens in every bed, and she discussed the colour effects to be achieved by planting against a lavender hedge. Rohde was an early member of the British Guild of Herb Growers and her book *A Garden of Herbs* appeared in 1920. Thereafter, until her death in 1950, she 'combined scholarship with practical gardening', *The Times* judging in her obituary that 'the mantle of Miss Jekyll,' another spinster, 'had fallen on her'.[6]

Plants define the gardens of the Clay family, three generations of whom have gardened in the south-eastern corner of the county around Ross-on-Wye. Little if anything survives of the garden at **Brockhampton Court** created by Alice Foster, who came to Herefordshire from Boston, Massachusetts, to settle with her Lancastrian husband, Arthur Wellesley Foster. Alice's yew garden, cricket ground and cricket pavilion are lost amongst the institutionalised grounds of the present-day Court. However, the gardens of the second and third generations of the Clay family, little more than a mile from the Court, are both in their prime. Heraldic beasts taken from the porch at Brockhampton Court make a defiant statement on the gate piers at the entrance to Mrs Clay's garden at **Fawley Court**,[7] while her stepson, Peter, working with Tim Stuart-Smith, has created a very different garden at nearby **Brockhampton Cottage**.

Fawley Court is unusual in that the village lane bisects the garden, with a terraced area close by the house and a much more expansive sector dramatised by pools on the other side. Mrs Clay has also adopted the lane on the approach to the house by planting it with a striking avenue of alternating variegated *Acer platanoides* 'Drummondii' and, as its name suggests, deep purple *Acer platanoides* 'Crimson King'. At the Court the three shallow terraces are planted with tiers of white Iceberg roses, dense herbaceous borders of whites, pinks and mauves and, at the top, a ring of Sorbus planted around 2000 to circle an Atlas supporting an openwork globe set on a richly pebbled base (*colour plate 54*). Across the lane a small ironwork gate gives access to a more private garden, inducing the sense of entering a secret enclosure. In early June, white and mauve irises introduce the first of the pools that dominate this part of the garden and echo subtly the floral colour palette of the terraces next to the house, before giving way to a greener, shrubbier, watery scene. A Millennium project was compulsory here, and a strikingly patterned boardwalk now stretches out to an island where a bronze resin statue of a young boy by Marion Smith, named *The Dreamer*, sits relaxed and cross-legged, gazing back towards the Court. A girl with her geese, modelled by the same artist, stands in the shallows. Both sculptures are from a series inspired by the 1979 International Year of the Child.

There are no sculptures at all at Brockhampton Cottage, where plants alone give definition and incident to the grounds around the house. For Peter Clay, 'agrarian stewardship is the key' to understanding what he and Stuart-Smith have created. Both are keen plantsmen – Stuart-Smith perhaps the most gifted of his generation, and Clay with an additional role as director of Crocus, a firm that has supplied plants for many of the Chelsea Flower Show gardens. When Clay inherited the property the garden consisted of a little more than a thuja hedge planted by his grandfather to exclude the wind from the hilltop site. As a result, it blocked all views of the landscape and his grandmother's small rose garden. Since 1999 Clay has torn up the hedge, demolished a modern bungalow, remodelled the original cottage and flung the garden open to embrace the surrounding countryside. In front of the cottage Stuart-Smith has designed the simple terrace of three wide shallow grass steps edged with stone that funnel the view in towards the cottage between two side-screen herbaceous borders. This anchors the building in its setting and makes sense of the ground to the north by providing a backdrop for yet more borders.

Clay has integrated garden and landscape by laying out 'dark green blobs' of planting that mirror the 'blobs of trees' in the landscape. Stuart-Smith's website describes the approach thus: 'the structure of the garden dissolves into a series of loose, globular plantings that bubble out from the landscape'. There was a deliberate decision to plant grasses to reflect the landscape. The red sandstone walls of the cottage have encouraged his limited colour palette and an avoidance of orange in the planting (*colour 55*). Close by the cottage is a purple border of double aquilegias, alliums, geraniums and thalictrum, punctured by towering spikes of white eremerus. Immediately in front of the cottage is a narrow border planted with *Astrantia major* 'Hadspen Blood' and 'Ruby Wedding' that have cross-fertilised. The walls of the cottage are clothed in ceanothus and roses. A line of eight topiary beech watchtowers, used here by Stuart-Smith for the first time, dominates the upper lawn on the north side of the cottage. The beeches overcome the feeling of vertigo that might otherwise draw the visitor down the precipice towards the Millennium Orchard. The Orchard also reflects the history of this landscape and was set out in a traditional planting pattern, using 300 perry pears of eighteen different

84 Quirky statuary and feathery planting combine to great effect at Grendon Court

varieties around one survivor from a long-lost perry orchard.

At **Grendon Court**, sited just above the A449 Ross to Ledbury road at Upton Bishop, Stuart-Smith's planting makes a courageous attempt to integrate the main house, a stuccoed early-nineteenth-century villa, into its sloping landscape. This was achieved by creating a new retaining wall of sandstone that separates the house from the drive, while excavating a balancing terrace to the north. The house now sits on a platform that allows the gardens to sweep round and envelop it on three sides. The south-facing courtyard garden is planted with deep purple alliums and lime green euphorbias that contrast well with the sandstone, and a gravel border is planted with cushions of thyme and box balls, adding a touch of formality close to the house.

To the rear a large open lawn extends to the west, ending in an appropriately soft and rural interpretation of a box parterre, punctured by spires of camassia. Its block-like outline establishes the trend for much of the rest of the garden, while a break in the surrounding sheltering beech hedges mimics a more formal *claire-voie*. A line of pillared yews punctuates the narrow border on the valley side of the lawn, while on the other side a beech hedge provides the backdrop to an animated sculptural group of a moorhen and her chicks (*84*). This group and a corrugated ram sculpted by Silvy Wetherall on the approach to the house make a welcome relief from the popular taste in children's garden statuary. Behind the hedge a pathway climbs up the gentle slope of the walled enclosure, which is engulfed by large blocks of planting. Grasses dominate until, at the top, they overcome any herbaceous competition, creating squares of miscanthus. Where flowers are allowed to intrude in this grassy green oasis, white foxtail lilies tower over the soft purples, pinks and whites of geraniums, astrantia and polygonum.

While Stuart-Smith's planting at Grendon is a symphony of whispering greens, his herbaceous borders at **Trippleton House** are ablaze with carefully coordinated colour.

Stuart-Smith was called in by his cousin, Domenica Dunne, making this an unusual commission. He was not closely involved with the planting design, but advised on the strategy and structure of the garden. Trippleton has now been taken over by Thomas and Henrietta Dunne, who moved here from Gatley Park, so they have inherited a mature garden. The lower terrace, with planting around the Pergola, is by Charles Chesshire, who is currently working for Domenica on the forecourt at Gatley Park. However, the upper terrace is by Stuart-Smith. Here there are four parallel grass terraces above borders of perennials and grasses, the borders decreasing subtly in their formality. The lowest and most formal of these has fastigiate yews and climaxes in a round white stone. The next has an avenue-style planting of paired small trees: two cherries opposite each other, two sorbus and so on. The following terrace is laid out as an orchard and the topmost has an arboretum-like planting of deciduous and conifer trees. Stuart-Smith's perennial and grass border includes *Stipa gigantea* and *Cephalaria gigantea*, as well as a dark maroon polygonum. Steps link this series of terraces to a large lawn, which has, to the side, a rectangular garden of borders set around an oval vase. This is planted mostly with pink and white roses and the nodding pink heads of *Dierama pulcherrimum*. Comparisons are insidious, but Chesshire's planting looks less inventive than Stuart-Smith's daring combinations. From here a gravel path climbs up the bank past a wooden seat, presumably brought from Gatley Park, and a potting 'room', which is far too neat and tidy to be called a shed, skirting a collection of bamboos to the kitchen garden.

If Tom Stuart-Smith is the current champion, together with Piet Oudulf, with whom he has collaborated, of the professional approach to design through plants, then Noel Kingsbury is surely this movement's most important theorist and chronicler.[8] Indeed, his small garden at **Montpelier Cottage**, tucked away in the folds of the land above the river near Whitney-on-Wye, is literally a seedbed for his experiments with plants. Kingsbury is like a latter-day John Evelyn with his 'elaboratorie', and had already created a garden along similar lines at Elmtree Cottage at Linton, near Ross-on-Wye, when he moved to the south-east facing slope at Montpelier in 2005. We were fortunate enough to be guided around the garden personally by Kingsbury when we made our site visit on a sultry July day in 2010.

Kingsley explained that Montpelier was 'almost a squatter's cottage' when he and his partner Jo bought it, and the ground about was only thistles and nettles. He has been writing on gardens for about twenty years now and refers to the Perennial Perspectives Seminar held at Kew on 29 June 1994 as the turning point that opened his eyes to a new way of planting.[9] Seminal also was his experience of Bratislava, where his partner was working, and the alternative ways of planting that he experienced travelling across Europe, particularly in Germany. But his meeting in Holland with Piet Oudolf was obviously the catalyst for a re-thinking of perennial planting. This can be seen in pockets around the charmingly ramshackle complex of cottage and office pavilion: a mix, as he calls it, of colonial hill station, American Indian Adirondack and railway station. In this terrain of fertile red soil containing sand and clay, which does not drain well, Kingsbury has created a series of research plots and other planting areas that, surprisingly given their diversity, cohere into a homespun whole. There is a purple-planted sector next to the cottage that includes *Knautia macedonica* and salvias. Further out box cubes are set in amongst the slabs, while nearby there are white nicotiana, red achillea and nasturtiums. Further down the slope there is a series of metre-wide strips, which read as a solid area of planting because the paths running between them are hidden.

Below this is a wild flower meadow where Kingsley is exploring self-sowing. He has a limited approach to weed control; he removes creeping buttercup, goose grass and some others, but leaves the rest to find their own dynamic. Self-seeding produces a hybrid swarm of geraniums. At the bottom of the meadow are pools and the ground is water-sodden; here he is attempting to prevent the horsetail encroaching further up the garden by using black matting. In this spot, which has had continuous habitation, there is sedge rush flora. He is aiming for a patchwork-quilt effect by nurturing nature: 'I'd like to have different mowing regimes in different areas and see what happened'. As well as a yurt, there is an obelisk-like stone slab with good calligraphy carved by local artist Catriona Cartwright. The stone came from the quarry at Talgarth and was commissioned by Kingsley's partner, Jo. In the spirit of Ian Hamilton Finlay, they are adding meaning to the garden; the quote is taken from T S Eliot's *Four Quartets*. Kingsley is thinking about using more plants with cultural allusions in the garden, such as cherries to denote Japan.

Moving back towards the cottage, Kingsley describes a patch of garden as 'Robinsonian', by which he means an attempt to get native and non-native species to work together. The boardwalk to his office pavilion cuts through the most problematic area of the garden (*colour 56*). Here he is gardening with self-sown plants such as *Verbena bonariensis*. The pavilion is surrounded by cherries, currants, grasses and gooseberries, while behind it is a box-edged area filled with annuals, which Kingsley admits is 'a departure for me'. He has recently been working in Mexico, so these are all plants with Mexican or Aztec origins. Further down the slope is his PhD plot – Kingsley received his doctorate from the University of Sheffield at the age of 51 – which concerned plant interactions. He believes that plant ecology is the new modern, and his objective is plant inter-selection for low maintenance, so that the gardener gets to tweak the planting without having to undertake major maintenance. Scattered all around the garden are red and pink flags that help identify small plants to avoid when weeding. The garden at Montpelier Cottage is no designed landscape, rather an ecological laboratory, but it merits a place in this survey for its significance in contemporary garden design.

There is more in the way of conscious planning and design at Veronica Cross' **Lower Hopton Farm** at Stoke Lacy, where there is a paved and hedged area by the house, which leads to trellised arbours, but plants dominate.[10] A eucalyptus shelterbelt borders an open lawn and there is a red lacquer bridge set across a stream in the grounds. However, unlike her enclosed formal design at Birtsmorton Court in Worcestershire, designed under her professional name of Veronica Adams,[11] here the grounds by the house have been laid out in semi-woodland style to provide planting beds for Cross' collection of hellebores. As well as drifts of these nodding blooms, Cross has a collection of over 200 peony cultivars, and in the late winter the garden is dusted with snowdrops. Further out beyond the confines of the woodland area there is a moated island with a recent Summerhouse and two tall giraffes trained out of yew.

The same amorphous, free-flowing approach has been taken by Charis Ward in laying out her gardens around **Abbey Dore Court**, though there is a large walled enclosure to the rear of the main house. While Lower Hopton Farm is a serious plant collector's garden, Abbey Dore is significant for the display of sculptural work by local craftsmen. This is signalled at the entrance by a dramatic metal unicorn's head by Walenty Pytel, a Polish sculptor who lives in the county. Other Herefordshire works by Pytel are the woodpecker at Bulmer's factory in Hereford and mallards coming in to land on the Wye beneath the Prospect in Ross. In a garden that Ward admits she cannot stop extending and altering, there is a curvy sculpture in the Walled Garden by Steve McCrae, who lives near Ledbury, and a simple bridge over the Dore, which marks the boundary of the site, by Peter Downing from nearby Pontrilas. Although Ward has designed most of the layout herself, she has been advised by Graham Stuart Thomas, particularly in the dark walk parallel to the river where he suggested a scheme that progressed through purple to gold to silver. In the silver area is a stunning *Romneya coulteri* with paper-white flowers and brilliant yellow centres.[12] The planting in the warm shelter of the Walled Garden (*colour 57*) includes pink dierama, blue nepeta and orange alstromeria. Clematis was tumbling everywhere here and elsewhere throughout the garden on our July visit; there were also creamy coloured phygelius and holyhocks. When asked how she got into gardening, Ward mentioned that her grandmother and mother were gardeners: 'I like my hands in the soil and I like colour'.

Sculpture also enlivens the tightly-packed garden at **Lower Hope**, just outside Leominster, where Clive Richards has placed bronzes of children all over the grounds. Close to the house, where two Victorian Wellingtonias once stood, there is a swirl of clipped box that creates a parterre of daffodils and tulips in which a girl strides purposefully, holding an umbrella. This is by Sydney Harpley and entitled *Rainy Day*. Next comes the White Garden of seasonally adjusted bedding and 'Frances Austin' and 'Margaret Merrill' roses, which fronts a gabled stone shrine with a statue of the Virgin Mary and a plaque with verses inscribed 'The Penitent'. Further on there is another young girl by Harpley who sits on a swing, its chains disappearing disconcertingly into the air, while across the beautifully manicured lawn a group of Harpley children loll beside the pool. Finally, sheltering under a pergola in the more productive area of the garden, which is dominated by a vast greenhouse-cum-butterfly house, there is a stone sculpture of Admiral Lord Nelson; Richards is a passionate collector of Nelson memorabilia.

Sculpture of a different kind – kinetic pieces and brilliant representational busts – enliven Angela Conner's **Monnington Court**, a beautiful small medieval house set at the end of a long avenue of evergreens. The tree-lined approach to the house is flanked by stables and paddocks with watchful horses. One of her most intriguing sculptures – the *Tipping Lady* – is set beside the drive (*85*). She has been cut through lengthwise and mounted so that she will move in the wind. Another ingenious device – the *Big Tipper* – is set on the lawn in front of the house. Water fills the plane of the sculpture and tips it gently, but the pattern of tipping and motion is different every time so its movement is unpredictable. Closer to the house by the kitchen door is a circle of seven heads comprising Conner, her husband and members of the Devonshire family; presiding over all is an amazingly life-like seated figure of Noel Coward. Around the lake there are other sculptural groups, including an avenue of bronze busts of mainly British worthies, which recalls Felix Denis' Garden of Heroes at Dorsington in Warwickshire.[13]

A more traditional layout is present at **Weston Hall**, Weston-under-Penyard, where there are three remarkable garden structures. The first two, both timber-framed – a Dog Kennel and a Tennis Pavilion developed from an existing barn – were designed by Henry Avray Tipping in the 1920s when he was extending the late sixteenth-century house. It may be that there is a lost sunken garden to the west of the house, also designed by Tipping. But it is the Millennium Folly, which looks like an ogee-topped Elizabethan banqueting house, designed by local architect Peter Gibbons, that catches the eye in the recently restored Walled Garden. This is some preparation for the new garden buildings in the Walled Garden at **Hampton Court**, which were commissioned by John van Kampen in about 2002 and contrived by the artist and garden designer Simon Dorrell. They comprise two identical timber-framed Summer-houses set over deep canals and a more appropriately Gothic stone Tower overlooking a maze. The Summerhouses are far too over-scaled for this essentially intimate space, but the colour-themed planting, blue in the South Garden, white and silver in the West, pink and silver in the East, is beautifully coordinated. This is a Dorrell signature, as too are the pleached avenues that give firm structure to the soft landscaping.

85 Angela Conner uses the forces of nature to animate her scupltures. On the approach to Monnington Court, where the grounds are laid out as a sculpture park, the delicately poised Tipping Lady twists and tilts in the breeze

If, as seems likely, the enclosure at Hampton Court was an attempt to recreate, in contemporary design terms, an element of the famous water gardens, then it has succeeded. However, Dorrell's own garden at **Bryan's Ground** near Presteigne is much more inventive and idiosyncratic, and in this sense it is closer to Veronica Cross' layout at Lower Hopton Farm. In the comfort of their own personal spaces both designers have allowed themselves to break free from the constraint of the usual client-practitioner relationship. As a result, Bryan's Ground, where Dorrell's partner David Wheeler has had an almost equal influence, particularly as regards plant selection, is an eccentric and whimsical layout, with extraordinary juxtapositions of formality and startling *bricolage* around every corner. Obviously it is an acquired taste, but as every garden should be, it is an intimate and engaging reflection of the minds and interests of its twin designers. At Bryan's Ground too, the house and the rooms that command views of the garden are important pointers as to what has been designed and planted: visual axes are demarcated by an

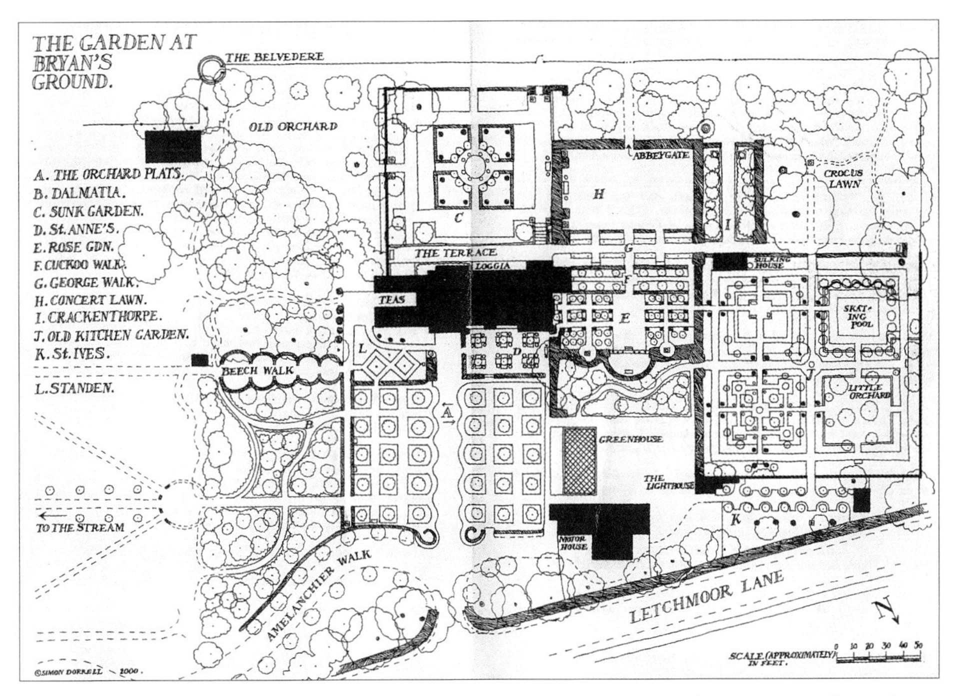

86 Simon Dorrell has drawn several versions of this plan as the garden rooms at Bryan's Ground have evolved since 1993. This 2000 edition captured the garden at the start of the Millennium. *By kind permission of Simon Dorrell*

avenue of red-twigged limes and yew hedges. It is as if Edwin Lutyens and Gertrude Jekyll had agreed to collaborate with William Heath Robinson to create an exuberant fantasy garden that never was.

Dorrell and Wheeler are garden makers, for this is not their first garden. Fleeing from modern housing and light industry, they came here in November 1993 from Rhayader in Wales, which Dorrell has captured in a Guisto Utens-like lunette that hangs inside the house. Their garden at Bryan's Ground maintains the Arts & Crafts aesthetic of the 1911 house, built for two spinster sisters, nieces of Sidney and Beatrice Webb of the Fabian Society, by Herefordshire's most important architects of the period, Groome and Bettington. There are now around twenty outdoor rooms spreading out into three acres of garden (*86*), as well as a five-acre arboretum known as Cricket Wood, begun on New Year's Day 2000.[14] The approach to Bryan's Ground consciously exudes welcome rather than the forelock-touching deference many visitors feel they have to adopt

87 The Dovecote at Bryan's Ground, modelled on one at Luntley Court, can be seen through the yew and box topiary of the Sunk Garden

when entering the hallowed sanctum of certain National Trust properties. A makeshift outdoor dresser full of found objects, bric-a-brac and potted plants leads on to the small courtyard where terracotta pots, garden tools, a milk churn and soil sieves are placed casually around. Everything about the garden is charmingly relaxed, encouraging the visitor to wander at leisure, whether through the formal Sunk Garden with its columnar Irish yews and box-hedged beds full of Abu Hassan tulips, fennel and nepeta (*87*), or the Old Kitchen Garden, which is alive with unexpected combinations of plants and architectural salvage. As Wheeler puts it: 'Like Beatrix Farrand....we relish symmetry and intimacy, hoping that the 20 or so garden "rooms" we've made since 1993 preserve the essential Arts-and-Crafts spirit. However, lacking the funds available to the likes of a Rockefeller, a Pierpont Morgan, or a Mildred Bliss at Dumbarton Oaks, we make do as best we can'.[15]

On our visit in April 2010 the serpentine canal in front of the house was the most recent addition. Now, in early summer, its flanking orchards are awash with blossom and the vertical blue accents of *Iris sibirica* 'Papillon' rising out of square beds (*colour 58*). Each new project – originally one per year – or architectural introduction is redolent of their personal and professional relationship. In 1995 the Sulking House was built by Dorrell with salvage from Cardiff Docks as a 50th-birthday present for Wheeler, and the Dovecote, which is based on the seventeenth-century pigeon house at Luntley Court, was constructed in 2006 to provide them with a summer dining room. The garden conveys a sense of shared enthusiasm, as do the intensely personal garden rooms around

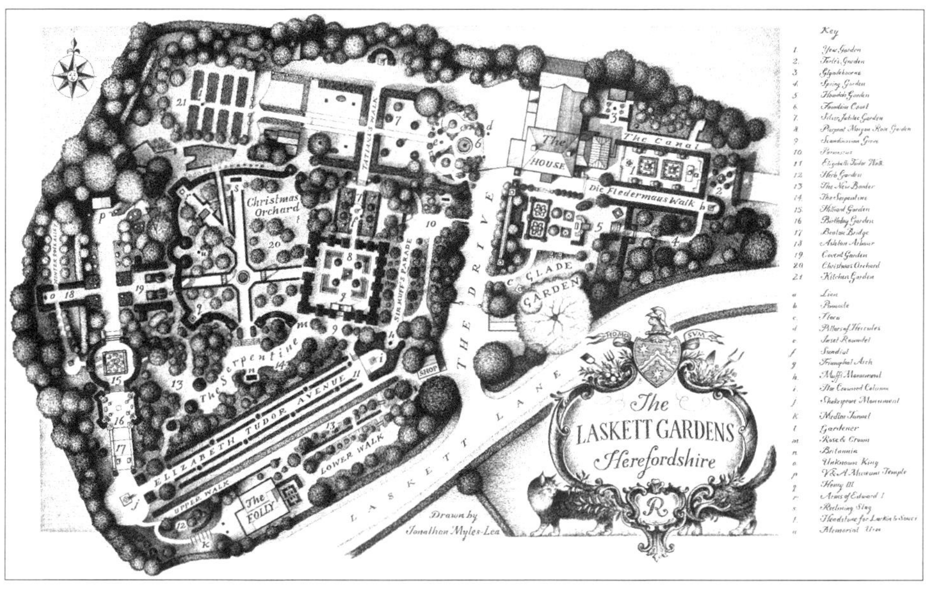

88 Jonathan Myles-Lea's plan of the grounds at The Laskett shows the profuse arrangement of garden spaces around the house, as well as the fascinatingly accretive nature of the whole complex. *By kind permission of Sir Roy Strong*

Sir Roy Strong's **The Laskett**.[16] But while Bryan's Ground features collections of 'junk', as Wheeler calls it, Strong's layout is in a different architectural register. Bryan's Ground has a delightful air of impermanence; indeed some of the salvage is actively decaying, while the architectural monuments of The Laskett have been built to last. Both, however, are significant layouts and deserve to be included here as cultural expressions of their time and historic gardens of the future.

This brings us back to Anne Wareham's recent diatribe on Strong's layout (*88*). She argues that it should not be perceived as 'a romantic garden, with historic and personal references', but 'seen as a conceptual garden where terror and chaos await you around every corner'. This might be an erudite analysis of Valentine Morris' mid-eighteenth-century Savage Picturesque layout at Piercefield near Chepstow, where horror does indeed lurk around every corner on that vertiginous ledge above the Wye, but it is hardly an appropriate description for Strong's multi-layered formality. Perhaps it is a question of competition, now that both The Laskett and Wareham's Veddw are both open regularly to the public; more likely it is provocative journalism for the sake of notoriety. Whatever the aim, this 'poisonous account' of The Laskett, as Andrew Lawson has termed it, is far too subjective and partial. But then, what should one's response be to such an individual garden? My own, for what it is worth, is that the visitor should approach any garden passively, simply enjoy its pleasures, and then engage with it actively in order to appreciate the motivations and interests of its creators. In this way, I shall never look at a honeysuckle again without thinking of David Wheeler's battle against cancer and the healing influence of his garden during the illness, about which he wrote so movingly in the *Daily Telegraph* when he was undergoing treatment in 2008.[17] Mortality is also starkly present at The Laskett, which can be viewed as much as a *memento mori* as a garden celebrating the lives and achievements of its designers. Indeed, the ashes of Strong's wife, Julia Trevelyan Oman, are contained in an urn placed within an orchard at the heart of the garden, the orchard being a typically Herefordian touch.

Just as most significant garden layouts, particularly of the eighteenth century, have an iconographical programme of meaning, that at The Laskett is the story of the life of its creators. It is a busy garden (*89*), full of historical and cultural references, as one would expect from a theatre designer and an expert on Tudor and Elizabethan culture and architecture. Perhaps its very overt erudition – Greek and Latin texts and mottoes feature on both the house and the garden buildings – is too much for the

89 This view through the Silver Jubilee Garden to the Pierpont Morgan Rose Garden with its Triumphal Arch emphasises the eclectic nature of both planting and garden furnishings at The Laskett

taste Gestapo. But then I have never heard anyone complain about the verses from Virgil's *Aeneid* at Stourhead, or Ian Hamilton Finlay's allusive, and at times wilfully obscure, Concrete Poetry at Little Sparta in Scotland. Perhaps, like Prince Charles' garden at Highgrove House in Gloucestershire, The Laskett is seen to be too self-aggrandising. However, I see it as the choreography, in plants and structures, of an intensely personal journey through life of two creative individuals; a journey that was once private, but is now open to everyone to share, just as at Bryan's Ground. In this way, the beautifully carved memorials to the family cats – The Lady Torte de Shell, Souci, Larkin and the Rev Wencelas Muff – are as poignant a reminder of shared lives as the stage setting of the Victoria & Albert Museum Temple celebrating Strong's tenure as Director, or the theatrical vista to the Monument commemorating the award to Strong of the prestigious Shakespeare Prize in 1980, which terminates the Elizabeth Tudor Avenue.

The garden's planting is a combination of controlled design and happy self-seeding. It begins with the box *parterre de broderie* adjacent to the house, signalling Strong's Tudor scholarship, and then leads through the fragrant rose quadrants to the exuberant textural and colourful planting of the deep herbaceous borders (*colour plate 59*). Aided by his dedicated gardeners, The Laskett is constantly evolving under Strong's lively and inventive mind. The garden's signature colours of turquoise and gold, which once highlighted the sculptures, have now been replaced by uniform terracotta. One of the most striking elements, which has evolved over the last ten years, is the wave-form hedge grown from a combination of beech below and yew above, leaving a narrow gap for views to the grounds beyond. The breathtaking concatenation of incidents is very like Clough Williams-Ellis' Portmeirion in North Wales, which has clearly influenced The Laskett, both delighting by their tightly-packed eclecticism. The garden at The Laskett is, without doubt, one of the most significant and beautiful of the late twentieth and early twenty-first centuries, as expressive of its time as it is of its twin creators.

Two further gardens, one of interest and the other of national importance, though relatively unknown as yet, strike a modernist note at the end of this chapter of plant innovation and traditional formalism. These are at **Knill Court**, in the far north-western corner of the county near Presteigne, and at **Lawless Hill**, which is in the south of Herefordshire, perched above the Wye at Sellack. Both have modernist parent houses, but while the terraced garden below Knill Court is relatively unassuming – planting threaded around little paths that take the contours of the site – the terrain around Lawless Hill is a dramatic interpenetration of house and landscape with water as its theme.

Knill Court is an excitingly bizarre place. To the wreck of a semi-demolished, late Victorian Gothic house has been added an angular modern brick structure, kept deliberately low to take the hilltop site (*90*). This was completed in 1980 for David and Helen Humphreys by their daughter Bridget and son-in-law Piers Ford. The surviving stone-mullioned bay

90 A thrilling sequence of terraces, devoid of barriers or balustrades, built by David Humphreys at Knill Court, imitates the cascade on the Hindwell Brook below

window openings of a long-lost reception room and the Victorian stone porch now act as an entrance screen to the new house beyond. The courtyard is laid out as a scree garden over the rubble-filled cellars of the lost house, with the miniature characteristics of the plants reflecting David Humphreys' role as the former Botanical Recorder for Radnorshire, during which time he engaged in a project to map the wild flowers of the British Isles in infinite detail. Inside the house, the open-plan living area has wide windows, giving views out south-west to Wales and down to the valley of the Hindwell Brook below. Humphreys' interest in wild flowers is evident in the planting. There are snakeshead fritillaries and white wood anemones; primroses have colonised the lawns of the former Victorian pleasure grounds, while brilliant yellow skunk cabbage, white trilliums and purple globes of candelabra primulas shine out from the banks of a slow branch of the stream that trickles through the shade of the garden deep below. The terraces between the house and the Hindwell Brook are planted with a rambling assortment of purple aquilegias, red poppies, comfrey, and the thistle-like flowers of centaurea.

Lawless Hill is also sited to give spectacular views, across a great bow in the Wye that encloses King's Caple. Unknown until research for this book began, the garden was given away by a line of cloud-pruned trees strung out along the horizon above the Wye.[18] A pair of anonymous, solid electronic gates and the absence of a letterbox maintained its privacy, but when the owner Keith Meehan was eventually contacted the visit could not have been more exciting. Meehan has used all the skills and contacts he has built up as a successful property developer to create a designed landscape on a vertical site, which is a stunning combination of the elemental nature of Frank Lloyd Wright's Falling Water and the calm of the Japanese gardens of Kyoto.

The garden begins quietly, but cleverly, with the driveway. Few would consider incorporating the ribbon of hard standing demanded by cars as a garden feature, but Meehan accomplishes it effortlessly with sweeps of granite sets laid out in a pattern inspired by an Italian trip and topped by a circular seat set around a tree. The seat stands on a metal grid that becomes a *lietmotif* in the garden and can be traced back to Meehan's commercial developments. The walls and buttresses of the terraces were built chiefly of Forest of Dean stone, constructed by a father and his son from Dorstone. Meehan recalls how they were the first craftsmen to arrive on site and the last to leave, five years later. He came back at weekends to find the terraces continuing to evolve upwards and outwards. Some are constructed from the largest stones that the quarry could provide and weigh up to eight tons. Other walls were on a smaller scale, such as that which surrounds a maquette of Alfred Hitchcock's head. The film director has no association with Herefordshire; the final version of the sculpture is in the courtyard of Meehan's scheme for redeveloping the former Gainsborough Film Studios in London. Anthony Donaldson, a founding figure of London's Pop Art scene in the 1960s, made the maquette

91 Anthony Donaldson's revolving Clouds are set against the backdrop of one of Herefordshire's most constant landscape features – the River Wye

92 The curved glass of the Summerhouse dulls reflections that would otherwise mar views back from the Wye into the vertiginous garden at Lawless Hill. The sauna bed in the basement aligns precisely on the water level

and also the pivoting sculpture of black, acid-etched clouds from which rain spears down in the form of steel rods (*91*). The artwork is sited on a second larger grassed platform on the opposite side of the house, just below the Japanese cloud-pruned pines. These, along with another 150 mature trees, were purchased from nurseries in Germany with advice from Juan Gaviria, Meehan's friend and a Venezuelan professor of botany.

A mirror pool and swimming pond are cantilevered from the rocky hillside beneath the house, and connected back to the battery of stone terraces by a Japanese-influenced dry river garden. Here, clipped box imitates water trickling between the rocks. The swimming pond is the technical *tour de force* of the garden and was inspired by a magazine article casually read during an aeroplane flight. Road construction techniques were necessary to build the roof of the games room that carries the pool. Its light well rises up dramatically through the water, while a curved glass and oak Summerhouse gives vistas out across the water (*92*). A steep pathway from this water sector twists unseen amongst the ferns that flourish beneath a magnificent display of magnolias and tree ferns. This leads to the lower boundary where candelabra primulas and gunnera enrich a second waterfall and a pool constructed from bold glacial rocks.

The sophistication and craftsmanship of the garden surrounding Lawless Hill shows that modern design can be sympathetically introduced within a picturesque landscape. It is a measure of the beauty of the garden that, as one walks its paths and explores its changes in level and atmosphere (*colour 60*), the Herefordshire landscape beyond is hardly noticed. On our visit in June 2010 the garden was private and not open to the public, but Lawless Hill now has a website and is offering bed-and-breakfast accommodation for either a 'romantic getaway' or just a 'relaxing holiday', not to mention the enjoyment of 'stunning gardens'.[19] This is fitting, for the garden is one of the most impressive in the country and should be much better known.

Chapter Notes Introduction & chapter 1

Introduction BORDER COUNTY OF LANDSCAPE AESTHETICS AND MELLOW FRUITFULNESS

1 Ronald Hutton, *Blood & Mistletoe: The History of the Druids in Britain*, (Yale University Press, 2009), pp.116-7.
2 The drawing is in Sir John Soane's Museum, Adam Volume 37, f.59. Stephen Astley, Curator of Drawings, is confident that this design was intended for Coxhall Knoll, whereas AA Tait argues in his *Robert Adam: drawings and imagination* (Cambridge, 1993), p.155, that it was a design for a 'decayed but magnificent romanesque camp doubling as an office court' for the Castle.
3 Christopher Morris (ed.), *The Illustrated Journeys of Celia Fiennes c.1682-c.1712*, 1982, p.64.
4 Ibid.
5 *A True Copy of a Letter from a person of eminence in London to his friend in Herefordshire giving a full account of the repeal of the Cyder Act and also a song sung by the members of the Herefordshire Society in London*, 1766, Hereford City Library, Herefordshire Tracts, vol.22.
6 Morris, *Fiennes*, p.64.
7 JN Jackson, 'Some Observations upon the Herefordshire Environment of the Seventeenth and Eighteenth Centuries', *Transactions of the Woolhope Naturalists' Field Club* (hereafter *TWNFC*), vol. 36, 1958, pp. 28-41; p.41.
8 Dorothy Stroud, *Capability Brown*, 1950, p.172.
9 JJ Cartwright (ed.), *The Travels through England of Dr Richard Pococke*, 2 vols (Camden Society, 1888-9), 2, p.222.
10 For these and other losses see Roy Strong, Marcus Binney & John Harris (eds.), *The Destruction of the Country House 1875-1975*, 1974.
11 Uvedale Price, *Essays on the Picturesque, as compared with the Sublime and the Beautiful*, 3 vols., 1810, 2, p.118.
12 Ibid., 2, pp.123-4. The watercolour by Robert Price, which shows the pedimented pavilion, is in a private collection. We are most grateful to David Davenport for an informed tour of the grounds at Foxley.
13 Ibid., 2, p.119.
14 We are most grateful to Edward Harley for permission to reproduce this image.
15 David Whitehead, *A Survey of Historic Parks & Gardens in Herefordshire* (Hereford & Worcester Gardens Trust, 2001).
16 David Whitehead, 'Brampton Bryan Park, Herefordshire: A Documentary History', in David Whitehead & John Eisle (eds.), *A Herefordshire Miscellany*, (Lapridge Publications, Hereford, 2000), pp.162-177; p.170.
17 J DU Ward, 'Fine Trees in a Castle Park', *Country Life*, 5 December 1957; Katie Fretwell, K Knox & DM Young, 'Croft Castle Park & Garden Survey', National Trust, 1986-7, pp.62-4.

chapter 1 CASTLES, TOURNAMENTS AND CHIVALRIC DISPLAY – IN SEARCH OF EARLY GARDENS

1 There are, of course exceptions, which bear some resemblance to pictorial prototypes, but never in such elaborate detail; for these see Sylvia Landsberg, *The Medieval Garden* (British Museum Press, no date), and *Medieval Gardens* (Dumbarton Oaks Research Library & Collection, Harvard University, Washington DC, 1986).

Chapter Notes chapter 1

2 See Timothy Mowl, *Historic Gardens of Gloucestershire* (Stroud, 2002), pp.15-20.

3 Public Record Office (hereafter PRO), C133/114.

4 Richard Barber & Juliet Barker, *Tournaments: Jousts, Chivalry and Pageants in the Middle Ages* (Woodbridge, Suffolk, 1989), p.31.

5 Juliet Barker, *The Tournament in England 1100-1400* (Woodbridge, Suffolk, 1986), pp.89-90.

6 Ian Mortimer, *The Greatest Traitor: The Life of Sir Roger Mortimer, 1st Earl of March, Ruler of England 1327-1330*, 2003, p.225.

7 We are most grateful to Carole and John Challis for their tour of this atmospheric site.

8 John Buchanan-Brown, 'The Natural History of Herefordshire: John Aubrey's Projected Tract', *TWNFC*, vol. 49, pt. 3, 1999, pp.379-403; p.387.

9 Hereford City Library, Pilley Collection, 2328.

10 David Lovelace, 'Bringewood Chase and surrounding countryside', April 2005, unpublished report for Forest Enterprise, Appendix 1.

11 *An Earthwork Survey and Investigation of Wigmore Castle, Herefordshire*, Archaeological Investigation Report Series A1/14/2002 (English Heritage, 2002), p.1.

12 PRO, C133/114.

13 William Dugdale, *Monasticon Anglicanum*, 6 vols., 1830, 6, pt.i, p.349.

14 C Taylor, P Everson, R Wilson-North & D Johnston, 'Bodiam Castle, Sussex', *Medieval Archaeology*, 34 (1990), pp.154-7.

15 Samuel & Nathaniel Buck, *Bucks Antiquities*, 2 vols., 1774, 1, plate 113.

16 Drawings based on these maps are illustrated in *Bronsil Castle, Eastnor, Herefordshire: A survey of the remains of a 15th century mansion, its surrounding moat, and ponds* (English Heritage, 2000), figs. 1 & 3 respectively. The maps are owned by Eastnor Castle Enterprises, Eastnor Castle.

17 HC Maxwell Lyte (ed.), *Calendar of Charter Rolls*, 1927, vol.6, p.137.

18 Lucy Toulmin Smith (ed.), *The Itinerary of John Leland in or about the years 1535-1543*, 5 vols., 1907, 4, p.133.

19 In his three *Country Life* articles on Hampton Court – 22 February, 1 & 8 March 1973 – John Cornforth illustrates the Bate painting, but does not discuss either the Elizabethan building it depicts or the garden enclosure. Sir Thomas warrants a paragraph but that is all. Apart from that the articles are devoted to the late-seventeenth- and early-eighteenth-century remodelling of both house and gardens.

20 JW Goodison, 'George Gower, Serjeant Painter to Queen Elizabeth', *The Burlington Magazine*, no.543, vol.90 (June 1948), pp.261-5.

21 Quoted in *Country Life*, 22 February 1973.

22 For the Nonsuch fountain see Martin Biddle, 'The Gardens of Nonsuch: Sources and Dating', *Garden History*, vol.27, no.1 (Summer, 1999), pp.145-83; fig.3.

23 Catherine Beale, *Hampton Court Guidebook* (Hampton Court Estate, Leominster, 2000), p.7.

24 Ian Atherton, *Ambition and Failure in Stuart England: The Career of John, first Viscount Scudamore* (Manchester, 1999), p.35.

25 The 1st Viscount's work at Holme Lacy is discussed in the following chapter of this study, as well as his connection with a designed landscape at Caradoc Court.

26 Quoted in Roy Strong, *The Cult of Elizabeth*, 1977, p.156. The poem was written on the occasion of the Philautia tilt of 1595.

27 JC Loudon, *Encyclopaedia of Gardening*, 1822, p.1238.

28 This is illustrated in Strong, *Cult of Elizabeth*, plate 76.

29 Ibid., p.159.

30 See John Harris, *The Artist and the Country House*, 1979, pp.164-5; plates 231-5 and colour plates 15, 16a & 16b.

31 Roy Strong, Marcus Binney & John Harris (eds.), *The Destruction of the Country House 1875-1975*, 1974, plate 55. John Harris, *Moving Rooms: The Trade in Architectural Salvages*, 2007, pp.196-7 discusses the shipment of the Julius Caesar Room to America.

32 Norman C Reeves (ed.), *The 1675 Thomas Blount Manuscript History of Herefordshire* (Lapridge Publications, Hereford, no date), p.55.

33 Illustrated in Harris, *Moving Rooms*, plate 195; quotation on p.196.

34 Reeves, *Blount Manuscript*, p.55.

35 Quoted in Whitehead, *Survey*, p.323.

36 See Timothy Mowl, *Historic Gardens of Dorset* (Stroud, 2003), pp.52-6; for other Bridgeman layouts featuring mounts see Peter Willis, *Charles Bridgeman and the English Landscape Garden* (Newcastle-upon-Tyne, 2002).

chapter 2 HARNESSED WATER, FORMALITY AND EARNEST HUSBANDRY – SEVENTEENTH-CENTURY GARDENS

1 David Whitehead, 'Some Connected Thoughts on the Parks and Gardens of Herefordshire', *TWNFC*, 1924, pp.193-223; p.217.

2 John Philips, *Cyder*, 1708, book 1, line 506.

3 FC Morgan, 'The Steward's Account of John, First Viscount Scudamore of Sligo (1601–1671) for the Year 1632', *TWNFC*, 1951, pp.155-84.

4 Hubert Reade, 'Some Account Books of the First Lord Scudamore and of the Hereford Craft Guilds', *TWNFC*, 1924, pp.119-133; p.119.

5 Whitehead, 'Connected Thoughts', pp.217-19.

6 David Whitehead, 'Holme Lacy House: a history of its architecture and garden', in Rosalind Lowe (ed.), *Essays in honour of Jim & Muriel Tonkin*, 2011, pp.69-92; p.73.

7 Ibid., p.70.

8 Speed's map is in Herefordshire Records Office (hereafter HRO), K38/D/2; the Frizell map is in the British Library, Add. MS. 36307 G24.

9 Whitehead, 'Connected Thoughts', p.219.

10 Ibid.

11 See Ron Shoesmith & Richard Morriss, 'Caradoc Court', in David Whitehead & John Eisle (eds.), *A Herefordshire Miscellany* (Lapridge Publications, Hereford, 2000), pp.272-86; plate 5.

12 David Whitehead, 'Caradoc Court, Sellack: Erection of six dwellings', *Hereford & Worcester Gardens Trust Newsletter*, no.33 (Summer, 2009), p.19.

13 Whitehead, 'Connected Thoughts', p.217.

14 Ibid.

15 Ibid., p.219.

16 Ibid.

17 British Library, Add. MS. 36307, G23; illustrated by Whitehead, 'Holme Lacy House', figure 10.

18 Ibid.

19 'Extracts from the Inventory for Sir John Ernle, 11 November 1686', Wiltshire & Swindon Archives, 1720/690. The 1797 map is archived at: 1720/589. We are grateful to Sandy Haynes for these references and for her help with Homme House.

20 Whitehead, 'Holme Lacy House', p.73; see also *Country Life*, 12 & 19 June 1909.

21 *Holme Lacy House: A History*, 1995, p.15.

22 EH Register entry.

23 See Robert Williams, 'Fortified Gardens', in Christopher Ridgway & Robert Williams (eds.), *Sir John Vanbrugh and Landscape Architecture in Baroque England 1690-1730* (Sutton Publishing, Stroud, 2000), pp.49-70.

24 Whitehead, 'Holme Lacy House', p.82.

25 *Country Life*, 12 June 1909.

26 Whitehead, 'Holme Lacy House', p.84.

27 Calendar of the Manuscripts of the Marquis of Bath preserved at Longleat, Wiltshire, *Historical Manuscripts Commission*, vol. 1 (1904), p.15; p.221.

28 Ibid., p.23; p.25.

29 Ibid., p.27.

30 David Whitehead, 'Brampton Bryan Park, Herefordshire: A Documentary History', in Whitehead & Eisle, *Herefordshire Miscellany*, pp.162-77; p.169.

31 Ibid., p.172.

32 Willis, *Charles Bridgeman* p.79; pp.176-7. The drawing is in Sir John Soane's Museum, where it is catalogued as attributed to James Gibbs, with whom Bridgeman was currently working.

33 Whitehead, 'Brampton Bryan Park', p.172.

34 Ibid.

35 Harley Papers, Brampton Bryan, Item A03. We are most grateful to Edward & Victoria Harley for a most instructive tour of the grounds at Brampton, and for their hospitality.

36 Whitehead, 'Holme Lacy House', p.80.

37 John Evelyn, *Sylva, or a Discourse of Forest-Trees*, 1664, Appendix: *Pomona*, pp.1-20.

38 See Peter Goodchild, '"No Phantastical Utopia but a Reall Place". John Evelyn, John Beale and Backbury Hill, Herefordshire', *Garden History*, vol.19, pt.2 (Autumn, 1991), pp.105-27; see also Timothy Mowl, *Gentlemen & Players: Gardeners of the English Landscape* (Sutton Publishing, Stroud, 2000), pp.23-34, and Michael Leslie, 'The Spiritual Husbandry of John Beale', in Michael Leslie & Timothy Raylor (eds.), *Culture and Cultivation in Early Modern England* (Leicester University Press, Leicester, 1992), pp.151-172.

39 John Beale, *Herefordshire Orchards, A Pattern For All England*, 1657, pp.6-7.

40 Ibid., pp.7-8.

41 Quoted in Clare Cross, 'Seventeenth-Century Orchards and Fruit Gardens', MA Dissertation, University of Bristol, November 2004.

42 Ibid., p.22.

43 Ibid.

44 Ibid.

45 Ibid.

46 Beale, *Herefordshire Orchards*, pp.38-39.

47 Ibid., p.37.

48 Ellen Beatrice Wood, *Rowland Vaughan His Booke*, 1610 (republished, 1897), title page.

49 See RE Kay, 'Some Notes on R Vaughan's "Waterworks" in the Golden Valley', *TWNFC*, vol.51 (1974), pt.2, pp.253-258.

50 Wood, *Booke*, p.133.

51 Whitehead, *Survey*, p.261. For Tackley see Timothy Mowl, *Historic Gardens of Oxfordshire* (Tempus, Stroud, 2007), pp.34-36.

52 Whitehead, *Survey*, p.276.

53 Christopher K Currie & Neil S Rushton, 'The Historical Development of the Court of Noke Estate, Pembridge, with an Archaeological assessment of the Canal-Like water features', *TWNFC*, vol.50 (2001), pt.2, pp.224-250.

54 See David Whitehead, 'The Purchase and Building of Stoke Edith Park, Herefordshire, 1670-1707', *TWNFC*, vol.43 (1980), pp.181-202; also *Country Life*, 6 June 1903 & 25 September 1909.

55 Ibid., p.183 & p.186.

56 HRO, Foley, E12/III/51.

57 Morris, *The Journeys of Celia Fiennes*, p.45.

58 Whitehead, 'Stoke Edith', p.186.

59 Ibid.

60 HRO, Foley, E12/III/724C.

61 HRO, Foley, E12/IV/173B/3.

62 HRO, Foley, E12/IV/173B/4 & HRO, Foley, E12/IV/173B/11.

63 HRO, Foley, E12/IV/173B/4.

64 Sir John Soane's Museum, vol.111/43. See colour plate 7.

65 Morris, *Celia Fiennes*, p.233.

66 Ibid., p.356.

67 Ibid.

68 Whitehead, 'Stoke Edith', pp.189-192.

69 John Harris & Gervase Jackson-Stops (eds.), *Britannia Illustrata, Knyff & Kip*, 1707 (Paradigm Press, Bungay, 1984), p.185.

70 All illustrated in John Harris, *The Artist and the Country House: A history of country house and garden view painting in Britain 1540-1870*, 1979, colour plates 15, 16a & 16b.

71 Deputy Keeper of the Records and the Public Record Office of Northern Ireland, D638/19.

72 John Harris, *William Talman: Maverick Architect*, 1982, p.43, writes: 'Generally, where Talman goes, London follows, or vice versa', and then lists Hampton Court as one site where they must have worked together. John Vanbrugh wrote to the Duke of Newcastle in 1703 of the 'vexation and disappointment' shared by many of Talman's patrons, including Lord Coningsby (Harris, *Talman*, p.20). There is, however, no surviving documentary proof that Talman designed the orangery and the summerhouse.

73 Nor is it present on a drawing by H Whittall of about 1704-1706, illustrated in *Country Life*, 22 February 1973.

74 John Cornforth, 'Hampton Court, Herefordshire-II', *Country Life*, 1 March 1973.

75 Catherine Beale & David Wheeler, *Hampton Court Castle Gardens* (Hampton Court, Leominster, 2009).

76 The former Victorian pleasure grounds to the west were once far more elaborate. They were decorated with urns and a blackamoor sundial, which may well have been a fugitive from the formal gardens; see *Country Life*, 29 June 1901.

chapter 3 Lost prospect towers and an unsung Rococo Garden

1 Public Record Office of Northern Ireland, 638/82/2.
2 William Alvis Brogden, 'Stephen Switzer and garden design in Britain in the eighteenth century', PhD, Edinburgh University, 1973, p.10.
3 Stephen Switzer, *An Introduction to a General System of Hydrostaticks and Hydraulicks, Philosophical and Practical,* 2 vols., 1729 (Garland Publishing, New York & London, 1982), Preface.
4 Ibid., 1, p.10.
5 Ibid.
6 Ibid.
7 Stephen Switzer, *Ichnographia Rustica or, the Nobleman, Gentleman, and Gardener's Recreation*, 3 vols., 1718, 1, Preface, p.pxviii.
8 C Bruyn Andrews (ed.), *The Torrington Diaries*, 4 vols., 1, 1970, pp.128-129.
9 HRO, LC Deeds 2443, no.18.
10 We are grateful to Michael Richardson for this information.
11 See John Cornforth, 'Langstone Court, Herefordshire', *Country Life*, 9 November 1967.
12 The survey is in a private collection. We are most grateful to Chris Jones for his hospitality at Langstone.
13 See John Buchanan-Brown, 'The Natural History of Herefordshire: John Aubrey's Projected Tract', *TWNFC*, vol.49 (1999), pt.3, pp.379-403; p.385.
14 *Country Life*, 27 January, 3 & 10 February 1966.
15 *Country Life*, 27 January 1966.
16 Castle Ditch is illustrated in Alistair Rowan, 'Eastnor Castle, Herefordshire-I', *Country Life*, 7 March 1968, fig.3.
17 Eastnor Castle Archives.
18 Brian Smith, *Herefordshire Map 1577 to 1800* (Logaston Press, Almeley, 2004), pp.25-27.
19 HRO, BN81.
20 Cartwright (ed.), *Travels*, 2, p.228.
21 For Pococke and the Rococo Garden see Timothy Mowl & Brian Earnshaw, *An Insular Rococo: Architecture, Politics and Society in Ireland and England, 1710-1770*, 1999, pp.73-87.
22 Cartwright (ed.), *Travels*, 2, pp.219-20.
23 For Robins see John Harris, *Gardens of Delight: The Rococo English Landscape of Thomas Robins the Elder*, 2 vol., 1978; for Bateman see John Harris, 'A pioneer in gardening: Dickie Bateman re-assessed', *Apollo*, October 1993.
24 WS Lewis (ed.), *The Yale Edition of Horace Walpole's Correspondence* (Yale University Press, New Haven & London), 48 vols., 1937-83, 10, p.43.
25 Ibid., 35, p.359.
26 HRO, G39/III/E/4-302. They seem to be have been aided at least by the gardener, Thomas Greening, who worked for William Kent at Claremont and for Queen Caroline at Richmond in the 1730s.
27 HRO, G39/III/E/326.
28 Howard Colvin, 'William Kent, Henry Flitcroft and Shobdon Church', in *Essays in Honour of John Frew* (ed. Jones & McKinstry, St Andrews, 2008).
29 For contemporary practice, especially as regards flower gardens, see Mark Laird, *The Flowering of the*

Landscape Garden: English Pleasure Grounds 1720-1800 (University of Pennsylvania Press, Philadelphia, 1999).

30 HRO, G39/III/163: Richard Bateman to Fallowes, 17 November 1747.

31 Illustrated in Laird, *The Flowering*, plate 107.

32 HRO, G39/III/E/218: Lord Bateman to Fallowes, 24 March 1749.

33 HRO, G39/III/E/237.

34 Laird, *The Flowering*, p.70.

35 HRO, G39/66 Box Maps.

36 HRO, G39/III/E/561

37 HRO, G39/III/E/563.

38 Worcestershire Record Office, Edward Knight, Garden Tour Notes.

39 David Whitehead & Ron Shoesmith, *James Wathen's Herefordshire 1770-1820: A collection of his sketches and paintings* (Logaston Press, Almeley, 1994), no pagination.

chapter 4 A failure of artificial Nature in the face of real scenery – the Brownian park

1 Entry 127 in Brown's Account Book reads: 'The Earl of Oxford at Eywood in Herefordshire a Journey there in August 1775'; the Account Book is on loan to the Lindley Library (a photocopy is catalogued at 994.5).

2 The plan is preserved at Lower Brockhampton.

3 For their collaboration in the county see Timothy Mowl & Marion Mako, *The Historic Gardens of England: Cheshire* (Redcliffe Press, Bristol, 2008), pp.75-77.

4 Letter from William Mason to Humphry Repton, published in Repton's *Sketches & Hints*, 1794, p.14.

5 HRO, AP25/2.

6 Christopher Hussey, 'Berrington Hall, Herefordshire-I-III', *Country Life*, 2, 9 & 16 December 1954; see also John Cornforth, 'Berrington Hall, Herefordshire', *Country Life*, 9 January 1992, and Nicholas Kingsley, 'Visions of Villas: The Work of Anthony Keck-II', *Country Life*, 27 October 1988.

7 HRO, microfilm of the tithe map for Berrington parish.

8 Account Book photocopy, Lindley Library 994.5

9 Banks Archive, Hergest Croft.

10 Dorothy Stroud, *Capability Brown*, 1950, p.196.

11 'Berrington Hall: Draft Report on the Historic Landscape', Land Use Consultants, March 1994, p.4.

12 John Cornforth, 'Berrington Hall, Herefordshire', *Country Life*, 9 January 1992.

13 Andrews, *Torrington Diaries*, 1, pp.129-130.

14 Nicholas Thompson, 'Moccas Court, Herefordshire-I & II', *Country Life*, 18 & 25 November 1976.

15 Brown's plan is in the Getty Center for the History of Arts and Humanities, Santa Monica, California, USA.

16 Stroud, *Capability Brown*, p.197.

17 The watercolour is preserved at the house. We are most grateful to Ben Chester-Master for allowing its reproduction here.

18 Account Book HRO, J56/IV/2. John Lambe Davis Survey c62/1

19 HRO, J56/IV/2-4.

20 HRO, J56/IV/2: 1777-1785.

21 John Phibbs, 'Reading the Landscape', in Paul T Harding & Tom Wall (eds.), *Moccas: an English deer*

park (English Nature, 1999), pp.69-79; p.74.
22 See *Country Life*, 12 January 1989.
23 HRO, A95/V/EL/510-521.
24 Ibid., Letter 512.
25 Ibid., Letter 513.
26 Ibid., Letter 517.
27 HRO, A95/V/EL/483.
28 Whitehead, *Survey*, p.4.
29 Ibid., p.88.
30 See David Whitehead, 'John Davenport and the Improvement Plan for Nanteos, Cardiganshire 1791', in *The Picturesque*, no.23 (Summer, 1998).
31 HRO, M5/6/14.
32 HRO, D52/8/2-3.
33 Whitehead, *Survey*, pp.233-234.
34 Ibid., p.234.
35 HRO, D52/8/2.

chapter 5 'In the enemy's quarters' – Repton and the pressure of the Picturesque

1 Uvedale Price, *Essays on the Picturesque, as Compared with the Sublime and the Beautiful*, 3 vols., 1810 (Thoemmes Press, Bristol, 2001), 3, 'A Letter to H Repton Esq. on the Application of the Practice as well as the Principles of *Landscape-Painting* to *Landscape-Gardening*', p.45.
2 Stephen Daniels, *Humphry Repton: Landscape Gardening and the Geography of Georgian England* (Yale University Press, New Haven & London, 1999), p.117.
3 Letter from Price to Lord Abercorn, quoted in Charles Watkins & Ben Cowell, 'Letters of Uvedale Price', *The Walpole Society*, vol.68 (Leeds, 2006), p.79.
4 Price, *Essays*, 3, p.31.
5 Ibid., p.30.
6 Ibid.
7 Daniels, *Humphry Repton*, p.117.
8 The Red Book is preserved at Garnons. We are most grateful to Harry Cotterell for permission to quote from it and to reproduce Repton's watercolours here.
9 The map is at Garnons; we are grateful to Harry Cottrell for permission to reproduce it here.
10 Under 'Situation', f.5.
11 This has been well chronicled by David Whitehead: 'John Nash and Humphry Repton: An Encounter in Herefordshire 1785-98', in *TWNFC*, vol. 48 (1991), pp.210-236.
12 Wilkins had already designed a crescent of cottages for the entrance to the park, which was finally built, but as a single cottage and gate.
13 HRO, D52/5/5.
14 HRO, D52/5/1.
15 HRO, D52/6/4.
16 HRO, D52/6/10.
17 HRO, D52/6/11. It is likely that the design was close to that which Repton prepared for a fishing pavilion at Longleat; see Timothy Mowl, *Historic Gardens of Wiltshire* (Tempus Publishing, Stroud,

2004), pp.117-119. Robert Ebbell, who is thought to have been a pupil of Atkinson, also played a part in the scheme to design a fishing lodge. As late as 1817 he submitted a sketch and plan for a rustic cottage with 'Cottagers Room', 'Pleasure Room' and a verandah with rustic seat (HRO, D52/1/8).

18 'Character', f.6.

19 'The House', f.7.

20 'Approach', f.11.

21 'Water', f.13.

22 'Of Deceptions', f.14.

23 'The Drive', f.18.

24 Whitehead, 'John Nash and Humphry Repton', p.227.

25 Hazel Fryer, 'Humphry Repton in Herefordshire', in Stephen Daniels & Charles Watkins (eds.), *The Picturesque Landscape* (University of Nottingham,1994), pp.80-5; p.84.

26 HRO, J56/IV/2.

27 Quoted in Hazel Fryer, 'Humphry Repton 1752-1818: A review of his work as a landscape gardener', PhD thesis, University of York, 2001, 114.

28 Phibbs, 'Reading the Landscape', in Paul Harding & Tom Wall (eds.), *Moccas: an English Deer Park* (English Nature, 1999), p.75.

29 Ibid.

30 Humphry Repton, *Observations on the Theory and Practice of Landscape Gardening*, 1803, p.139.

31 Repton recalled this partnership in his *Memoir*; see Ann Gore and George Carter (eds.), *Humphry Repton's Memoir* (Michael Russell, Wilby, 2005), pp.75-6.

32 Michael Mansbridge, *John Nash*, 2004, p.112.

33 See Nigel Temple, 'Pages from an Architect's Notebook', *TWNFC*, vol.45, pt.3 (1987), pp.743-750. There is said to be a date of 1825 incised on the porch. It is known that Charles Heather had worked for Nash at Ingestre Hall in Staffordshire before coming to Homend and was also working with Smirke at this time. The current belief is, therefore, that the Lodge is possibly by Heather in Nash's style.

34 David Verey, *Herefordshire: A Shell Guide*, 1955, p.48.

35 Quoted in George Carter, Patrick Goode & Kedrun Laurie (eds.), *Humphry Repton, Landscape Gardener: 1752-1818*, 1982, p.153.

36 There is a copy in HRO, BE37.

37 Luke Booker, *The Hop-Garden A Didactic Poem* (Newport, 1799), no pagination.

38 Anon., *The Life and Amours of Lady Ann F-l-y: The whole of her intrigues, from the time of her Marriage with the Hon. EDWARD FOLEY, in October 1778, till the present Time PARTICULARLY WITH Lord M—— Col. F——zp——k, Captain L——d, Mr St——r, the Earl of P——h, and others. INCLUDING The whole substance of the TRIAL for Crim. Con. Between the Hon. Mr F——y and the Earl of Peterborough,* London, 1778, pp.7-9.

39 Quoted by Sarah Lloyd, 'Amour in the Shrubbery: Reading the Detail of English Adultery Trial Publications in the 1780s', *Eighteenth-Century Studies*, vol.39, no.4 (2006), pp.421-42; p.421. Mrs Arabin's husband had taken out another high profile prosecution for adultery in June 1785.

40 Rev Stebbing Shaw, *Tour to the West of England in 1788*, 1789, p.154.

41 Under 'The House', watercolour 1; quotation on f.5.

42 'The Parsonage', f.7.

43 'View to the South', f.10.

44 'The Approach', f.14.

45 HRO, B/30/1, nos. 11 & 12. These plans have now been withdrawn from the Record Office and their whereabouts unknown.

46 'The Village', f.16.

47 Ibid.

48 A double cottage and the cider mill are illustrated in Daniels, *Humphry Repton*, plates 124 & 125.

49 Repton, *Observations* (2nd ed., 1805), p.147.

50 HRO, E12/III/620.

51 HRO, E12/III/620.

52 The Red Book for another Foley estate, Prestwood in Staffordshire, made in January 1791, closed with a watercolour of Stoke Edith, indicating that Repton had already made a visit to the Herefordshire property. A payment of £21 by Edward Foley on account to Repton in July 1790 has also been interpreted by Dorothy Stroud as being in respect of Stoke Edith (Stroud, *Humphry Repton*, 1962, p.51).

53 Red Book, 'Other Views from the House', f.13.

54 Ibid.

55 Booker, *Hop-Garden*.

56 See Malcolm Andrews, *The Search for the Picturesque: Landscape Aesthetics and Tourism in Britain 160-1800*, 1989.

57 Jane Austen, *Northanger Abbey*, 1818 (Penguin Books, Harmondsworth, 1972), p.125.

58 HRO, BB41: Red Book facsimile.

59 Quoted in Daniels, *Humphry Repton*, p.127.

60 *A Sketch from the Landscape.*

61 See Temple, 'Pages from an Architect's Notebook', p.743.

62 For Belmont see David Whitehead, 'Belmont, Herefordshire: The Development of a Picturesque Estate, 1788-1827', *The Picturesque*, nos.11, 12 & 13 (Summer, Autumn & Winter, 1995), pp.1-8, pp.1-11 & pp.10-22 respectively.

63 The house was rebuilt to designs by James Wyatt between 1788 and 1790.

64 Quoted in Timothy Mowl & Brian Earnshaw, *Trumpet at a Distant Gate: The Lodge as Prelude to the Country House*, 1984, p.68.

65 Whitehead, 'Belmont, Herefordshire', no.12, p.3.

66 There is an undated group of surveys of Belmont in HRO, C38/49/2/5/C, which shows the grotto as a circular structure at the east end of a long, thin circuit walk through a shrubbery running parallel with the Wye.

67 Charles Heath, *The Excursion down the Wye from Ross to Monmouth*, 1799, p.96.

68 HRO, B34: facsimile of Red Book, under 'An apology'.

69 'Views from the house'.

70 'Of Landscape Gardening'.

71 Richard Payne Knight, *The Landscape, a Didactic Poem*, 3 books (2nd ed., 1795), 1, lines 271-274.

72 Price, *Essays on the Picturesque*, 1, pp.16-17.

73 Ibid., p.17.

74 William Gilpin, *Observations on the River Wye, and several parts of South Wales, &c. relative chiefly to Picturesque Beauty*, 1782, Section 1.

75 Stephanie Macdonald, 'The Honourable Daines Barrington "On the Progress of Gardening" 1782', MA Dissertation, Department of History of Art, University of Bristol, 2002.

76 *Archaeologia*, vol.7 (1785), pp.113-130.

77 Ibid., p.130.

78 Ibid.
79 Susan Sloman, *Gainsborough in Bath* (Yale University Press, New Haven & London, 2002).
80 Price, *Essays on the Picturesque*, 2, p.368.
81 George Sherburn (ed.), *The Correspondence of Alexander Pope*, 5 vols (Oxford, 1956), 3, p.290.
82 Whitehead, *Survey*, p.225.
83 Nikolaus Pevsner, *The Buildings of England: Herefordshire*, 1963, p.281.
84 Heath, *Excursion*, p.23.
85 Ibid., p.25.
86 John Cornforth, 'Hill Court, Herefordshire_I', *Country Life*, 27 January 1966.
87 Revd Charles J Robinson, *A History of the Mansions & Manors of Herefordshire*, 1872, p.271.
88 Watkins & Cowell, 'Letters of Uvedale Price', p.11.
89 Ibid., p.10. The Robert Price drawing is illustrated at fig.4.
90 From a commemorative stone in the building.
91 Cartwright (ed.), *Travels*, 2, pp.224-5.
92 Watkins & Cowell, 'Letters of Uvedale Price', p.14.
93 Ibid., pp.23-25.
94 Edward Wedlake Brayley & John Britton, *The Beauties of England and Wales*, 1805, 6, pp.581-2.
95 A full account of the controversy is given in Andrew Ballantyne, *Architecture, Landscape and Liberty: Richard Payne Knight and the Picturesque* (Cambridge, 1997), pp.86-109.
96 Quoted in Watkins & Cowell, 'Letters of Uvedale Price', p.30.
97 Ibid.
98 Payne Knight, *The Landscape*, 1, lines 239-244.
99 For Payne Knight in general see Ballantyne, *Architecture, Landscape and Liberty*; see also Nicholas Penny's two articles in *Country Life*: 28 January & 4 February 1982.
100 The watercolours are in a private collection. We are most grateful to Mrs Angela Lawson for permission to reproduce them here.
101 HRO, BL35. The survey has a pencil date of 1780.
102 MW Thompson (ed.), *The Journeys of Sir Richard Colt Hoare through Wales and England 1793-1810* (Alan Sutton Publishing, Gloucester, 1983), p.109.
103 Payne Knight, *The Landscape*, 2, lines 284-287.
104 Uvedale Price, *An Essay on the Picturesque as compared with the Sublime and the Beautiful*, 1794, p.15.
105 Edmund Burke, *A Philosophical Enquiry into the Origin of our Ideas of the Sublime and Beautiful*, second edition, 1759 (Scolar Press, Menston, 1970), pp.58-59.
106 While Andrew Ballantyne, his biographer, has written the most definitive account of Payne Knight's achievements at Downton, a handy illustrated pamphlet has been produced by Barney Rolfe-Smith, *Notes on Bringewood Forge and The Downton Walks* (Leintwardine History Society, Leintwardine, 2009).
107 We are most grateful to Tom Wall for a wonderfully atmospheric and informed tour of the circuit. The general public are not allowed entry.
108 HRO, J53/IV/24.
109 Quoted in Rolfe-Smith, *Notes*, p.33.
110 British Library, MS 43230: Aberdeen Papers, ff.47-47v.
111 British Library, MS 43230: Aberdeen Papers, f.48. We are most grateful to Christopher Francis for help with the translation.
112 As a rider to this argument, it should be noted that Payne Knight paid for 200 rose trees to be

planted among the trees at the rear of the Castle as early as 1772. It seems, therefore, that he saw a place for something close to the fussy Gardenesque on the ground, but chose to ignore it in his writings in order to strengthen his attack upon Brown.

chapter 6 REGENCY ECLECTICISM AND THE POST-PICTURESQUE

1 Frederic G Kenyon (ed.), *The Letters of Elizabeth Barrett Browning*, 2 vols., 1898, 1, pp. 158-161; p.158.
2 Simon Avery & Rebecca Stott, *Elizabeth Barrett Browning* (Pearson Education, Harlow, 2003), p.26.
3 Sandra Blutman, 'Hope End, Herefordshire: Childhood Home of Elizabeth Barrett Browning', *Country Life*, 19 September 1968.
4 Margaret Reynolds (ed.) *Aurora Leigh by Elizabeth Barrett Browning* (Ohio University Press, 1992), p.186
5 Quoted by Anna Sproule, *Lost Houses of Britain* (David & Charles, Newton Abbot, 1982), p.176.
6 *Country Life*, 19 September 1968.
7 See Nigel Temple, 'Humphry Repton, Illustrator, and William Peacock's *Polite Repository* 1790-1811', *Garden History*, vol.16, no.2 (Autumn, 1988), pp.161-173. One such image was of Hampton Court, where Repton probably undertook some work in 1794, though the extent appears limited.
8 Repton sent Lord Somers his trade card in the hope of obtaining a commission. It is included in Elizabeth Banks Associates Ltd., 'Eastnor Castle Landscape Restoration Plan', vol.1, June 1992, 15.0; the original is in the archives at Eastnor Castle.
9 Timothy Mowl, *Historic Gardens of Gloucestershire* (Tempus Publishing, Stroud, 2002), pp.117-121.
10 Anne Anderson, 'Wordsworth and the Gardens of Coleorton Hall', *Garden History*, vol.22, no.2 (Winter, 1994), pp.206-207.
11 John Claudius Loudon, *Encyclopaedia of Gardening*, 1822, p.1238.
12 Cited in Whitehead, *Survey*, p.216.
13 Mary Southall, *A Description of Malvern and it's concomitants: including a guide to the drives, rides, walks and excursions*, 1822, p.155.
14 British Library, Maps 137.a.1(8): sale catalogue, 24 July 1867.
15 There is a small, open Doric temple housing an urn in the Quarry Garden of indeterminate date.
16 Jane Bradney, 'Donald Beaton and the Walled Garden at Haffield' in Fiona Grant & Jane Patton (eds.), *The walled Gardens of Herefordshire*, (Logaston Press, Almeley, 2009), pp.59-68; p.59.
17 *Gardener's Magazine*, 1836, p.114.
18 Ibid., p.115.
19 Watkins & Cowell, *Letters*, p.290.
20 Bradney, 'Donald Beaton and the Walled Garden at Haffield', p.63.
21 Alistair Rowan, 'Eastnor Castle, Herefordshire-I, II & III', *Country Life*, 7, 14 & 21 March 1968.
22 Thomas Love Peacock, *Nightmare Abbey*, 1818 (Penguin Books, Harmondsworth, 1969), p.42.
23 Oliver Garnett, *Croft Castle* (National Trust, 2004), p.29. Arthur Oswald gives an illustration of the Wall in one of his two articles on Croft in *Country Life*, 28 April & 5 May, but does not venture a date.
24 HRO, 098/LC/5506.
25 Revd TD Fosbroke, *The Wye Tour or Gilpin on 'The Wye'*, 1838, p.52.
26 For Scott and Meyrick see Clive Wainwright, *The Romantic Interior: The British Collector at Home* (Yale University Press, New Haven & London, 1989); see also Mark Girouard, *The Return to Camelot: Chivalry and the English Gentleman* (New Haven & London, 1981), pp.39-54 and Rosalind Lowe, *Sir Samuel Meyrick and Goodrich Court* (Logaston Press, Almeley, 2003).

27 Thomas Love Peacock, *Crotchet Castle*, 1831 (Penguin Books, Harmondsworth), 1969, p.163.
28 Quoted in Lowe, *Sir Samuel Meyrick*, p.108.
29 Ibid., p.94.
30 HJE Grierson (ed.) *The Letters of Sir Walter Scott*. 12 vols, (1932-79) 8, p.91.
31 In 1831 Meyrick was described as moving trees 'a la Stewart'. National Library of Wales, MSS 6655C, f.20.
32 Henry Steuart, *The Planter's Guide*, 1828, p.10.
33 Lowe, *Sir Samuel Meyrick*, p.124.
34 National Library of Wales, MS. 6655C, f.28.
35 Lowe, *Sir Samuel Meyrick*, p.136.
36 Hugh Meller, 'The Architectural History of Goodrich Court, Herefordshire', *TWNFC*, vol.42, pt.2 (1977), pp.175-185; p.182.
37 Charles Nash, *The Goodrich Court Guide*, 1845, p.31.
38 Ibid., p.36.

chapter 7 Pines, parterres and a Pulhamite rockery – Victorian excess

1 John Claudius Loudon, *The Landscape Gardening and Landscape Architecture of the late Humphry Repton* (Gregg International, Farnborough, reprint, 1969), p.347.
2 Miles Hadfield, 'The Exotic Trees of Eastnor', *Country Life*, 20 June 1968.
3 Ibid.
4 Ibid.
5 Douglas Silvanus-Davis, former archivist, Eastnor Castle writing to Sophieke Piebenga, 15 October 2002, with information from the Castle's cash accounts. WJ Bean points out that almost always during the nineteenth century, and therefore presumably in this case, the *Picea* and *Abies* genus were transposed. WJ Bean, *Trees and Shrubs Hardy in the British Isles*, 1976, 4 vols., 3, p.177.
6 *Country Life*, 20 June 1968. In 1884 Brown was Keeper of the Botanical Department at the British Museum.
7 *Gardeners' Chronicle*, 26 January 1878, p.107.
8 *The Garden*, 21 April 1888, p.358.
9 *Gardeners' Chronicle*, 23 January 1892, pp.103-104; p.103.
10 Ibid.
11 Ibid., p.104.
12 John Rankin, *A History of our firm being some account of the firm of Pollock, Gilmore & Co and its offshoots and connections 1804-1920*, 1921.
13 Shirley Evans, 'William Andrews Nesfield (1793-1881): Artist and Landscape Designer' (PhD thesis, Falmouth University, 2007), 2 vols., 1, p.47.
14 In 1864 Richard Snead-Cox noted in one of his journal entries the passing of his 'old and beloved friend....Mrs Salvin Dowager of Croxdale'. Croxdale is three miles south of Co Durham and on the doorstep of Brancepeth, the youthful home of the architect Nesfield and his brother-in-law, Anthony Salvin. The Journal is in a private collection.
15 Evans, 'William Andrews Nesfield', dates Nesfield's report on Garnstone to October 1845 and to October 1848: vol.2, p.356 and p.259. However, the series of annual timber sales held on the Garnstone estate between 1846 and 1849 indicates that Nesfield's advice to reduce the trees was given in

October 1845: HRO, BS28/1/9.

16 Ibid., 2, p.112.

17 Ibid., 2, p.116.

18 HRO, M5/33/20: sale particulars of 1887.

19 See CJ Bradney, 'The Italian Garden in England 1787-1863', PhD thesis, University of Bristol, 2008.

20 Snead-Cox, Journal.

21 Ibid.

22 Ibid.

23 Private collection.

24 Snead-Cox, Journal.

25 Evans, 'William Andrews Nesfield', p.146.

26 Snead-Cox, Journal.

27 Ibid.

28 It does, however, raise the question as to whether Nesfield was involved in the decision to bring Belmont's Hereford Drive back into use in the 1860s. This has previously been raised by Whitehead in 'Belmont, Herefordshire', p.19, with respect to Nesfield's son, Arthur Markham Nesfield, who also undertook some unidentified landscape design work for Wegg Prosser in 1866 and 1870.

29 In November 1853 he made suggestions for the colours and patterns to be used in the saloon, the library, the Painted Hall and Lady Emily's private sitting room: HRO E12/IV/173B6.

30 Nesfield refers to a bill from Veitch, whom he describes as 'a respectable man' in a letter to Lady Emily written on 8 March 1854: HRO, E12/IV/173B6.

31 See for example his notes on the planting of box edging for a parterre that accompanied his plan of January 1854: HRO, E12/III/737.

32 He referred to his dealings with Seeley of the statuary and garden ornament manufacturers, Austin & Seeley, in several letters to Lady Emily, including those dated 4 October 1853, 13 October 1854, 8 November 1859 and 28 November 1859: HRO, E12/ IV/173B6.

33 Ibid., 4 October 1853.

34 See Christopher Ridgeway, 'William Andrews Nesfield: between Uvedale Price and Isambard Kingdom Brunel', *Journal of Garden History*, 13, 1993, pp. 69-89, pp. 76, 78. Evans has also discussed the scrapbook of designs in her unpublished thesis on Nesfield.

35 HRO, E12/IV/173B6: 2 January 1854.

36 HRO, E12/IV/173B5: William Andrews Nesfield, Plan No V: 'arrangement of colours for beds', October 1854.

37 Ibid.

38 HRO, E12/IV/173B6: 26 September 1855.

39 HRO, Foley, E12/IV/173B: Robertson, 'Expenses attending the construction of three new Flower Gardens and otherwise carrying out the designs furnished by Mr Nesfield – 1854'.

40 Elliott, *Victorian Gardens*, p.138.

41 HRO, E12/IV/173B6: 26 September 1855.

42 Ibid.

43 HRO, E12/IV/173B: 8 March 1858.

44 E12/IV/173B6: 22 December 1859.

45 HRO, E12/III/726: William Andrews Nesfield, 'Stoke Edith Park No 1 Detailed Plan of Proposed Geometric Treatment for Terrace, Parterres &c', December 1853.

46 HRO, E12/IV/173B6: 1 February 1860.

47 *Journal of Horticulture and Cottage Gardening*, 3 June 1862, p.177. Shirley Evans' research into the Nesfield family archive in Victoria, Australia, corroborates his involvement. Evans, 'Nesfield', 2, p.16.

48 J Robson, 'The Royal Horticultural Garden at Kensington', *Journal of Horticulture and Cottage Gardener,* 5 November 1861, pp.113-14. Donald Beaton, 'The Planting Out at the Royal Horticultural Society's Garden at South Kensington in 1862', *Journal of Horticulture and Cottage Gardener,* 19 August 1862, pp.387-389.

49 *Journal of Horticulture and Cottage Gardener,* 3 June 1862, pp.177-178.

50 Evans, 'Nesfield', 2, p.16.

51 Ivor Pfeull, *A History of Shobdon* (Ivor Pfuell, London, 1994), p.88.

52 Evans, 'Nesfield', 2, p.17.

53 *Journal of Horticulture and Cottage Gardener*, 28 June 1877, pp.484-86; p.481.

54 The residents remain unconvinced about this venture and the Hall and its gardens are becoming an increasingly successful wedding venue.

55 See Bradney, 'The Italian Garden in England', 1, pp.248-59; also Richard Garnier, 'Alexander Roos (*c.*1810-1881)', *Georgian Group Journal*, vol.XV (2007), pp.11-68 and Howard Colvin, 'Introducing Alexander Roos' in Ian Gow and Alastair Rowan (eds.), *The Scottish Country House 1600-1914* (Edinburgh, 1994), pp.277-284.

56 Elliott, *Victorian Gardens*, pp.128-132.

57 Katie Fretwell (ed.), 'Brockhampton Park Survey', unpublished report, 1989, pp.14-15. Fretwell points out that Thomas' plan is titled for the attention of H J Barneby Esq. This was John Habington Barneby, who changed his surname to Lutley in 1864.

58 See Elliott, *Victorian Gardens*, pp.145-147. Evidence also exists for his involvement at Mentmore Towers, Buckinghamshire; Henham Hall, Suffolk; Patshull House, Staffordshire; Westonbirt, Gloucestershire and, interestingly given the parallel with Roos, Hadzor Hall.

59 See Julia Ionides, *Thomas Farnolls Pritchard of Shrewsbury* (Dogrose Press, Ludlow, 1999), p.100 for a reproduction of Mrs Balwyn Childe's sketch. The whereabouts of the original album of sketches is now unknown, following its return to its owner from Worcestershire Record Office around 1985.

60 Simon Jervis, 'Whitbourne Hall, Herefordshire II', *Country Life*, 27 March 1975.

61 Ibid.

62 See Mowl and Barre, *Staffordshire*, p.236.

63 The architectural historian, HS Goodhart-Rendel, coined this phrase for architects who combined styles without regard to their history or nationality. Pevsner's description was quoted by Paul Thompson, 'Building of the Year: 33-35 Eastcheap, City of London, 1868', *Victorian Studies*, vol. 12 (September, 1968), pp.101-103; p.103.

64 Evans family private collection.

65 Ibid.

66 We are gratefully to Lady Mynors for her most informative and efficient tour.

67 *Littlebury's Directory and Gazetteer of Herefordshire,* 1876-77, p.323.

68 For more on Edward Milner see Elliott, *Victorian Gardens*, pp.171-73.

69 HRO, M5/5/44:1898 Sale particulars for Robbins, Billings & Co, London.

70 HRO, M5/5/45:1925 Sale particulars for Edwards, Russell & Baldwin.

71 HRO, F99/168.

72 Barney travelled widely in Canada in the 1880s, which may have further inspired his interest in North

American conifers. See W. Henry Barneby, *Life and Labour in the Far, Far West being notes of a tour in the western states, British Columbia, Manitoba and the North West Territory*, 1884. This was dedicated to his friend and travelling companion, Charles Maysey Bolton Clive, of Whitfield, Herefordshire, who died during the trip. Also W Henry Barneby, *The New Far West and the Old Far West*, 1889.

73 Field Trip Report, Ross, for the British Camp on Little Doward and King Arthur's Cave August 25, *TWNFC*, 1884, pp.210-19; p.213.

74 See JN Rimmington, Little Doward Camp, unpublished report 229, HSM 45003, Herefordshire Archaeology, and Mark Bowden, Little Doward, Ganarew, Herefordshire Analytical Earthwork Survey of the Hill Fort and Rapid Landscape Investigation, unpublished report 72 (English Heritage, 2009).

75 Whitehead, *Survey*, p.247.

76 Ibid.

77 For more about Charles Watkins see Ron Shoesmith, *Alfred Watkins: A Herefordshire Man* (Logaston Press, Almleley, 1990).

78 HRO, M5/15A/71:1921 Sale Particulars.

79 James Pulham, *Picturesque Ferneries, and Rock-Garden Scenery, in Waterfalls, Rocky-streams, Cascades, Dropping Wells, Heatheries, Caves or Cavernous Recesses for Boathouses, &c, &c*, 1877, p.79.

80 For more on Edward Newman see Martin Rickard, 'Edward Newman (1801-1876) in the Welsh Marches', *Pteridologist*, vol. 2, pt. 3 (1992), pp.130-32.

81 Death of Mr Henry Newman, *Leominster News*, 5 June 1908.

82 Ibid.

chapter 8 PURITAN DAWN TO HAWAIIAN SUNSET – THE EDWARDIANS

1 Timothy Mowl, *Historic Gardens of Worcestershire* (Tempus Publishing, Stroud, 2006), p.163-165.

2 One of these, at Malvern Wells, is called Cob Nash.

3 Mary Miers, 'In harmony with the landscape: Perrycroft, Colwall', *Country Life*, 20 July 2011.

4 Wendy Hitchmough, *C F A Voysey*, 1995, p.67.

5 Ibid., p.69.

6 Ibid., plate 9 on p.71.

7 He returned to make alterations to the house and lodge in 1907, 1914 and 1924.

8 Voysey's drawings for Perrycroft are in the Royal Institute of British Architects Drawings Collection at the Victoria & Albert Museum; we are most grateful to Gillian Archer, the current owner of Perrycroft, for showing us copies of his plans and for sharing with us her knowledge of the building.

9 'The Revival of English Domestic Architecture VI: The Work of Mr C F A Voysey', *The Studio*, vol.11, no.51 (June, 1897), pp. 16-25; p.18.

10 Quoted by Hitchmough, *CFA Voysey*, p.60.

11 The photograph is in English Heritage's National Monuments Record in Swindon.

12 Hugh Meller, 'The Architectural History of Goodrich Court, Herefordshire', *TWNFC*, vol.42, pt.2 (1977), pp.175-185; p.183.

13 Pevsner, *Herefordshire*, p.83.

14 Thomas Mawson, *The Life and Works of an English Landscape Architect*, 1927, p.135. Mawson's record for 1907 opens with his commission for Moffatt; glass lantern slides and some photographs held in the Cumbria Record Office illustrate this work. Mawson also enhanced the planting of the herbaceous

borders and added a procession of typically Edwardian rose arches to one walk.

15 We are most grateful to Roger Lee for making these albums available for study and for allowing us to reproduce the photographs here.

16 Clayton's design is in one of the family albums.

17 It has featured little in architectural literature, but David Wheeler published an article on the gardens and their planting entitled 'Rise up among the Roses' in *Country Life*, 17 July 1997.

18 Whitehead, *Survey*, p.42.

19 See Lucy Archer, *Raymond Erith: Architect*, 1985, pp.160-163.

20 Whitehead, *Survey*, p.128.

21 Whitehead, *Survey*, p.54.

22 See Helena Gerrish, *Edwardian Country Life: The Story of H Avray Tipping*, 2011, pp.140-147.

23 Whitehead, *Survey*, p.55.

24 Gerrish, *Edwardian Country Life*, p.141.

25 Ibid., p.147.

26 See Jane Brown, *The Art & Architecture of English Gardens* (Rizzoli, New York, 1989), p.212.

27 RIBA Drawings Collection, Folder 27: RAN/36/G/1.

28 Ibid.

29 Richard Hollins Murray, *Dinmore Manor and the Commandery of the Knights Hospitaller of St John of Jerusalem at Dinmore, Herefordshire*, 1936; Clive Aslet, 'Dinmore Manor, Herefordshire', *Country Life*, 18 April 1985; Noel Kingsbury, 'A Garden Glows at the Valley's Edge', *Country Life*, 15 October 1998.

30 *Aslet*, *Country Life*, 18 April 1985.

31 Ibid.

32 Hollins Murray, *Dinmore Manor*, pp.13-14. Architectural drawings for Bethington & Son show the layout of the Cloister Garden including the pools (HRO, E44/3/i-x).

33 Kingsbury, *Country Life*, 15 October 1998.

34 For Friar Park see Timothy Mowl, *Historic Gardens of Oxfordshire* (Tempus Publishing, 2007), pp.119-132.

35 They are the late George Harrison and his wife Olivia.

chapter 9 EXOTICS, DAFFODILS, ECLECTIC GARDEN BUILDINGS AND A PIONEERING PLANTSMAN

1 Lawrence Banks, *Hergest Croft Gardens* (Kington, Herefordshire, 2010), p.4.

2 Ibid; see also Tony & Vicky Schilling, 'Arboreal Glories', *Country Life*, 4 January 1996, and Miles Hadfield, 'A Garden of Collectors' Pieces', *Country Life*, 27 February 1975.

3 Lawrence Banks, 'W L Banks, Gardening in the Age of William Robinson: Hergest Croft, Kington, 1896-1910', *The Radnorshire Society Transactions*, 1999, pp. 34-47.

4 See Timothy Mowl, *Historic Gardens of Oxfordshire* (Tempus Publishing, Stroud, 2007), pp.127-129.

5 Jan Dalton, 'From banks to bulbs', *The Garden*, vol.122 (March, 1997), pp.156-158; see also Peter Davis, 'The Backhouses of Weardale, Co. Durham, and Sutton Court, Hereford: Their Botanical and Horticultural Interests', *Garden History* Vol.18, pt.1 (Spring, 1990), pp.57-68.

6 Dalton, 'From banks to bulbs', p.158.

7 Ibid., p.159.

8 Davis, 'The Backhouses', p.64.

9 Ibid.

10 The current owner, who is descended from the Backhouse family, was not at home on our site visit.

11 Whitehead, *Survey*, p.235.

12 Leslie A Marchand, (ed.), *Byron's Letters and Journals*, 6 vols., 1973, 2, p.237.

13 Harley Papers in Banks Archive, Hergest Croft, 'Waste Book 1793', f.36.

14 Ibid., f.271.

15 Whitehead, *Survey*, p.236, citing HRO, R63/IV/61/492.

16 We are most grateful to Sue Wood for allowing access to the grounds.

17 For Arkwright see Catherine Beale, 'A Notable Narcissus Nursery', *Hortus*, no.81 (Spring, 2007), pp.15-24.

18 Ibid., p.21.

19 *ODNB*.

20 Adam Munthe, *Hellens: A Guide to the House and its History* (Hellens, Much Marcle, 2005), p.5; see also James Bettley, 'Hellen's, Herefordshire', *Country Life*, 29 September 1988.

21 Munthe, *Hellens*, p.5. For more biographical information on Munthe see Bengt Jangfeldt, *Axel Munthe* (Centraltryckereit Ab, Borås, Sweden, 2001).

22 The festivities are described in Malcolm Munthe, *Hellens: The Story of a Herefordshire Manor* (Pennington-Mellor-Munthe Charitable Trust, 1957), pp.124-129.

23 A photograph of the plan is in the archives of the Landscape Institute, which are now deposited at the Garden Museum. It is reproduced in Geoffrey Jellioce, *The Guelph Lectures on Landscape Design* (University of Guelph, Ontario, 1983), p.5.

24 See *Country Life*, 3 February 1966, fig.8.

25 William Hooker, *Pomona Londiniensis*, 3 vols., 1818, 3, no pagination.

26 Borthwick Institute, University of York, JR/1/127.

27 This and other biographical information on Russell is taken from *The Times*, Obituary, 13 May 1996, and Anthony Pugh-Thomas, 'James Philip Cuming Russell 1920-1996', *Somerset Gardens Trust Newsletter*, no.40 (Spring, 2009); see also Steven Desmond, 'Great British Garden Makers: James Russell 1920-1996', *Country Life*, 20 March 2010.

28 Sir Thomas and Lady Henrietta Dunne have recently completed a house swap with their son Philip and his wife Domenica. They have moved to nearby Trippleton House, where they have inherited herbaceous terraces influenced by Tom Stuart-Smith, which will be discussed in the next chapter.

29 This, and the following quotations, is taken from Russell's papers at the Borthwick Institute.

30 Hadfield Papers, University of Reading, 1408, 14/29.

31 All information on Dillon's Orchard is taken from the Hadfield Papers at the University of Reading. For Moraston see Miles Hadfield, 'Gardens of the Golden Age: Family Memories before 1914', *Country Life*, 6 April 1967.

32 Miles Hadfield, 'Flowers in the Grass: A Planting Guide for Lawn-haters', *Country Life*, 28 August 1975.

33 Ibid.

34 Ibid.

35 Charlotte Johnson, 'Percy Cane (1881-1976): Garden Designer', Thesis, Architectural Association, London, 1995.

36 Fenja Gunn, 'Reviewing Percy Cane', *The Garden*, vol.121, pt. 9 (September 1996), pp.571-75; p.571.

37 Borthwick Institute of Archives, University of York, JR/1/117: De Quincey to Russell, 26 June 1951.

38 Ibid., De Quincey to Russell, 16 April 1951.

39 Ibid., De Quincey to Russell, 14 January 1954.

40 Ibid., De Quincey to Russell, 21 November 1952.

Chapter Notes chapter 10

chapter 10 'TASTE GESTAPO' VERSUS ESTABLISHMENT – THE LATEST GARDENS

1 Anne Wareham, 'Gardens Need Critics', *Garden Design Journal*, 10 March 2011.
2 Anne Wareham, 'The emperor's new weeds', *The Spectator*, 29 October 2011.
3 Andrew Lawson, *The Spectator*, Letters, 5 November 2011.
4 The notebook was in the possession of Hinck & Wall, an antiquarian bookseller in Cambridge, in September 2004; see catalogue number 56.
5 Ibid.
6 *ODNB*.
7 The gardens at Fawley are kept immaculately by Steven Redding and his team. Redding came to Fawley from Hergest Croft in 1997.
8 He has been involved with Anne Wareham in setting up 'The thinkin*G*ardens Group', whose website describes it as a forum 'for people who want more than gardening from gardens'; http://thinkingardens.co.uk accessed on 4 December 2011. Since 2008 he has also, in collaboration with the garden journalist, Tim Richardson, chaired the 'Vista Debates' at the Garden Museum in London. For papers related to these debates see Tim Richardson & Noel Kingsbury (eds.), *Vista: The culture and politics of gardens*, 2005.
9 For an account of the Seminar see Jill Billington & Lucy Gent, 'The Perennial Problem', *Vitis: The Journal of the Society of Garden Designers*, Autumn, 1994, pp.9-11; see also Brita von Schoenaich, 'The end of the border?', *Landscape Design*, no.229 (April, 1994), pp.9-14.
10 We were also fortunate to be taken around the garden by Cross, who was fresh from planting and weeding.
11 See Timothy Mowl, *Historic Gardens of Worcestershire* (Tempus Publishing, Stroud, 2006), pp.16-19.
12 See Fred Whitsey, 'Hard Work and a Great Triumph: Abbey Dore Court Garden, Herefordshire', *Country Life*, 23 April 1987.
13 See Timothy Mowl & Diane James, *The Historic Gardens of Warwickshire* (Redcliffe Press, Bristol, 2011), pp.259-260.
14 For writings on the garden see David Wheeler (ed.), *The Penguin Book of Garden Writing*, 1996, Introduction, pp.xvi-xviii; David Wheeler, 'Arts-and-Crafts gardens welcome the spring', *Country Life*, 21 April 2010, and Stephen Lacey, 'Past Glories', *Telegraph Magazine*, 21 May 2011.
15 *Country Life*, 21 April 2010.
16 See Roy Strong, *The Laskett: The Story of a Garden*, 2003; see also Patrick Bowe, 'Fantasy from a Common Field', *Country Life*, 16 January 1997.
17 David Wheeler, 'How my garden healed me', *Daily Telegraph*, 1 August 2008.
18 We are grateful to Sandy Haynes, who spotted them while walking along the Wye.
19 http://lawlesshill.com

Gazetteer

The following is a list of the gardens of significant historic importance that are covered in this book and open to the public.

Abbreviations

EH	English Heritage
GC	Golf Course
H	Hotel, holiday home, B & B
W	Wedding venue
NCH	Open by appointment as a National Collection Holder
NGS	Privately owned but open occasionally as part of the National Gardens Scheme
NT	National Trust
P	Privately owned but open occasionally or regularly
PP	Public Park
P-to-P	Point-to-point venue
S	Spa and health club
WT	Woodland Trust

Abbey Dore Court	P/NGS	www.abbeydorecourt.co.uk
Belmont	GC	www.belmont-golf.co.uk
Berrington Hall	NT	www.nationaltrust.org.uk
Brinsop Court	H	www.brinsopcourt.com
Broadfield Court	P	www.broadfieldcourt.co.uk
Brockhampton Cottage	NGS	www.ngs.org.uk
Brockhampton Estate	NT	www.nationaltrust.org.uk
Brockhampton Park *see* Brockhampton Estate		
Broxwood Court	H	www.broxwoodcourt.co.uk
Bryan's Ground	P/NGS	www.bryansground.co.uk
Burton Court	W	www.burtoncourt.com
Caradoc Court	W	www.caradoccourt.co.uk
Castle Ditch *see* Eastnor Castle		
Court of Noke	P	
Croft Castle	NT	www.ngs.org.uk
Eastnor Castle	P	www.eastnorcastle.com
Elton Hall	NCH	www.nccpg.com
Fawley Court	P	
Garnons	P-to-P	www.pointtopoint.co.uk
Grendon Court	NGS	www.ngs.org.uk

Hampton Court	P	www.hamptoncourt.org.uk
Hellens	P/NGS	www.hellensmanor.com
Hergest Croft	P	www.hergest.co.uk
Holme Lacy	H/NGS	www.warnerleisurehotels.co.uk
Holmer Park	S	www.holmerpark.co.uk
Homme House	W	www.hommehouse.co.uk
How Caple Court	P/W	www.howcaplecourt.co.uk
Kinnersley Castle	P	www.kinnersleycastle.co.uk
Knill Court	P	
Langstone Court	P	
Laskett, The	P/H	www.thelaskettgardens.co.uk
Lawless Hill	H	www.lawlesshill.com
Lwr Brockhampton House *see* Brockhampton Estate		
Lower Hope	NGS	www.ngs.org.uk
Luntley Court	H	www.luntleycourt.co.uk
Moccas Court	W	www.moccas-court.co.uk
Monnington Court	NGS	www.ngs.org.uk
Newport House	NGS	www.ngs.org.uk
Perrycroft	H/NGS	www.ngs.org.uk
Ross on Wye Prospect	PP	
Sufton	P	
Treago Castle	H	www.treago.co.uk
Weir, The	NT	www.nationaltrust.org.uk
Weston Hall	NGS	www.ngs.org.uk
Whitbourne Hall	W	www.whitbournehall.com
Wigmore Castle	EH	www.english-heritage.org.uk
Wyastone Leys	WT	www.woodlandtrust.org.uk

The Gardens

Not all gardens shown are open to the public

Index Page numbers in **bold** refer to illustrations and captions

Page numbers in **bold** refer to illustrations and captions

'Mowl is determined to tramp over every piece of uneven grassland and through every bramble-tangled woodland, looking for clues' Ursula Buchan *The Spectator*

The Historic Gardens of England

from Redcliffe Press
buy online at: www.redcliffepress.co.uk or call 0117 973 7207

Cheshire

the eighth title in Tim Mowl's celebrated series
TIM MOWL AND MARION MAKO
From the Duke of Westminster's Eaton Hall to Lord Leverhulme's Thornton Manor and his noted garden village at Port Sunlight, there is a swagger and grandeur about the landscape and garden experiments in Cheshire.

Staffordshire

the ninth title in Tim Mowl's celebrated series
TIM MOWL AND DIANNE BARRE
Staffordshire is usually associated with the Potteries and the Black Country, the industrial heartland of the Midlands, yet it is also a county of gently rolling landscape with some of the most eccentric gardens in the country. Nothing is quite what it seems.

Somerset

the tenth title in Tim Mowl's celebrated series
TIM MOWL AND MARION MAKO
Somerset is still a county of deep-delved country lanes, textured manor houses and small market towns that remains agrarian and refreshingly old-fashioned. Rich in medieval deer parks, its period of greatest garden activity was the eighteenth century when a group of aesthetic rivals laid out circuits of exotic garden buildings in and around the Quantocks.

Warwickshire

the eleventh title in Tim Mowl's celebrated series
TIM MOWL AND DIANE JAMES
Warwickshire is a county rich in history, one that has constantly recycled the legends of its heroes. It maintains a deep sense of nostalgia for the past and a traditional approach to garden design, yet modernism briefly peeps through.

Coming soon...

Cambridgeshire

the thirteenth title in Tim Mowl's celebrated series
TIM MOWL AND LAURA MAYER
Cambridgeshire has every style of historic landscape, from the remains of a seventeenth-century water garden at Hamerton to a 1979 recreation of a Gothick trellis at Abbots Ripton. There are an astonishing 300 moated sites – the legacy of a constant battle to drain the fens and channel the surplus waters. A book to enlighten and inspire the visitor.